Research Handbook on Diversity and Corporate Governance

T0342287

Edited by

Sabina Tasheva

Professor, University of Sydney, Australia and Copenhagen Business School, Denmark

Morten Huse

Professor Emeritus, Department of Communication and Culture, BI Norwegian Business School, Norway

EE Edward Elgar
PUBLISHING

Cheltenham, UK • Northampton, MA, USA

Published by
Edward Elgar Publishing Limited
The Lypiatts
15 Lansdown Road
Cheltenham
Glos GL50 2JA
UK

Edward Elgar Publishing, Inc.
William Pratt House
9 Dewey Court
Northampton
Massachusetts 01060
USA

Paperback edition 2024

A catalogue record for this book
is available from the British Library

Library of Congress Control Number: 2022950772

This book is available electronically in the **Elgar**online
Business subject collection
http://dx.doi.org/10.4337/9781800377783

ISBN 978 1 80037 777 6 (cased)
ISBN 978 1 80037 778 3 (eBook)
ISBN 978 1 0353 4058 3 (paperback)

Printed and bound by CPI Group (UK) Ltd, Croydon, CR0 4YY

Contents

Figures

Tables

RESEARCH HANDBOOK ON DIVERSITY AND CORPORATE GOVERNANCE

Contributors

Carl Åberg is Associate Professor at the Department of Business, Strategy and Political Sciences at the University of South-Eastern Norway. He completed his PhD at the Chair of Management and Governance at Witten/Herdecke University. His research interests are in the areas of corporate governance, boards of directors, strategy, digitalization and dynamic capabilities. Beyond his academic work, Carl has worked as a consultant in various leadership, strategy and corporate governance projects, in both the public and private sector.

Abdullah Al-Mamun is a Senior Lecturer of Accounting in the School of Business at the University of Wollongong, Australia. Abdullah plays the role of academic program director for the Master of Profession Accounting (MPA). His research focuses on corporate governance and corporate social (ir)responsibility based on emerging economies, in particular Asian economies. More specifically, his research interests include board characteristics and leadership structure, and their influences on firm outcomes in the form of corporate social responsibility (CSR). Abdullah regularly presents these research findings to high-profile conferences, including the Academy of Management, Academy of International Business and the International Corporate Governance Society. Abdullah has also published his research work in internationally reputed journals such as *Emerging Markets Review*, *Meditari Accountancy Research*, *Journal of Asian Business Studies*, *Accounting Research Journal*, and *Thunderbird International Business Review*.

Audur Arna Arnardottir is a clinical psychologist and an associate professor in the Department of Business Administration at Reykjavik University. She has worked in academia over twenty years and her areas of teaching and research fall under organizational behavior and psychology, with focus on group and board dynamics and effectiveness, effects of gender quota on boards, leadership development, work–family balance, stress and burnout, and job performance. Her publications can be found in journals such as *Journal of Business Ethics*, *Academy of Management Learning & Education*, and *International Journal of Productivity and Performance Management*.

Sarosh Asad is an assistant professor at the Department of Innovation Management and Strategy in the Faculty of Economics and Business, University of Groningen (the Netherlands). She received her PhD from Copenhagen Business School (Denmark). Her research focuses on the influence of CEOs, top executives, and boards of directors on firms' strategic decisions and organizational outcomes.

Andrea D. Bührmann has held the position of full professor at the University of Göttingen since 2011. In 2013 she became the founding director of the Göttingen

Diversity Research Institute. Bührmann was a visiting professor at the University of California, Berkeley, at the University of Klagenfurt and at the German Institute for Japanese Studies Tokyo. From 2015 to 2017, Bührmann was University Vice President for Studies and Teaching, and, following her re-election, she was University Vice President for Studies and Teaching, Equality and Diversity from 2017 to 2021. Since 2021 Bührmann has become an auditor of the Stifterverband's "Diversity Audit" for the development and implementation of university-specific diversity strategies.

Vartika Chandra Saman is a postdoc scholar at Johns Hopkins University, USA. Previously, she was a lecturer at Indian Institute of Management Rohtak (IIM Rohtak). She received her doctoral degree from Jawaharlal Nehru University (JNU), New Delhi. Her research interests span across diversity and inclusion in organizations, intersectionality in business and business ethics. Before joining IIM Rohtak, she worked with IIM Bangalore, XLRI Jamshedpur and NIDM (Ministry of Home Affairs, Government of India). Her work has been published with Springer Nature Switzerland and Sustainability. Her report "COVID-19 Third Wave Preparedness: Children's Vulnerability and Recovery", published by NIDM (Ministry of Home Affairs, Government of India), was highlighted by all the leading newspapers and news channels in India. Dr Vartika has presented her research work at various international and national platforms including University of British Columbia, Witten/ Herdecke University and Jawaharlal Nehru University. She is also a reviewer for the journal *Management and Labour Studies*, SAGE Publications. She writes on social and contemporary issues in various e-newspapers. She is an honorary consultant for the NGO Women's Empowerment in Indian Villages (WEIV), which works in the field of women's education and adolescent health and well-being in Bihar, India.

Sara De Masi is Senior Assistant Professor of Management at University of Florence and Lecturer at New York University (Florence campus). She holds a PhD in Economics, Markets and Institutions from IMT – Institute for Advanced Studies. She has been a visiting scholar at NYU, Stern School of Business in 2010 and in 2012. Her research has been published in international journals such as *Corporate Governance: An International Review, Journal of Technology Transfer, Business Strategy & Environment* and *The Leadership Quarterly*. Her current research interests focus on corporate governance, boards of directors, board diversity, women on boards, strategy and sustainability.

Cihat Erbil, PhD, is currently a Research Assistant in the Department of Business Administration at Ankara HBV University in Ankara, Turkey. His research centres on social innovation, social entrepreneurship and critical management studies. In his studies, he aims to give voice to "others" and make them visible.

Hilde Fjellvær is Associate Professor at NTNU Business School. She completed her PhD at the Norwegian School of Economics at the Department of Strategy and Management. Her research interests are in the areas of corporate governance, boards of directors and diversity, particularly in the context of venture capital and private equity. She also studies pluralistic organizations, dual leadership and institutional logics.

Patricia Gabaldón is an Associate Professor of Economic Environment at IE Business School and Academic Director of Economics at the School of Global and Public Affairs, at IE University. With a PhD in Economics, she has developed her research around the role of women in the economy and its effects on economic growth and sustainability. She works on the importance of women and gender diversity in leadership positions and boards, focusing on the relevance of women on the impact on goals and processes at the board and later, on the sustainable side of boards, firms, and economies. Her work has been published in journals such as *Journal of Business Ethics*, *Corporate Governance: An International Review* and *Long Range Planning*, among others.

Jeremy Galbreath is an Associate Professor of Strategy and Business Sustainability in the School of Management and Marketing at Curtin University, Australia. His career spans nearly 40 years in both business and academia and, as an academic, he has established himself as a top 2% ranked global scientist with over 7,000 citations and almost 200 publications. Associate Professor Galbreath serves on various editorial boards, including the *Journal of Management & Organisation*, and has received over AU$1M in research funding, including a prestigious Australian Research Council (ARC) Grant and several industry-based grants. Jeremy's research specialisation intersects boards of directors, strategy, innovation and sustainability, and he has spent years studying the Australian wine industry. He holds a PhD (Curtin University) from Australia and MBA (Colorado State University), MSc (Ball State University) and BSc (Ball State University) degrees from the United States.

Dimitrios Georgakakis holds a Chair in Strategy and International Business at the University of York, Management School (United Kingdom). In the past, he held permanent and visiting positions at the University of St Gallen (Switzerland) and Texas A&M University (USA). His research has been published in several academic outlets, including the *Journal of Management*, *Journal of Management Studies*, *Journal of World Business*, *Leadership Quarterly*, *Long Range Planning* and the *Academy of Management Discoveries*. He has received research awards from several international academic organizations – such as the Latsis Foundation, the Academy of Management, the Strategic Management Society, Emerald Publishing and the European Institute of Advanced Studies in Management.

Katrin Hansen was a professor at Westfalian University of Applied Sciences in Germany from 1994 until 2021. She has held positions as Vice-President of the university (1996–2001, 2008–2020). Currently she is the vice-chairwoman of Käte Ahlmann foundation, dedicated to entrepreneurial mentoring. Since 2016 she serves as auditor to support German universities during the audit process "Vielfalt gestalten" (Shaping Diversity) organized by the "Stifterverband für die Deutsche

Wissenschaft". Katrin is a researcher in the fields of Organizational Development, Women Entrepreneurs, Diversity Management, Intercultural Management and Entrepreneurial Diversity, active at the international field. Katrin has published many books (some together with colleagues), book chapters and articles.

Mariano L.M. Heyden is Professor of Strategy & International Business at the Monash Business School in Australia, where he also serves as Director of PhD Degrees in the Department of Management. His internationally published research tackles the characteristics of senior business leaders that enable innovation and change, and appears in leading scholarly journals such as Journal of Management, Journal of Applied Psychology, Research Policy, Organization Studies, Journal of Management Studies, The Leadership Quarterly, Human Resource Management, and Long Range Planning. He serves on numerous editorial review boards, such as the *Journal of Management, Journal of Management Studies*, and *Corporate Governance: An International Review.* Professor Heyden is a Trustee of the Society for the Advancement of Management Studies (UK), a Representative-at-Large of the Strategic Management Society (US), and previously served on the Scientific Board of the *European Academy of Management*, as well as the Membership Engagement Committee of the STR Division of the *Academy of Management* (US). His thought leadership on topic issues has been covered by *ABC News, The Australian, Business Insider, Harvard Business Review, MIT Sloan Management Review, The Conversation, Sydney Morning Herald, Manage Magazine,* and the *World Economic Forum.* He has received over AU\$700,000 in international and domestic research funding, including the prestigious Australian Research Council's Discovery Early Career Research Award (DECRA-17).

Morten Huse is Professor Emeritus at BI Norwegian Business School, Department of Communication and Culture. His research has covered many issues related to boards of directors, including stakeholder issues, gender issues and behavioural perspectives. His 2020 book *Resolving the Crisis in Research by Changing the Game: An Ecosystem and a Sharing Philosophy* illustrates his present agenda against the existing publish or perish culture in academia. He has signed the DORA declaration and endorsed RRBM. He is a former president of EURAM, and from 2019 to 2022 he was member of the board of governors at AOM.

Hildur Magnúsdóttir is a PhD fellow at the University of Iceland, School of Business. Her doctoral work explores corporate governance and strategic management. She holds an MSc degree in strategic management from the University of Iceland (2018–2020) and a BSc in business administration from Reykjavik University (2006–2008). Alongside her PhD, Hildur is affiliated with the Danish software company DecideAct. Hildur has previously published on her research within board of directors and nomination committees. She has also cooperated with agencies such as the Icelandic Chamber of Commerce on, for example, providing guidelines for nomination committees.

Esha Mendiratta is an assistant professor at the Global Economics and Management Department, Faculty of Economics and Business, University Groningen, Netherlands. Her research focuses on corporate governance and strategic leadership, specifically the antecedents and consequences of board of director and top management team composition.

Caitlin Harm Nam is an undergraduate student at the University of the South Pacific (USP), studying a Bachelor of Commerce majoring in Economics, with a Bachelor of Law. She was born and raised in Fiji and is of Chinese ethnicity. Alongside her undergraduate studies, Caitlin has had experience working with local women NGOs, developing a keen interest in the area of women's economic empowerment.

Ana Naulu is a graduate student of the School of Accounting, Finance and Economics at The University of the South Pacific (USP). She hopes to further her research interests in the field of economics governance and financial intelligence in the South Pacific. She participated in the Summer Global Youth Forum 2021 by the International Training Centre of the International Labour Organization (ITC-ILO) and other international training on Sustainable Development Goals (SDGs).

Jana Oehmichen is a Full Professor of Organization, Human Resources, and Management Studies at the Johannes Gutenberg University (JGU) Mainz and an Honorary Professor of Leadership & Governance at the University of Groningen. In her research, she is interested in corporate governance, ownership structure, incentive systems, board composition, strategic change and digital strategy and leadership. Her work has been published in journals such as *Strategic Management Journal, Leadership Quarterly, Global Strategy Journal, Journal of Management Studies, Human Resource Management, Journal of Business Ethics* and *International Business Review*.

Mustafa F. Özbilgin is Professor of Organisational Behaviour at Brunel Business School, London. He also holds two international positions: Co-Chaire Management et Diversité at Université Paris Dauphine and Visiting Professor of Management at Koç University in Istanbul. His research focuses on equality, diversity and inclusion at work from comparative and relational perspectives. He has conducted field studies in the UK and internationally and his work is empirically grounded. His research is supported by international as well as national grants. His work has a focus on changing policy and practice in equality and diversity at work. He is an engaged scholar, driven by values of workplace democracy, equality for all and humanisation of work.

Michael Seamer was an Associate Professor in Accounting with the Faculty of Business and Law at the University of Newcastle, Australia. On his departure, after 25 years at Newcastle, he was also serving as the Deputy Head (Teaching and Learning) of the Newcastle Business School and the Director of Undergraduate Programs. Michael completed his PhD in 2009, investigating links between corporate governance and management-perpetrated fraud and failures in corporate disclosure. Michael's current research interests continue to focus on the relationship between effective corporate governance and enhanced firm performance and stakeholder outcomes, with a particular focus on developing economies. His research has been published in several A-ranked international journals; Michael is an award-winning teacher and PhD supervisor.

Cathrine Seierstad is Professor at the Department of Business, History and Social Sciences at the University of South-Eastern Norway. Her research explores the fields of equality, diversity and inclusion at work, leadership, women on boards, HRM, corporate governance and CSR. Her recent research has investigated the wider effects of using gender quotas on corporate boards in a variety of countries.

Throstur Olaf Sigurjonsson is a professor at University of Iceland. His areas of research are corporate governance, business ethics, policymaking and policy implementation. Olaf has published more than 50 articles, books and book chapters in the last decade. He is also a permanent part-time academic at Copenhagen Business School. Olaf leads two international research projects in the field of corporate governance: on the impact of digital development on governance and on impact of economic and social shocks on the dissemination of content in the field of governance, towards companies, institutions and teaching.

Baljeet Singh is a Senior Lecturer of Economics at The University of the South Pacific (USP). He is also the Coordinator of the Discipline of Economics at USP. His research interest is in the field of development economics and climate change in the South Pacific region. He has published several articles in reputed international refereed journals. His research has been supported by competitive grants from institutions such as the Global Development Network (GDN). He has participated in several international workshops and conferences.

Agnieszka Slomka-Golebiowska is Professor of Corporate Governance at Warsaw School of Economics; a former Fulbright Fellow at Haas Business School, University of California, Berkeley; and has cooperated with Professor Oliver Williamson and is an Alexander von Humboldt Fellow (Hertie School of Governance). She holds a PhD in Financial Economics from Warsaw School of Economics and Habilitation in Economics and Management from the same university. She was a visiting scholar at a number of universities: New York University, Ronald Coase Institute at Cambridge (MIT) and Tucson (UOA), Munster (WWU), Copenhagen (CBS), Birmingham (BBS), Berlin (HSoG), Genoa (UoG – Law School), Vienna (WU), Florence (UniFI) and Oslo (BI). She is the author of numerous research articles in professional journals, among others: *Business Strategy and the Environment, Management Decision, Emerging Markets Review* and *Journal of Management and Governance*, and books on corporate governance and sustainability. She is Associate Editor at the *International Review of Financial Analysis*. Agnieszka has almost two decades of extensive experience on boards of directors of large international publicly listed and private companies, as well as international organizations such as UN WFP.

As a purpose-driven academic, board member, and mentor, she advises companies in fulfilling their commitments to social sustainability through profitable strategies.

Sabina Tasheva is Professor of International Business at Copenhagen Business School and Professor of International Management at University of Sydney Business School. She further holds an adjunct Professorship with the University of South Pacific and a Visiting Professorship at Harvard University. She received her PhD from University of St Gallen, Switzerland and was visiting scholar at University of Washington, Seattle and University of Technology Sydney, Australia. Sabina's research focuses on the composition, dynamics and decision-making of top management teams and boards of directors and has appeared in *The Academy of Management Review, Strategic Management Journal, Journal of International Business Studies, Journal of Management Studies, Journal of Organizational Behavior, Journal of World Business* and *Strategic Organization*, among others. Sabina conducted the 2012 Census of Women in Leadership in Australia and is currently leading a team conducting the first Census of Women in Leadership in the South Pacific. She is passionate about diversity in all of its expressions and has conducted research on the topic in various countries around the world.

Hans van Ees is Emeritus Professor of Corporate governance and institutions at University of Groningen. In his research he is interested in comparative corporate governance, agency and stewardship perspectives on corporate governance, corporate purpose and corporate governance and board composition and board dynamics. His work has been published in journals such as *Strategic Management Journal, Journal of International Business Studies, Journal of Management, Journal of Management Studies, Corporate Governance: An International Review, Journal of Business Ethics* and *International Business Review*.

Alana Vandebeek is a Postdoctoral Research Fellow at KU Leuven (Belgium), Faculty of Economics and Business, in the Department of Accounting and Finance. Her research focuses on corporate governance with a strong emphasis on group dynamics and diversity on boards. She holds a PhD in Business Economics from Hasselt University (Belgium). Alana has participated in several international conferences, and has published in *Journal of Family Business Strategy* and *Corporate Governance: An International Review*.

Michelle Weck is a PhD candidate of corporate governance at the University of Groningen. She is interested in social and psychological processes in corporate governance. Her work has been published in the journal *Long Range Planning*.

Preface

Morten and I met in 2004, sharing an interest in how boards work, particularly the processes and dynamics that shape their behaviour. At the time, diversity in corporate boards was not even a topic. Norway was about to introduce its first ever (and first worldwide) quota for women on the boards of publicly listed companies, yet the hype around the topic was still in its infancy. Morten was a well-established scholar in the field of boards and governance, who was particularly supportive of young scholars and their ideas. And he was never shy of extending his networks and supporting people with similar interests to connect and work together. So, when we both discovered we had interest in gender diversity, we decided to write an article. Yet, none of us had an idea of the impact it would have. The one thing we had in common is that we were not interested in the link to financial performance. Instead, we wanted to know what happens when a woman joins the corporate board. How does it affect the board effectiveness and behaviour? How does it affect the perceptions and behaviour of both men and women and of board chairs, CEOs and board members? So, we ventured in an exploration beyond the surface; we did not have expectations that our results will support or not the presence of women in corporate boards. We simply wanted to understand how women may impact board decision-making and behaviour.

Today our article "Women on corporate boards: going beyond the surface" has more than 1,000 citations. Yet, for both of us it is not so much about the impact it has in terms of citations; it is rather about the inspiration that this article has provided to other research to delve underneath the surface, to understand the social psychological foundations of human behaviour and how they affect the work of diverse boards. To ask the real questions, even when the answers are not straightforward. Over the years, we have collaborated on a number of projects. And we have not always agreed on the directions and purpose; there have been times that we have walked in different directions in terms of intellectual debates. And in the true spirit of diversity, we have not agreed because we did not need to. After all, the purpose of diversity is to raise different knowledge, perspectives and opinions. And in the spirit of diversity, sometimes it is about expression of ideas rather than agreement.

Today, we are proud to present the latest result of our collaboration: a vastly diverse collection of scholarly contributions that differ in terms of disciplinary origin, use of theories and methodologies. Even the language and structure of each contribution is unique; and this is exactly the collection of cutting-edge research that we would like to present to you. It has been incredible to witness the advances of diversity research in the context of Corporate Governance over the past two decades, ever since, for example, the introduction of the Sarbanes–Oxley Act and the Guidance for Corporate Governance around the world that focuses on directors characteristics, probing deeper into who boards of directors are, what they do and why they do it. It has been intellectually challenging and rewarding to witness the discussion move beyond director independence to the human capital, social capital and demographic characteristics of corporate directors to diversity in all of its expressions. And we are proud to present a collection of articles that deal with issues of gender beyond the dichotomy, intersectionality of gender and other important characteristics such as cast and ethnicity, and novel theoretical dimensions such as dynamic capabilities and digital expertise. Furthermore, this collection contains a number of studies that delve deeper into the way that boards are working by exploring demographic fault lines and theories of proportions; and contributions that integrate insights across disciplines and decades of research into a historical overview and multilevel framework of diversity and Corporate Governance. We hope you will enjoy this collection of insightful contributions. And we hope it will inspire you to think about diversity differently and ask different questions.

We thank Edward Elgar Publishing for letting us make a contribution with this volume. We further thank all contributors for their efforts and willingness to participate and share their ideas. We have been learning a lot from your contributions. All chapters in this book have been subject to peer review.

Sabina Tasheva and Morten Huse
July 2022

1. Introduction to *Research Handbook on Diversity and Corporate Governance*

Sabina Tasheva and Morten Huse

BOARD DIVERSITY AND CORPORATE GOVERNANCE: PAST, PRESENT AND FUTURE

Past, present and future are the concepts that have guided this *Handbook* on research about diversity and corporate governance. We have in this *Handbook* tried to present alternative ways of exploring and understanding diversity and corporate governance that fit the contemporary discussions in the field. We have used a critical approach to mainstream research on the topic, and we argue for new and alternative ways to explore diversity and corporate governance.

In Chapter 2, one of the editors Sabina Tasheva reviews theoretical and empirical advancements in the field of diversity and corporate governance. Diversity discussions have advanced significantly since the start of the century and our understanding of diversity has both expanded and become more focused. While ten years ago, board diversity was mostly referring to women on corporate boards, both the corporate landscape and academic literature have changed significantly since. Not only have boards become more diverse since, but our understanding of diversity is continuously expanding. Tasheva discusses the many advances in the field and proposes directions for future research.

DIVERSITY AND CORPORATE GOVERNANCE: BEYOND HUMAN CAPITAL, SOCIAL CAPITAL AND DEMOGRAPHIC CHARACTERISTICS

Most research about diversity and corporate governance has been about women on boards. In Part II, we have six chapters focusing on boards and diversity, but they all go beyond mainstream understandings and measures about board diversity. We have thus labelled this part 'Beyond human capital, social capital and demographic characteristics'.

In Chapter 3, Cathrine Seierstad, Carl Åberg and Hilde Fjellvær comment on the board diversity debate in Norway that followed the acceptance/introduction of the gender quota law in 2003/06. They argue that the meaning of board diversity can be considered contextual, contested and temporal. In the Norwegian context, they argue that while there was an implicit expectation that the gender quota law for public limited companies (PLCs) would increase diversity both within and beyond the PLC boards, the board diversity debate and achievements in Norway have been and still are predominantly focusing on gender and the PLC context. Seierstad, Åberg and Fjellvær argue in this chapter that there is a need for a wider board diversity debate.

In Chapter 4, Mustafa Özbilgin and Cihat Erbil expand our understanding of gender diversity with a discussion of LGBT+ in the boardroom and introduce a rainbow agenda. They lean on the theory of heteronormativity and show how it clashes with the talent potential and human rights of LGBT+ individuals in the workplace. Focusing on the boardroom, where heteronormativity is most pronounced, they explain what makes LGBT+ inclusion an international imperative for boardroom diversity. At the end of the chapter, they outline how LGBT+ inclusion could manifest in the boardroom.

Board diversity can be understood beyond diversity among board members. One of the unique features in Chapter 5 is that Carl Åberg, Hilde Fjellvær and Cathrine Seierstad make a distinction between diversity within a board and diversity among boards. They ask whether board diversity among board members impact entrepreneurial activities. By integrating discussions about diversity and boards, they debate the impact question by leaning on three entrepreneurial resource perspectives: dynamic capabilities, absorptive capacity and ambidexterity. They show how diversity must be used to achieve corporate entrepreneurship, competitive advantage and value creation. In utilizing these three perspectives as moderators, they show how diversity can contribute to corporate entrepreneurship. Job-related diversity is a focus in this chapter.

Firms in emerging economies vary greatly in their corporate social responsibility (CSR) engagement. To extend research in this field, Abdullah Al-Mamun, Michael Seamer, Jeremy Galbreath and Mariano L.M. Heyden draw in Chapter 6 on resource dependence theory to hypothesize the association between board of director international experience and CSR engagement in three emerging economies in Asia. They argue that the foreign economic contexts in which directors have accumulated international experience, matters for understanding the local board–CSR relationship in emerging economies. Their findings show that a board's international experience in developed economies is positively related to their firm's CSR engagement. They conclude that the specific international experience is important for understanding local CSR engagement in emerging markets.

Jana Oehmichen, Michelle Weck and Hans van Ees present empirical evidence from the Netherlands about board diversity and the board members' digital experience in Chapter 7. Given the recent corporate governance, strategy and information systems literature, they propose that the digitalization of our economy can have consequences for the tasks for non-executive board members. Firms need digital expertise within their boards. This might influence overall board diversity. They ask whether firms bring digital experts into the boards, and whether these experts are different with respect to non-job-related and job-related diversity dimensions. The results show that the group of non-digital board members is more diverse than the group of digital board members.

In Chapter 8, Hildur Magnúsdóttir, Throstur Olaf Sigurjonsson, Audur Arna Arnardottir and Patricia Gabaldón assess Nomination Committees (NCs), building on the results of a study conducted in Iceland, a country where board gender quota and NCs have relatively recently been established. The study aims to explore NCs role in the selection process of corporate board members and whether those processes promote increased board diversity, above and beyond the emphasis on gender diversity which legislation demands. This is done by conducting 13 interviews with investors, board members and NCs members, using the lenses of agency theory and social identity theory. Findings are that the emergence of NCs has promoted and enhanced improved selection processes of board members, the transparency of that processes and increased gender diversity on boards.

ADVANCES IN INTERSECTIONALITY

Intersectionality is one of the most recent advancements in diversity research and whereas many researchers shy away from its complexity, we have several valuable contributions in this *Handbook*.

In Chapter 9, Sarosh Asad and Dimitrios Georgakakis explore the notion of intersectionality in the context of corporate boards to argue that dual minority status in corporate boards (e.g. representation of directors with both gender and ethnic minority status) triggers a higher number of governance-related shareholder resolutions, a prominent form of shareholder activism. Their work further sheds some light on the career disadvantages that dual minority directors may face due to shareholder resolutions – stressing that duality of minority status may associate with greater barriers at the board–shareholder interface. The chapter contributes to the growing body of research suggesting that firms need to simultaneously consider the multiple configurations of board diversity.

Vartika Chandra Saman presents an interesting exploration of intersectionality in the Indian context in Chapter 10. By focusing on boards of contemporary Indian businesses, this chapter examines the ways in which caste, class and gender intersect with the market and the implications these different combinations of attributes hold for entrepreneurial prospects of dalit women. The author argues that focusing on intersectionality is necessary in order to understand diversity beyond gender in business as intersectional discrimination is paramount to understanding the experience of dalit women. There is a paucity of literature in the area and this chapter sets an agenda for a new wave of diversity research. The chapter investigates a number of important questions such as: Are social caste hierarchies being replaced by competing equalities? What has been the experience of dalit women as entrepreneurs? What happens when there are overlapping identities? Why is it important to understand diversity in the context of different identities? The study is based on an extensive literature review and some in-depth interviews with dalit women entrepreneurs. The findings suggest that studying overlapping identities helps to understand and advance the concept of diversity.

In Chapter 11, Caitlin Harm Nam, Ana Naulu, Baljeet Singh and Sabina Tasheva investigate the intersectionality of board of directors in the largest Fijian firms. By utilizing unique hand-collected data through survey and secondary sources in an under-researched context, they offer some novel insights on how gender and ethnicity of corporate directors intersect in the context of the South Pacific. They argue that current conceptualizations and investigations of board diversity need to progress beyond gender and focus on other relevant attributes in conjunction with gender being race, nationality, ethnicity, and so on. This pioneering study offers some insights by looking at the intersectionality of gender and ethnicity in the context of Fijian boards of directors. By building upon insights of the cross-cultural and national differences in gender diversity, they explore and explain how the specificities of the context of the South Pacific, and Fiji in particular, influence the gender and ethnic composition of Fijian boards of directors. The authors propose to inspire further research on intersectionality in under-researched regions in the South Pacific and beyond.

HOW DO WE UTILIZE THE BENEFITS OF DIVERSITY? RESEARCH ON BOARD DIVERSITY, PROCESSES AND DECISION-MAKING

In Chapter 12, Alana Vandebeek introduces the concept of fault lines in boards of directors and discusses current trends and future directions. By synthesizing the literature in the field, a number of aspects are highlighted regarding the fault line literature in corporate boards. The author reviews the fault line attributes mostly examined within board research, the most commonly used measures and methods and the underlying fault line mechanisms and outcomes. The chapter further outlines the role of contingencies in the way group fault lines unfold in corporate boards. The chapter presents a thorough review of prior research since its inception, and further provide insights and inspirations for future research to guide future explorations into the role of group fault lines in boards of directors.

Esha Mendiratta further advances the discussion of group fault lines in board research by delving into underlying theories and specific methodological issues in Chapter 13. She argues that corporate governance scholars have shown an increasing interest in the concept of fault lines, that is, the hypothetical dividing lines that fracture a group into two or more homogeneous subgroups based on the alignment of multiple individual-level characteristics, and that the research has advanced significantly over the years. By reviewing the literature on board and top management team level fault lines and their influence of board- and firm-level outcomes, she synthesizes the emerging literature along the lines of theoretical background, empirical findings and methodological focus. Based on this synthesis and in the context of pressures faced by boards due to societal challenges, she argues that fault lines may be a crucial perspective for corporate governance research on board composition going forward. Specifically, she suggests that research could benefit from (a) drawing theoretically from other disciplines, (b) exploring management of fault line-related dynamics in light of new corporate governance developments and (c) methodological considerations. Her contribution offers valuable insights for current and aspiring scholars exploring board dynamics by offering in-depth perspectives and analysis of the theoretical and empirical dimensions of the literature.

In Chapter 14, Sara De Masi and Agnieszka Slomka-Golebiowska discuss proportions of diversity in the context of corporate boards. They argue that proportions are important when exploring the benefits of diversity and that each set of board tasks requires different dynamics. Specific states of board dynamics are trigged by specific proportions between a minority and a majority subgroup. The authors suggest that the numerical proportions between a majority and a minority subgroup can be seen as a source of perceived power whereas minority members gain trust and legitimization when their numerical representation increases. This power and legitimation of the minority is not vested in a single person, but it is vested in the minority as a group. Hence, when applying the theory of proportions to studies of boards, we need to understand how a proportion of various types of diversity triggers board dynamics and thus enhances board tasks. Their argument suggests that we need to step back from the idea of *one size fits all*. Understanding the proportions required for each set of board tasks helps the board to increase their effectiveness and exploit the benefits of diversity.

CONSEQUENCES FOR RESEARCH AND PRACTICE

There are two chapters in the final part of the *Handbook*. These chapters challenge existing research and practice, and identify and suggest questions about diversity and corporate governance that should critically be readdressed in future research and practice.

Many studies on workforce and board diversity focus on one isolated research level. Thus, they risk failure by abstracting from other relevant contexts that are necessary to fully understand the impact of diversity. Andrea D. Bührmann and Katrin Hansen argue in Chapter 15 that a multi-level examination of diversity research is important for understanding the dynamics between the different levels and forms of diversity in and beyond organizations. Accordingly, Bührmann and Hansen develop a conceptual heuristic for discussing an intersectional framework for multi-level research on diversity. First, they show that diversity, particularly actual and perceived human capital diversity, is not given, but the effect of diverse practices. With this in mind, contexts become very important. Secondly, they distinguish different forms of diversity and their intermediations. Thirdly, they introduce a framework for a multi-level research approach. Bührmann and Hansen discuss the different approaches to responding to diversity on different levels. In this chapter, they identify further and alternative research perspectives.

Finally, Morten Huse addresses the question about excellence in research in Chapter 16. He suggests three approaches of doing meaningful and groundbreaking diversity and corporate governance research. He introduces programmatic research, polymorphic research and introspection. First, programmatic research. The overall contribution of this book illustrates programmatic research on diversity and corporate governance. He argues that the value of the book goes far beyond each individual chapter. Second, the book also illustrates polymorphic research. With polymorphic research, we challenge mainstream and formulaic approaches to research. He also argues that we use the potential of a book format to bring to the market what we believe in. Finally, through introspection he openly interprets, evaluates and reflects on the findings based on his own previous experiences. These three approaches can help us to present research that is important, interesting and innovative. Why should we aim at something that is not groundbreaking?

PART I

BOARD DIVERSITY AND CORPORATE GOVERNANCE: PAST, PRESENT AND FUTURE

2. Diversity on corporate boards as a multi-dimensional and multi-level phenomenon: from duality to unity of theoretical and practical perspectives

Sabina Tasheva

INTRODUCTION

This work reviews and synthesizes theoretical and empirical advancement in the area of diversity and corporate governance since 2012. The aim is to present an update from the review published in the *Sage Handbook of Corporate Governance* (Nielsen, 2012). While 10 years ago, board diversity was an emerging topic in the field and mostly referred to women on corporate boards, both the corporate landscape and academic literature have changed significantly since. Not only have boards become more diverse since but our understanding of diversity is continuously expanding. This chapter discusses the many advances in the field and proposes directions for future research.

DELVING DEEPER INTO DIVERSITY OF WHAT?

In contrast to 2012, empirical contributions on board diversity are abundant in 2022. While in the early years of diversity and governance discussions, attention has mostly been devoted to board gender diversity, the nature of the discourse has changed significantly. The predominance of gender studies has led in the past many to associate the term "board diversity" with gender diversity or women directors. Yet, recently scholars have moved beyond narrow conceptualizations of diversity and focused on the consequences of different types of diversity in the context of boards.

One of the main changes in the discourses of boards and governance over the past decade is the focus on the individual rather than the organization or business perspective. The often cited "business case for diversity" is now largely established in the academic literature and business practice due to the wide acceptance of the McKinsey Diversity Reports (Barta, Kleiner & Neumann, 2012; Dolan et al., 2020; Hunt et al., 2018; Hunt, Layton & Prince, 2015). Organizations no longer need to argue why we should hire women or other diverse individuals; rather, the focus is on the unique perspectives and experiences that they bring along.

The discussion has further expanded to incorporate foreigners on top management teams and boards of directors (Nielsen, 2010; Nielsen & Nielsen, 2013; Oxelheim et al., 2013) and racial and ethnic minorities (Buse, Bernstein & Billimoria, 2016; Guest, 2019) and various forms of international experience (Al Mamun et al., Chapter 6 in this *Handbook*; Rivas, 2012). In 2013, Johnson, Schnatterly and Hill (2013) demonstrated the increased focus on directors' characteristics rather than independence and systematically reviewed the literature according to the categorization of diversity in human capital, social capital and demographic characteristics. Tasheva and Hillman (2019) further developed the arguments for why these three specific sources of diversity matter and how they may have different implications depending on the type of tasks we are looking into and the interactions among different levels of theory and analysis.

Furthermore, recent advances in the diversity and inclusion literature advocate broader conceptualizations of diversity encompassing various forms of "humanness" and human experience such as visible and invisible disability, neurodiversity, mental health, parental policies, sexual harassment and domestic violence. While these issues have rarely been discussed in the context of boards and corporate governance, with the increasing transparency and use of social media, they offer fruitful avenues for future research on diversity and corporate governance.

DUALITY VS SPECTRUM

One of the most recent advances in the diversity and corporate governance literature is the conceptualization of diversity as a multi-level construct that exists not only within the board or top management team (TMT) but also within the individual (Tasheva & Hillman, 2019). While diversity is typically defined at the team level of analysis, between individuals within the team, the definition of diversity as intra-personal diversity captures the variety of individual characteristics or experiences. Specifically, intra-personal diversity or personal range allows us to investigate the impact of multiple individual traits and experiences on individual and team-level behaviour. Tasheva and Hillman (2019) argue that while we often classify individuals based on their predominant characteristics, many of us have a personal range in various characteristics/experiences and that such personal range needs to be account for theoretically.

For instance, in the early days of research on board diversity, the gender discussion has been largely focused on women vs men categorization, predominantly arguing that women face significant barriers in reaching TMT and board positions and thus need to be supported and given equal opportunities (Ibarra, Ely & Kolb, 2013). In this context, discussion of gay and lesbian directors was very limited. As Özbilgin and Ebril (Chapter 4 in this *Handbook*) note, "LGBT+ equality has been called 'the last acceptable prejudice' since the early 2010s" (Noga-Styron, Reasons & Peacock, 2012). However, with the increasing theoretical advancements (Tasheva & Hillman, 2019) and increasing acceptance of the rights of the LGBQT+ individuals, we can create greater awareness and understanding of the phenomenon of board gender diversity. Gender diversity can no longer be defined and measured as a simple dummy variable accounting to 0 or 1 but needs to be understood and studied in all of its complexity.

The gender discussion has further been driven by arguments regarding social role theories (Eagly & Steffen, 1984; Ibarra et al., 2013), suggesting that we often associate women with predominantly female attributes and men with predominantly male attributes. As such, we expect women and men to behave in certain ways, without accounting for the fact that there is a variation between individuals within a certain gender; that is, some women may exhibit predominantly male characteristics and vice versa, some males may exhibit predominantly female attributes and behaviour. Consequently, we need to recognize that even within the men vs women categorization, we all range within a spectrum rather than representing two opposite categories, or duality. The implication of this realization for board diversity is that we no longer need to focus on whether a director is male or female by gender. Rather, we need to explore the extent to which each individual presents a range of successful leadership characteristics regardless of whether we perceive such characteristics as female and male attributes. Moreover, research can demonstrate how individuals can successfully balance the somewhat opposing values and attributes within themselves before learning how to balance these gender dynamics within the board/team.

More importantly, the increasing awareness and acceptance of LGBTQ+ or non-binary employees, opens new avenues for conceptualizing and studying diversity. When Amy Hillman and I published our *Academy Review* article on "Integrating diversity at different levels of analysis" (Tasheva & Hillman, 2019) we were aware of the complexities of personal range in gender. Yet, we shied away from theorizing about it in what was already a complex theory piece. However, it challenged us to list as a limitation what is indeed a very significant phenomenon that we have been trying to sweep underneath the carpet: both in our society and in academic and corporate leadership. Discussion of intra-personal diversity or personal range in gender seemed too hard to bring on the table both in terms of theoretical and practical implications. Will the personal range in gender increase the variety of perspectives and inclusion in team? And would gender-diverse individuals serve as bridges between individuals representing the two polarities? Or would such intra-personal diversity rather trigger even stronger social categorization that will actually prevent them from sharing their unique experience and perspectives? These are the questions we asked, to which we did not have an immediate answer. Mustafa Özbilgin and Cihat Ebril (Chapter 4 in this *Handbook*) offer a wonderful overview of the complexity of the topic. It is only through recognizing the variety within an individual or the personal range that we can adequately study and understand the true dynamics of diversity in the context of corporate boards.

The discussion of duality vs spectrum is not limited to gender. Race, nationality and ethnicity are further avenues in which we need to allow for spectrum rather than duality if we mean to be inclusive in the context of corporate governance. LaFramboise et al. (1993) presented five theoretical models of second culture acquisition and recognized the complex consequences of bi- and multi-culturalism for the individual. While bi-culturalism may often lead to a sense of psychological divide and suffering, it also offers the benefits of double-consciousness or switching between different models of cultural consciousness and behavior. Piaskowska and Trojanowski (2014) conducted one of the first explorations of the impact of bi-culturalism at the apex of organizations where demands on executive decision-makers' cognitions are extremely high. Their study suggests that TMT international orientation can positively moderated the negative impact of cultural differences and host country risk on acquisition ownership stakes. Hence, bi-culturalism and multi-culturalism of top executives can bring significant benefits for multinational corporations' (MNCs) global strategy. Future research needs to further explore the impact of bi-culturalism and multi-culturalism on the decision-making and performance of individual directors and collectively the board of directors.

MULTI-DIMENSIONALITY

Beyond identifying relevant dimensions, there has been an increasing understanding in the literature that we need to consider multiple characteristics simultaneously. While previously this has been done by interacting diversity dimensions at the team level (Pelled, Eisenhardt & Xin, 1999), the current advancements in the field suggest that the interactions may occur at both individual and team levels of analysis (Tasheva & Hillman, 2019). We as individuals are multidimensional; and whereas certain characteristics such as human and social capital may be relevant to the board roles, we also bring other characteristics to the team that may play an important role in both social categorization and information-processing.

At the same time, with the increasing pressures for including minorities, there has been too much emphasis on directors' demographics such as gender and race while their highly relevant human capital and social capital characteristics have been neglected. Nielsen and Huse (2010a) demonstrate that it is not the gender of women directors per se but their values and human capital that determine their contribution to board decision-making and strategic involvement. By the same token, Mendiratta (2019) demonstrates that in the context of US S&P 500 boards, gender may not have direct effect on performance but demographic fault lines based on gender and human capital are likely to determine the performance implications of board composition.

Nielsen (2012) suggested the use of demographic fault lines in boards and governance research and they have been successfully integrated in board research and advancing our understanding of board dynamics. Theory and research on demographic fault lines (Lau and Murnighan, 1998), which considers simultaneously multiple aspects of individual members' characteristics, theorizes and estimates the probability of forming sub-groups based on similarity in more than one attribute. Empirical studies confirm that group fault lines are a powerful predictor of team dynamics and performance (Lau & Murnighan, 2005; Thatcher & Patel, 2011, 2012) and hold great promise for uncovering the simultaneous effects of multiple group composition aspects. Mendiratta (Chapter 13) and Vanderbeek (Chapter 12) in this *Handbook* offer comprehensive reviews of theory and research on fault lines in the concept of boards. Their contributions unequivocally suggest that if we are to understand the composition and dynamics of corporate boards, we need to move from uni-dimensional to multi-dimensional conceptualizations and measures of diversity.

INTERSECTIONALITY

Another great advancement in the boards and governance literature is the discussion of intersectionality. Intersectionality plays an important role in conceptualizing board composition, as individuals who are disadvantaged on more than one dimension (e.g. gender and nationality, age and disability) are likely to experience higher degree of discrimination and harassment. Nkomo et al. (2019) note that most researchers shy away from the complexities of intersectionality while the rare exceptions provide evidence that stereotypes associated with multiple characteristics combine to influence the perception of employees (Hall et al., 2019). Delving deeper into the individual level of analysis requires paying close attention to issues of personal range and intersectionality and their implications for individual behaviour and performance in the workplace. Specifically, future research needs to focus on how individuals who are minorities on more than one characteristic (e.g. gender and social status or experience or education) can navigate the corporate landscape and not only secure positions on corporate boards but are also able to exert influence on board decisions in the context of board decision-making. Prior research suggests that networks may be a mechanism through which individuals can mitigate minority status (Westphal & Milton, 2000); hence researchers may explore how internal and external social capital can help overcome disadvantages associated with intersectionality.

MULTI-LEVEL PERSPECTIVES

Diversity is a multi-level phenomenon that needs to be approached from a multi-level perspective both theoretically and empirically. Typically, prior research applying a multi-level lens has considered the multi-level contextual moderators on the diversity–performance relationship. Scholars have increasingly recognized that the consequences of diversity are shaped not only by the individuals and teams involved but also by the broader social context such as organizational and national contexts. As witnessed with the corporate governance reforms and guidelines, decision-makers at the national level can implement policies and practices that reduce the negative attitudes towards diversity. Based on this criticism of the individual approach to understanding diversity, attention is increasingly being paid to the different layers of context in which diversity is embedded, and the influence that factors at individual, group, organizational and societal levels may exert on the consequences of diversity (Jackson, Joshi & Erhardt, 2003).

More importantly, researchers are increasingly recognizing the upward multi-level influences in research on diversity in boards and governance. Theoretically, we need to account for the fact that certain individuals may have more influence on decision-making than others and that models of board diversity need to model such influences in board members interaction. More significantly, with the advent of movements such as Black Lives Matter and #MeToo, we increasingly recognize that individuals can have an influence on organizational and societal outcomes as well. This too needs to be integrated in future research on diversity and corporate governance by applying novel theories and methodologies that account for modelling of such megatrends and events.

FUTURE OF BOARD DIVERSITY RESEARCH

An important direction for future research on diversity and corporate governance is the exploration of the impact of hybrid board meetings on the dynamics of power and politics in corporate boards. Whereas prior to the Covid-19 pandemic, most board meetings required physical presence, the future of corporate boards is likely to represent the movement towards hybrid modes of working. This may have important implications for board dynamics and behaviour. Past research suggests that many of the important decisions are taken outside the boardroom, in the social context. If, due to travel restrictions and modified mode of working, social interactions are limited, this may play out significantly in terms of power and influence and social dynamics and sub-group formations in corporate boards. Innovative research methods will be needed to explore the implications of this trend for the dynamics and effectiveness of corporate boards and particularly how diverse individuals can make valuable contributions in the context of hybrid board meetings.

Moreover, with the increasing role of social media in creating networks and disseminating information, big data availability and timely availability of data may have important implications. Researchers may have access to real-time data and observe and conceptualize team-level heuristics in decision-making. At the same time, data availability may suggest real-time monitoring of decision-making and their implications for individuals, business and societies. Such developments may have important implications for the way we conceptualize and measure board accountability and the role that diversity plays in corporate governance and such processes.

Last but not least, real-time access to data my allow research to catch up with reality and rather than documenting what happened in the past, researchers may be able to inform practice in a timely manner. Moving from explanatory modes of research based on past data to predictions of the future may increase the applicability of academic research for board decision-making.

REFERENCES

Barta, T., Kleiner, M., & Neumann, T. (2012). Is there a payoff from top-team diversity? *McKinsey Quarterly*, 12(April), 65–6.

Buse, K., Bernstein, R. S., & Bilimoria, D. (2016). The influence of board diversity, board diversity policies and practices, and board inclusion behaviors on nonprofit governance practices. *Journal of Business Ethics*, 133(1), 179–91.

Dolan, K., Hunt, V., Prince, S., & Sancier-Sultan, S. (2020). Diversity still matters. *McKinsey Quarterly* (May), 1–7.

Eagly, A. H., & Steffen, V. J. (1984). Gender stereotypes stem from the distribution of women and men into social roles. *Journal of Personality and Social Psychology*, 46(4), 735–54.

Guest, P. M. (2019). Does board ethnic diversity impact board monitoring outcomes? *British Journal of Management*, 30(1), 53–74.

Hall, E. V., Hall, A. V., Galinsky, A. D., & Phillips, K. W. (2019). MOSAIC: a model of stereotyping through associated and intersectional categories. *Academy of Management Review*, 44, 643–72.

Hunt, V., Layton, D., & Prince, S. (2015). Diversity matters. *McKinsey & Company*, 1(1), 15–29.

Hunt, V., Prince, S., Dixon-Fyle, S., & Yee, L. (2018). Delivering through diversity. McKinsey & Company, https://www.mckinsey.com/capabilities/people-and-organizational-performance/our-insights/delivering-through-diversity.

Ibarra, H., Ely, R., & Kolb, D. (2013). Women rising: the unseen barriers. *Harvard Business Review*, 91(9), 60–66.

Jackson, S. E., Joshi, A., & Erhardt, N. L. (2003). Recent research on team and organizational diversity: SWOT analysis and implications. *Journal of Management*, 29(6), 801–30.

Johnson, S. G., Schnatterly, K., & Hill, A. D. (2013). Board composition beyond independence: social capital, human capital, and demographics. *Journal of Management*, 39(1), 232–62.

LaFromboise, T., Coleman, H. L., & Gerton, J. (1993). Psychological impact of biculturalism: evidence and theory. *Psychological Bulletin*, 114(3), 395.

Lau, D. C. & Murnighan, J. K. (1998). Demographic diversity and faultlines: the compositional dynamics of organizational groups. *Academy of Management Review*, 23, 325–40.

Lau, D. C. & Murnighan, J. K. (2005). Interactions within groups and subgroups: the effects of demographic faultlines. *Academy of Management Journal*, 48, 645–59.

Mendiratta, E. (2019, July). Not just a woman or a man: influence of team faultlines on board gender diversity-firm performance. *Academy of Management Proceedings*, 2019(1), 14224.

Nielsen, S. (2010). Top management team diversity: a review of theories and methodologies. *International Journal of Management Reviews*, 12(3), 301–16.

Nielsen, S. (2012). Diversity among senior executives and board directors. In T. Clarke & D. Branson (eds), *The SAGE Handbook of Corporate Governance*, Thousand Oaks, CA: Sage, pp. 345–62.

Nielsen, S. & Huse, M. (2010a). The contribution of women on boards of directors: going beyond the surface. *Corporate Governance: An International Review*, 18(2), 136–48.

Nielsen, S. & Huse, M. (2010b). Women directors' contribution to board decision making and strategic involvement: the role of equality perception. *European Management Review*, 7(1), 16–29.

Nielsen, B. B. & Nielsen, S. (2013). Top management team nationality diversity and firm performance: a multilevel study. *Strategic Management Journal*, 34(3), 373–82.

Nkomo, S. M., Bell, M. P., Roberts, L. M., Joshi, A., & Thatcher, S. M. (2019). Diversity at a critical juncture: new theories for a complex phenomenon. *Academy of Management Review*, 44(3), 498–517.

Noga-Styron, K. E., Reasons, C. E., & Peacock, D. (2012). The last acceptable prejudice: an overview of LGBT social and criminal injustice issues within the USA. *Contemporary Justice Review*, 15(4), 369–98.

Oxelheim, L., Gregorič, A., Randøy, T., & Thomsen, S. (2013). On the internationalization of corporate boards: the case of Nordic firms. *Journal of International Business Studies*, 44(3), 173–94.

Pelled, L. H., Eisenhardt, K. M. & Xin, K. R. (1999). Exploring the black box: an analysis of work group diversity conflict and performance. *Administrative Science Quarterly*, 44(1), 1–28.

Piaskowska, D. & Trojanowski, G. (2014). Twice as smart? The importance of managers' formative-years' international experience for their international orientation and foreign acquisition decisions. *British Journal of Management*, 25(1), 40–57.

Rivas, J. L. (2012). Board versus TMT international experience: a study of their joint effects. *Cross Cultural Management: An International Journal*, 19(4), 546–62.

Tasheva, S. & Hillman, A. J. (2019). Integrating diversity at different levels: multilevel human capital, social capital, and demographic diversity and their implications for team effectiveness. *Academy of Management Review*, 44(4), 746–65.

Thatcher, S, & Patel, P. C. (2011). Demographic faultlines: a meta-analysis of the literature. *Journal of Applied Psychology*, 96(6), 1119.

Thatcher, S. M. & Patel, P. C. (2012). Group faultlines: a review, integration, and guide to future research. *Journal of Management*, 38(4), 969–1009.

Westphal, J. D. & Milton, L. P. (2000). How experience and network ties affect the influence of demographic minorities on corporate boards. *Administrative Science Quarterly*, 45(2), 366–98.

PART II

DIVERSITY AND CORPORATE GOVERNANCE: BEYOND HUMAN CAPITAL, SOCIAL CAPITAL AND DEMOGRAPHIC CHARACTERISTICS

3. Gender quotas on boards 20 years on: a useful tool for increased wider diversity? Achievements, "broken promises" and blindspots in the Norwegian board diversity debate

Cathrine Seierstad, Carl Åberg and Hilde Fjellvær

Around the turn of the millenium, Ansgar Gabrielsen, the Norwegian Minister of Trade and Industry, 'famously' claimed to be sick and tired of the lack of diversity and the old boys club dominating the business sector in Norway. He proposed the introduction of a gender quota law for boards of Public Limited Companies (PLCs)[1] in 2002. Now, we can discuss whether, 20 years down the line, Gabrielsen's ambition of creating more diversity in the upper echelons, particularly in corporate boards, has succeeded.

Internationally, there has been an increased focus on board diversity, in particular in regard to gender diversity on boards. The international domino or snowball effect (Machold, Huse, Hansen and Brogi, 2013) in terms of increased focus on and use of strategies to increase the share of women on boards (WOB) is extensively documented (Heidenreich and Storvik, 2010; Teigen, 2012; Terjesen et al., 2015; Kirsch, 2018; Mensi-Klarbach and Seierstad, 2020). Nevertheless, the focus on gender is a relatively narrow diversity indicator. There are some notable exceptions in some countries where the board diversity focus and initiative have stretched to other dimensions. An example is the UK where, following from the Lord Davies Report (Davies, 2011) focusing on gender in the FTSE100/250 boards, the government initiated and funded the Parker Review focusing on ethnic diversity on UK boards (Parker Review, 2017). The same extended board diversity focus has largely been missing in other countries, Norway included.

Diversity as a concept is multifaceted and tricky in the sense that the meaning of diversity and what it entails is unclear. Kirton and Green (2015: 2) illustrate how diversity can be a descriptor of the workforce or group that can refer to a wide range of differences. These can be either at social group level, such as gender, race/ethnicity, age, religion, disability or sexual orientation, or they can be individual characteristics, such as qualifications, background, lifestyle, personality, interest, talents, values, experiences and many others. Diversity can also be described as having visible or invisible dimensions or be at the surface level (such as demographic differences) or deep-level differences (such as personal differences). Hence, when organisations and/or politicians (or governance scholars for that matter) talk about diversity, what they mean is often unclear. Tatli, Vassilipoulou, Ariss and Özbilgin (2012), building on the work of Lombardo et al. (2009, 2010), argue that the meaning of diversity and the types of initiatives (in their study of diversity management) is contextually bound, which indicates that meanings and dimensions of diversity and acceptance of initiatives is context (country) specific. They argue that "diversity has no universal fixed meaning but is contextual, contested and temporal. Temporarily fixed definitions and frames of diversity are path-dependent and shaped by the regulatory context. Thus, unique national histories and the context of regulation are key determinants of the ways in which the concept is redefined as it crosses national and regional borders" (Tatli et al., 2012: 293). Tatli et al. (2012) also emphasise how concepts are stretched, fixed, shrunk and bent to the specific context they operate in. In addition, they acknowledge that in considering questions about diversity, it is important to be aware of taboos, the 'blindspots' of what is missing from the debates in the different contexts.

In this chapter we aim to reflect on the board diversity debate in Norway. We propose that the gender quota law has very much started and shaped the board diversity debate in Norway, and hence take that as our starting point. We will comment on the wider diversity effects of the gender quota law, the understanding of diversity in the Norwegian board context as well as highlight some of the blind spots in the board diversity debate. We will also reflect on some of the 'broken promises'/the implicit expectations of domino effects. Does board diversity mean the same thing in different countries? Does it mean the same within the board context as in other parts of society? What kind of diversity is desired and sought after?

The chapter is organised as follows; first, we will comment on the background for and introduction of the quota law. Next, we will present a reflection on the diversity effects of the quota law 20 years on, followed by a reflection on its wider effects. Finally, we will present a discussion and conclusion.

THE INTRODUCTION OF THE QUOTA LAW

The underrepresentation of women in senior positions in the private sector, particularly at board level, has received an increased interest since the 1980s in Norway (Seierstad and Huse, 2017). A wide range of initiatives and policies were introduced at different stages, much pushed forward by women in politics and the civil service (Seierstad, Warner-Søderholm, Torchia and Huse, 2017). The nature of the initiatives varied, from soft initiatives such as board-ready women programme, networks and databases to the introduction of the quota law. In 2003, the parliament ratified the quota law, as proposed by Ansgar Gabrielsen. With Gabrielsen, the proposed quota law was supported and rationalised not only by justice case arguments, which had dominated the board debate prior to 2002, but also with business case arguments and ideas around value creation (Sørensen, 2011, 2013; Seierstad et al., 2017). The requirement of the gender quota law dictates a gender balance on PLC boards of 40 per cent (ranging from 33 per cent to 50 per cent for smaller boards).[2] The gender quota law was implemented from 2006 for new companies, with a two-year grace period ending in 2008 for existing PLCs. Hence, it has been applicable to all PLCs since January 2008.

When the gender quota law was ratified, the share of women on PLC boards was only around 8 per cent. The law was controversial and heavily debated in politics and in the private sector. For example, the Confederation of Norwegian Enterprises (NHO) were negative to a gender quota law, and due to the relatively strong opposition, the gender quota law was introduced as a 'sunset law', a law that would never be put in place/enforced, if companies (PLCs) voluntarily increased the share of women on their boards. In 2005, after two years of the voluntary increase period, the share of women had increased to around 17 per cent, not enough for the law to be withdrawn; hence, from January 2006 it was enforced. The gender quota law in Norway has strong penalties for non-compliance; hence, the quota target was met shortly after the introduction. While heavily debated when introduced, the gender quota law has been widely accepted and to a large extent, the quota has support both in politics and in the private sector. This might be due to the contextual setting of Norway, with a long history of using quotas in areas of the labour market and in politics (see Seierstad and Huse, 2017).

Reflections on the Gender Quota Law: Twenty Years On

Being the first country to introduce a gender quota law for board positions and consistently being ranked amongst the most gender-equal countries of the world, internationally, Norway has received a lot of attention and praise for their equality/diversity achievements. Nevertheless, there are many nuances to Norway's achievement in terms of both gender balance and diversity. In this section we comment on some of the effects and lessons learned from the Norwegian case.

Narrow compliance
As mentioned earlier, the requirement of the gender quota law in Norway varies from 33 per cent to 50 per cent depending on board size, but with 40 per cent being the requirement for boards with ten or more directors. The gender quota law is a gender-neutral law; the wording in the law is 'minimum representation of each sex'. Kanter (1977) suggests that a balanced group has a ratio from 60:40 to 50:50, while a tilted group has a ratio of 65:35, a skewed group 85:15 and a uniform group only has one type (i.e. men or women). The Norwegian gender quota law indicates a balanced group, a characteristic of which is that you no longer have in–out groups; thus one might expect that once groups becomes balanced, we might observe a further increase beyond minimum requirement (40 per cent), to fully balanced (50 per cent). The gender quota law has strong penalties/sanctions for non-compliance (litigation) and consequently the quota target was met shortly after the introduction. Nevertheless, while we have observed a modest increase beyond the minimum requirement, PLC boards have not yet reached the stage of full balances. Le Bruyn and Seierstad (2020) found that as of 2019, the share of women on PLC boards was

around 43 per cent. This indicates compliance with the gender quota law, yet perhaps not full embracement of completely gender diverse boards.

Decline of PLCs

When the gender quota law was implemented in 2006, there were around 445 PLC companies in Norway. In 2019, this number had declined to less than 200 (Le Bruyn and Seierstad, 2020). As Le Bruyn and Seierstad (2020) demonstrate, as of 2019 there were more than 340,000 companies in Norway, less than 1 per cent (0.06) of which are PLCs and affected by the gender quota law.[3] This is interesting as there is a wide acceptance of the quota law for PLC boards, yet the number of companies affected is very low. Originally, quota proponents predicted a voluntary spill-over to private sector companies not affected by the law (limited companies) (Seierstad et al., 2021a). However, as of 2019, this was not the case and the share of women on limited companies had a very modest increase from around 16 per cent to around 18 per cent (Le Bruyn and Seierstad, 2020). Another interesting factor is that for the companies that changed company form from PLC to limited, one can observe an increase in the share of women to around 30 per cent in 2008, followed by a sharp decrease to around 16 per cent by 2019.

Taken together, this may indicate that company boards in general do not fully embrace the idea that increased gender diversity is important for good board work and corporate governance, and the applauded board diversity initiative in Norway is rather narrow in reach, limited to a decreasing number of PLC boards. Thus, despite the success on PLC boards, the use of gender quotas and contribution/importance of gender diversity on boards in general can be interpreted as contested.

Women directors: golden skirts, the decline of the golden skirts and diversity

One of the early findings following the introduction of the gender quota law was the increase of a group of directors holding multiple PLC directorships, 'prominent directors' (Seierstad and Opsahl, 2011). In 2002, before the introduction of the gender quota law, seven of the 91 directors holding more than one PLC directorship were women. After the introduction of the gender quota law, the level of prominence levelled out with 107 women and 117 men holding two or more directorships. Seierstad and Opsahl (2011) also looked at the level of prominence within this group and found that in 2009, after the full implementation of the quota law, all directors holding seven or more directorships were women and the maximum number of directorships one director had was nine. The group of women holding multiple directorships received a lot of attention in the media as well as in academic circles. This group was often referred to as the 'golden skirts' (particularly by the media). The 'golden skirts' was a sign that although gender diversity on boards increased, the actual diversity of directors on boards decreased as there was some recycling of the same women. In 2016, the maximum number of directorships one director held had decreased to five, around the same level as before the introduction of the law. Hence, 'the golden skirts' were, as Seierstad and Opsahl (2011) proposed, only an early effect of the gender quota law.

Within research, media and the private sector, there has also been an interest in who the women that retained seats on boards following the introduction of the gender quota law are. Huse (2013) investigated the characteristics and identified four clusters of women who got directorships shortly following the introduction: younger women, experienced businesswomen, women with experience in politics and women who already had board positions following the introduction of the law. Following Huse (2011), Seierstad, Tatli, Aldossari and Huse (2021b) took a Bourdieuian approach and investigated the life and career trajectories of 31 women characterised as prominent directors. They examined to what extent the forced structural changes (in this case the quota), challenged what are considered appropriate and legitimate capital(s) on corporate boards (the field in Bourdieu's term). They suggest that the external push through state-imposed quota regulations has broadened the field (corporate board context) to become more gender inclusive. As a result, a much wider set of experiences and backgrounds, social and cultural capital, are considered legitimate.

Professionalism of the board nomination/recruitment process
Finally, Seierstad, Healy, Le Bruyn and Fjellvær (2021a) found that over a ten-year period following the introduction of the gender quota law, directors on PLC boards reported increased formalisation and professionalism in the recruitment/nomination process, more transparency and increased focus on board skills and competencies. Seierstad et al. (2021a) reported an increased focus on competence, experience and fit for directors and on boards as a unit, more use of board evaluations to provide information on "what they have and what they need", as well as more use of head-hunters. These factors are considered positive and important for attracting and maintaining a more diverse board focusing on diversity also beyond gender. However, this has yet to be studied on a larger scale. To further an enlarged diversity focus, there is a potential for increased focus and understanding of how these dimensions may be influenced.

Wider Effects of the Gender Quota Law

As pointed out at the outset of this chapter there were implicit expectations from stakeholders that the implementation of the gender quota law should not only change gender diversity on PLC boards, but that over some time one should also observe significant spill-over effects to other domains of the corporate world. In the following section we discuss how particularly in the Norwegian context we can instead observe a development of equality silos and a narrow understanding of diversity.

Equality/quota silo
The gender quota law supporters envisioned a spill-over effect of increased diversity. However, such effects have been difficult to prove (Bertrand et al., 2019; Seierstad et al., 2021a). Seierstad et al. (2021a) set out to investigate to what extent the gender quota law for board positions led to a positive equality reach, both internally (PLC board context) and nationally, but concluded that the equality reach is limited to what

they refer to as a PLC equality silo. They found increased internal equality reach within the board setting, where the proportion of women as chair and deputy chair, what they refer to as "access to power and influence", has increased. Moreover, the increased diversity within the boardroom is experienced as positive, valuable and accepted. Still, Seierstad et al. (2021a) suggest that the quota silo has a hard casing as they only observe moderate changes, or spill-over effects, to other private sector boards (limited) and the wider organisational setting (focusing on CEO positions). Nevertheless, considering that change takes time, the potential for a wider diversity spill-over will be an important area to continue to study.

Narrow understanding of diversity
It is apparent that the diversity debate in Norway tends to be centred around gender, which is largely due to the introduction of the gender quota law and the international and national attention on this dimension. For example, the Norwegian Code of Conduct for Corporate Governance (NUES) (2018) highlights how diversity is an important element for good corporate governance. It suggests: "The composition of the board of directors should ensure that the board can attend to the common interests of all shareholders and meets the company's need for expertise, capacity and diversity" (NUES, 2018: 31). Interestingly, the NUES goes on from a rather generic mention of diversity to demonstrate and specify gender: "The composition of the board of directors as a whole should represent sufficient diversity of background and expertise to help ensure that the board carries out its work in a satisfactory manner. In this respect due attention should be paid to the balance between male and female members of the board. The board is responsible as a collegiate body for balancing the interests of various stakeholders to promote value creation by the company. The board should be made up of individuals who are willing and able to work as a team" (NUES, 2018: 32).

Both Huse (2011) and Seierstad et al. (2021b) found that, among the group of women entering boards following the introduction of the gender quota law, there was some heterogeneity in terms of dimensions such as age, education, industry and so on. However, there are few studies that have looked at the group of male PLC directors following the introduction of the gender quota law or increased diversity beyond gender. It would be interesting to know if the gender quota law also had consequences on the representation of male directors in terms of diversity dimensions such as age, educational/industry background.

Taken together, the gender quota law and Code of Conduct for Corporate Governance focus on a rather narrow understanding and focus of board diversity and we know little beyond gender diversity and within the group of women. This understanding can perhaps have the unintended consequence that other forms of diversity, or intersectionality (the interlink between different forms of diversity) is missing from political and organisational debates, meaning that Norway, which was originally seen as the 'leader' of board diversity, might be lagging behind.

The use of quotas to increase board diversity internationally

In Europe, as of 2018, ten European countries have introduced gender quota laws for corporate boards (Norway, Spain, Iceland, France, Italy, Belgium, the Netherlands, Germany, Austria and Portugal), yet with great diversity in terms of design and coverage. Mensi-Klarbach and Seierstad (2020) analysed all gender quota laws and demonstrated great variety among the 'quota countries' both in terms of hardness (e.g. level of sanctions for non-compliance) and progressiveness (ambition of the quota law). In Europe, there is an increase in focus on initiatives to increase diversity, mainly focusing on gender, and there has been an increased acceptance of using radical initiatives, such as quotas, to speed up that process. Nevertheless, as we found in the case of Norway, the reach of companies is often rather limited (largest companies), and the success of the quota very much relies on penalties for non-compliance.

In addition to the use of gender quota laws to increase gender diversity, several other countries have introduced initiatives such as voluntary targets (Seierstad, Gabaldon and Mensi-Klarbach, 2017). Interestingly, also within these countries, the focus tends to be on gender, hence a rather narrow understanding and focus of diversity. As mentioned, one notable exception is the UK where the Lord Davies Report (2011) and Hampton Alexander Review (2016) focusing on gender was followed by the Parker Review (2016) focusing on ethnic diversity. Hence, while there was originally a focus on gender diversity, this has developed into a wider diversity focus which also includes ethnicity in the UK setting. Contextually, this makes sense considering the UK diversity climate and history with a strong focus on ethnicity (Tatli et al., 2012). This exemplifies the potential temporal and developmental dimension of the board diversity debate within a country.

DISCUSSION AND RESEARCH AGENDA

Discussions about the importance of board diversity will increase in intensity following discussions of the importance and push for sustainability, diversity and good corporate governance, including pressure from UN, EU and national levels. In this chapter, we have mainly focused on the board diversity debate in Norway and the introduction of the gender quota law as a backdrop to understanding the board diversity debate and climate.

The achievements of the gender quota law are notable. First, the gender quota law target was met, and qualified women entered Norwegian boardrooms. Moreover, although not a direct effect of the gender quota law, there is an increase in the use of board evaluations. These can be very useful in identifying the skills and competences of boards and what is missing. Thus, the use of board evaluations can potentially reveal a lack of diversity and an active search for more diversity. Further, an increased use of executive search advisors and nomination committees has promoted a professionalism of board recruitment and nomination procedures. Moreover, both the feeling of equality and acceptance of women directors and also initiatives to increase diversity have increased. Finally, Norway can take the credit for the increased focus on and use of strategies to increase gender board diversity internationally.

Nevertheless, while the gender quota law has been a success in terms of creating increased internal gender equality and have an international equality reach (Seierstad et al., 2021a), spill-over effects to other types of private sector boards have been rather modest. Moreover, the board diversity debate in Norway is highly dominated by the gender focus, leading us to question if what we have is increased gender diversity and what do we know about other types of diversity, including diversity among men? For example, is this group more homogeneous following the introduction of the quota law? Hence, we question whether the acceptance of success in terms of increasing gender diversity on boards has acted as a smokescreen for discussions of other types of diversity.

Elements of the framework from Lombardo et al. (2010) and Tatli et al. (2012) can help us sum up the Norwegian board diversity debate. To remind you, they argue that concepts, such as equality/diversity/diversity management, are contextual, contested and temporal. In the case of the Norwegian board diversity debate, it is clear the context and history of focusing on gender equality and the use of quotas in areas of the public sector and politics was important for the acceptance of a gender quota law, also within the PLC context and this has further shaped the board diversity debate. We suggest that the construction of the meaning of the board diversity debate in Norway is currently *fixed* around the notion of gender diversity, which has historically been important in the Norwegian equality debate and within political strategies and initiatives. It is *stretched* to an acceptance of quotas as a tool to increase gender diversity, also in the private sector. It is *bent* away from social and individual justice case rationales, which dominated the board diversity debate prior to the acceptance of the gender quota law, to business case and value creation logic. Finally, the board diversity debate is *shrunk* to a rather narrow (and decreasing) PLC board context with little focus on other areas, such as limited companies, which is the largest company form.

Our analysis also reveals several blind spots in the Norwegian board diversity debate. The rather narrow understanding of board diversity (gender) means that those other forms of diversity, both at group and individual level, are ignored. Moreover, we argue that the rather narrow focus on the shrinking number of PLC boards is a blind spot as gender board diversity in limited companies has been relatively stable (and low) since the introduction of the quota law, which is largely missing from the Norwegian 'success story' of diversity on boards.

Research Agenda

We suggest that there is time and room for the Norwegian board diversity debate to be revisited and revaluated, and to critically ask what needs to be done to further increase board diversity. This can be done at multiple levels and from multiple actors, including political (initiatives), amendments to the Norwegian Code of Conduct, academic discussion and knowledge as well as led by organisations. Recent discussions on public opinion suggests that there may be change underway in how Norwegian companies and their boards consider how diversity issues concern them. Thus, researchers should cast a wide net to study where and how such initiatives are surfacing, so that we can uncover the blind spots. In particular, we suggest that there is a need for research focusing on the following areas:

- Can we observe any increased diversity or diversity focus within the Norwegian board setting?
- The group of male directors: are they still 'male, pale and stale', or do we see more diversity within this group?
- To what extent does the use of board evaluation result in more and different forms of diversity (beyond gender, age, ethnicity, highly job-related diversity dimensions and so on)?
- Is the board diversity focus on compliance or value creation?
- Shareholder/stakeholders views and perceptions on the importance of diversity: do the owner(s) push for diversity or is it the wider stakeholders?
- Diversity (focus and achievements) on limited companies' boards (not affected by the gender quota law).
- Wider gender diversity in organisation (beyond boards).
- Diversity as part of organisational sustainability focus and agenda.
- International/comparative studies of board diversity initiatives (quotas and other softer regulations).
- How board diversity debates and initiatives are, for example, contextual, contested and temporal in other countries.

CONCLUSION

In this chapter, we set out to comment on and discuss the board diversity debate in Norway with a focus on the gender quota law for PLC companies as a backdrop. In particular, we commented on to what extent the gender quota law has been a useful tool for wider board diversity, what the achievements of the gender quota law are and to what extent there have been 'broken promises' and blind spots in the Norwegian board diversity debate. Moreover, we have highlighted important areas for further research. Taken together, we argue that there is time and opportunity to broaden the board diversity debate in Norway and move beyond the rather narrow gender diversity and PLC context focus which has dominated the board diversity debate over the last decades.

NOTES

1. We refer to it as the Quota. Formally, it was an adjustment of an existing law, the Company Act.

2.   For the board of a public limited company, both sexes shall be represented as follows:
     1.   If the board has two or three members, both sexes must be represented.
     2.   If the board has four or five members, each gender shall be represented by at least two.
     3.   If the board has six to eight members, each gender shall be represented by at least three.
     4.   If the board has nine members, each gender shall be represented by at least four, and if the board has several members, each gender shall be represented by at least 40 per cent (Ot.prp.nr 97. (2002–03) *Odelstingsproposisjon nr 97*).
3.   Since 1981, the Equality Act (section 21) has regulated gender representation (similar to a quota) on public boards, committees and councils. Gender representations regulations were also implemented in other companies, such a state and municipal companies and cooperatives. Limited companies on the other hand are not affected by quota regulations (see Le Bruyn and Seierstad, 2020).

REFERENCES

Bertrand, M., Black, S., Jensen, S. & Lleras-Muney, A. (2019). Breaking the glass ceiling? The effect of board quotas on female labor market outcomes in Norway. *The Review of Economic Studies*, 86(1), 191–239. https://doi.org/10.1093/restud/rdy032.

Davies, M. (2011). *Women On Boards – The Davies Report* (No. URN 11/745). London: GEO/BIS.

Hampton-Alexander Review (2016). FTSE women leaders improving gender balance in FTSE leadership. https://assets.publishing.service.gov.uk/government/uploads/system/uploads/attachment_data/file/613085/ftse-women-leaders-hampton-alexander-review.pdf.

Heidenreich, V. & Storvik, A. E. (2010). *Rekrutteringsmønstre, erfaringer og holdninger til styrearbeid blant styremedlemmenes representanter.* Tabellrapport fra survey undersøkelse, ISF Rapport 2010, 11. Oslo: Oslo Institute for Social Research.

Huse, M. (2011). The golden skirts: changes in board composition following gender quotas on corporate boards. Australian and New Zealand Academy Meeting, Wellington, NZ.

Huse M. (2013). Characteristics and background of the Norwegian women directors. In: Machold, S., Huse, M., Hansen, K., et al. (eds), *Getting Women on Corporate Boards: A Snowball Starting in Norway.* Cheltenham, UK and Northampton, MA, USA: Edward Elgar Publishing, 69–77.

Kanter, R. M. (1977). *Men and Women of the Corporation.* New York: Basic Books.

Kirsch, A. (2018). The gender composition of corporate boards: a review and research agenda. *The Leadership Quarterly*, 29, 346–64.

Kirton, G. & Green, A. M. (2015). *The Dynamics of Managing Diversity: A Critical Approach*, 4th edn. Abingdon: Routledge.

Le Bruyn, E. G. & Seierstad, C. (2020). *Kjønnsmessig sammensetning av toppledere I forskjellige styringsformer etter kjønnskvotering i styrer i Norge.* MAGMA.

Lombardo, E., Meier, P. & Verloo, M. (2009). *The Discursive Politics of Gender Equality: Stretching, Bending and Policymaking.* London: Routledge.

Lombardo, E., Meier, P. & Verloo, M. (2010). Discursive dynamics in gender equality politics: what about 'feminist taboos'? *European Journal of Women's Studies*, 17: 105–23.

Machold, S., Huse, M., Hansen, K. & Brogi, M. (eds) (2013). *Getting Women on to Corporate Boards: A Snowball Starting in Norway.* Cheltenham, UK and Northampton, MA, USA: Edward Elgar Publishing.

Mensi-Klarbach, H. & Seierstad, C. (2020). Gender quotas on corporate boards: similarities and differences in quota scenarios. *European Management Review.* https://doi.org/10.1111/emre.12374.

NUES [The Norwegian Code of Conduct for Corporate Governance] (2018). https://nues.no/wp-content/uploads/2018/10/NUES_eng_web_okt2018_2.pdf.

Ot.prp.nr 97 (2002–03). *Odelstingsproposisjon nr 97*. Om lov om endringer i lov 13. juni 1997 nr. 44 om aksjeselskaper, lov 13. juni 1997 nr. 45 om allmennaksjeselskaper og i enkelte andre lover (likestilling i styrer i statsaksjeselskaper, statsforetak, allmennaksjeselskaper mv.).

Parker Review (2017). A report into ethnic diversity on UK boards. https://www.gov.uk/government/publications/ethnic-diversity-of-uk-boards-the-parker-review.

Seierstad, C., Gabaldon, P. & Mensi-Klarbach, H. (eds) (2017). *Gender Diversity in the Boardroom: European Perspectives on Increasing Female Participation – The Use of Different Quota Regulations*. Basingstoke: Palgrave Macmillan.

Seierstad, C. & Huse, M. (2017). Gender quotas on corporate boards in Norway: 10 years later and lessons learned. In: Seierstad, C., Gabaldon, P. & Mensi-Klarbach, H. (eds), *Gender Diversity in the Boardroom: European Perspectives on Increasing Female Participation – The Use of Different Quota Regulations*. Basingstoke: Palgrave Macmillan.

Seierstad, C. & Opsahl, T. (2011). For the few not the many? The effects of affirmative action on presence, prominence, and social capital of female directors in Norway. *Scandinavian Journal of Management*, 27, 44–54.

Seierstad, C., Healy, G., Sønju Le Bruyn Goldeng, E. & Fjellvær, H. (2021a). "A quota silo" or positive equality reach? The equality impact of gender quotas on corporate boards in Norway. *Human Resource Management Journal*, 31, 165–86. https://doi.org/10.1111/1748-8583.12288.

Seierstad, C., Tatli, A., Aldossari, M. & Huse, M. (2021b). Broadening of the field of corporate boards and legitimate capitals: an investigation into the use of gender quotas in corporate boards in Norway. *Work, Employment and Society*, 35(4), 753–73. https://doi.org/10.1177/0950017019892835.

Seierstad, C., Warner-Søderholm, G., Torchia, M. & Huse, M. (2017). Women on boards: beyond the institutional setting – the role of stakeholders and actors. *Journal of Business Ethics*, 141(2), 289–315.

Sørensen, S. Ø. (2011). Statsfeminismens møte med næringslivet. *Tidsskrift for kjønnsforskning*. (ISSN 0809-6341)(2), 102–10.

Sørensen, S. Ø. (2013). *Likestilling uten kjønn?: En studie av hvordan kjønnskvotering til bedriftsstyrer ble montert som politisk reform*. Doktoravhandlinger ved NTNU, 1503–8181.

Tatli, A., Vassilopoulou, J., Ariss, A. A. & Özbilgin, M. (2012). The role of regulatory and temporal context in the construction of diversity discourses: the case of the UK, France and Germany. *European Journal of Industrial Relations*, 18(4), 293–308. https://doi.org/10.1177/0959680112461092.

Teigen, M. (2012). Gender quotas in corporate boards: on the diffusion of a distinct national policy reform. In: Engelstad, F. & Teigen, M. (eds), *Firms, Boards and Gender Quotas: Comparative Perspectives* (Comparative Social Research Series). Bingley: Emerald.

Terjesen, S., Aguilera, R. V. & Lorenz, R. (2015). Legislating a woman's seat on the board: institutional factors driving gender quotas for boards of directors. *Journal of Business Ethics*, 128, 233–51.

4. LGBT+ in the boardroom: a rainbow agenda for change

Mustafa F. Özbilgin and Cihat Erbil

The theory of heteronormativity posits that contemporary institutions cater to the values and needs of heterosexual individuals (Schlit & Westbrook, 2009). Therefore, heteronormativity is a hegemonic order that enforces normative pressures and social expectations through an individual's life course (Öztürk & Özbilgin, 2014), based on the norms of dominant gender identity (i.e. cisgender) and sexual orientation (i.e. heterosexuality) (Lasio et al., 2019). Warner (1991) refers to how prevailing social mores and norms explicitly and tacitly enforce heterosexuality on individuals as compulsory heterosexuality. There has been growing recognition that dominant social expectations based on heterosexual and cisgender standards undermine the talent potential and human rights of LGBT+ (Lesbian, Gay, Bisexual, Transgender, and others) individuals (Özbilgin & Soytemel, 2020). This normative pressure pushes LGBT+ to society's margins, denigrating their potential contribution to work and life (Özbilgin, 2017). LGBT+ is the social movement that emerged to combat the human rights breaches and exclusion that individuals experience due to the heteronormative and cisgender impositions in social, economic and political life (Roseneil et al., 2013).

LGBT+ equality and inclusion are the future challenges in international equality, diversity and inclusion agendas. In a historic speech at the State Department in February 2021, Joe Biden promised to further LGBT+ rights through the diplomatic efforts of the USA:

> To further repair our moral leadership, I'm also issuing a presidential memo to agencies to reinvigorate our leadership on the LGBT+ issues and do it internationally. [...] We'll ensure diplomacy and foreign assistance are working to promote the rights of those individuals, included by combating criminalization and protecting LGBT+ refugees and asylum-seekers. (Alper & Shalal, 2021: 1)

This speech marks an essential step towards legitimation of sexual orientation diversity at work and life as a protected category internationally. LGBT+ equality has been called 'the last acceptable prejudice' since the early 2010s (Noga-Styron et al., 2012). Since the early 2010s, much progress has been made to legalise LGBT+ relationships and marriages and protect fundamental equal rights for LGBT+ individuals. These achievements were set against the considerable religious and politically inspired backlash, which became rampant against all forms of diversity and inclusion (Saba et al., 2021). Fifty-two years after the Stonewall uprising in New York, there is partial progress in achieving fundamental human rights for LGBT+ individuals internationally (Duberman, 1993). ILGA (2020a) research shows that less than half of the countries in the world have legal protections for LGBT+, and 81 countries have legal protection for LGBT+ in employment. The criminalisation of LGBT+ and concomitant hate crimes against LGBT+ remains unchallenged in many countries.

Although institutional forms of discrimination have reportedly harmed the school and university experience of LGBT+ individuals, Wimberly et al. (2015) identify that their attainment levels match those of heterosexual and gender binary students. Although schools and universities now graduate students who openly identify as LGBT+, their access to jobs and their ability to remain authentic in their careers is hampered by the strength of the heteronormativity in the labour market (Fric, 2017). What remains unattended in LGBT+ rights has been the challenge of promoting LGBT+ inclusion in positions of power and influence. Only a limited number of studies to date have explored LGBT+ in the boardroom. Even fewer scholars have suggested that boardroom diversity should also include sexual orientation as a diversity category (e.g. Nourafshan, 2017). There is only one remarkable example of regulation to date that covered LGBT+ inclusion in the boardroom: California State legislated that the publicly traded corporations should have either minority ethnic or LGBT+ individuals in their boardrooms (Guynn, 2020). Boardroom diversity, which started initially with demands for more women in the boardroom, has been gaining an intersectional character in recent years (Sanchez-Hucles & Davis, 2010; Samdanis & Özbilgin, 2020), and sexual orientation diversity will add to the complexity of theorisation and practices of boardroom diversity soon. Byington et al. (2021) showed that LGBT+ issues are on a meteoric rise in management studies. In this chapter, we contribute to this fast-growing field of work, asking why it is essential to have sexual orientation equality in the boardroom, and what it means to have LGBT+ in the boardroom. Finally, we offer a roadmap for organisations to capture LGBT+ talent in the boardroom.

WHY IS IT IMPERATIVE TO CONSIDER SEXUAL ORIENTATION DIVERSITY IN THE BOARDROOM?

Multiple factors render sexual orientation diversity an imperative for the boardroom. First, there is great *potential to capture top talent* if organisations consider sexual orientation as part of the boardroom diversity. As we explained above, heteronormativity permeates every aspect of institution-making. The human capital of LGBT+ is often undervalued in a heteronormative context. Inclusion of the LGBT+ individuals could help organisations tackle sexual orientation-based bias and stigma in defining notions such as talent and merit. Talent is traditionally defined as individuals with high levels of human capital (Florida, 2002). Considering the Bourdieusian expansion of capitals with social capital, cultural capital and symbolic capital (Bourdieu & Wacqant, 2013), combating bias and stigmatisation of LGBT+ individuals could help unleash their human, social, economic and cultural capital at work, offering them equal footing with heterosexual staff. Proofing of the definition of talent against bias and stigma is essential for inclusive talent practices. The low representation and invisibility of LGBT+ talent today is causing significant talent waste and exit in traditional sectors such as finance and asset management (Morrissey et al., 2018) which defines talent in narrow ways. New graduates reportedly do not wish to work in these lucrative sectors, which operate with traditional norms of compulsory heterosexuality and toxic masculinity (Griffin, 2013; Predmore, 2020). New sectors, which come with inclusive talent practices, such as the high-technology sector (Hewlett, 2011), can compete with and attract talent that the traditional sectors discourage due to their inflexible approaches that fail to provide inclusive environments. The competition between sectors for diverse talent is becoming a critical issue for the sustainability and longevity of all sectors of work and employment.

Thanks to the widening of higher education, talented people today come from highly diverse backgrounds. If nurtured in the right way, diverse talent may bring cognitive and experiential richness to organisations (Özbilgin et al., 2016; Roberson et al., 2017). Based on a calculation of 50 per cent women, 60 per cent non-Christian, 20 per cent with a disability, 13 per cent non-white, 7 per cent non-heterosexual making up the overall population in the UK (ONS, 2019), the traditional talent pool of white, able-bodied, young, middle/upper class, heterosexual men from dominant religious group constitute less than 20 per cent of the national talent pool in the UK today. Companies that only recruit from the traditional talent pool miss out on over 80 per cent of the talent pool. The proportion of talented workers from traditional backgrounds is even smaller in cosmopolitan cities, which host higher diversity across all categories (Kucukaltan & Özbilgin, 2019). Further, Florida et al. (2008) demonstrated that promoting and protecting sexual orientation diversity plays a decisive role in developing talent in the 'creative class', a concept used to define highly talented individuals. In this context, organisations must consider LGBT+ talent as part of their efforts to widen their talent pools.

Second, legitimation of sexual orientation diversity in the boardroom will allow LGBT+ board members to *experience authenticity at work*. Authenticity can be defined as "owning one's personal experiences, be they thoughts, emotions, needs, wants, preferences, or beliefs, processes captured by the injunction to know 'oneself'" (Harter, 2002: 384). Restricting authentic self-expression in the workplace causes individuals to make extra effort to hide themselves and to limit their thoughts and actions (Van den Bosch & Taris, 2014). The fact that individuals have to hide suppresses their talents and creativity. Beyond the inclusion of gender and sexual identities, the presentation of the authentic self allows individuals to use their abilities (Levitt & Ippolito, 2014) and spend the energy they would otherwise waste in passing as cis-hetero in the boardroom.

Third, the sexual orientation diversity in the boardroom can *help transform organisations* that are constrained by dysfunctional and redundant gender and sexuality hierarchies. Organisations are not neutral settings. Masculine norms widely structure relationships within organisations, and gender and sexuality hierarchies perpetuate male supremacy (Acker, 1990; Öztürk et al., 2020). While gender issues are often tackled by headcounts in boardroom decisions, ignoring the complexity of masculine domination in cultures and structures (Bourdieu, 2001; Acker, 2012), LGBT+ representation in the boardroom could bring idiosyncratic complexities such as removing the need for passing as cis-hetero at work and freedom to disclose LGBT+ identity, which could help organisations to move beyond headcounts in diversity interventions and to start tackling cultural and structural changes that allow for diversity and inclusion. For example, in a conservative industry, Allyn L. Shaw's board membership as Chief Operations Officer (COO) of the Bank of America is a striking example that could help LGBT+ inclusion in the boardroom be considered in the future. While Yahoo! Finance included Allyn L. Shaw on the Outstanding Executives list in 2020 (OUTStanding.com, 2020), his company increased the gender balance from 30 per cent to 41 per cent. Also, Shawn emphasised that being on the board as openly gay encouraged employees to exist with their diverse identities (SALT, 2019). This example highlights the complementarity between gender and sexual orientation diversity, which helped promote the former.

Fourth, representation at the top (e.g. in the boardroom), is of significant symbolic importance for organisations in showing their commitment to *capturing changing moral and social demands*. There has been a substantial push for social justice regarding LGBT+ equality (ILGA, 2020b). Leadership diversity is an intersectional concern. Leaders play significant roles in crafting their organisations' moral and cognitive worlds (Mergen and Özbilgin, 2021). Lack of leadership diversity in any category may render the organisation less desirable for talented atypical candidates and their well-being at work. Özbilgin and Erbil (2021) demonstrated a significant benefit for organisations to capture the demands of social movements such as #BlackLivesMatter, #MeToo and #LGBT+pride in securing well-being work. Therefore, boardroom diversity signals two important commitments internally and externally. The organisation captures the moral and social changes in its immediate environment.

Fifth, as Slootmaeckers et al. (2016) argued, LGBT+ inclusion is now *the litmus test* for all industries, as LGBT+ inclusion often indicates a commitment to other diversity and inclusion categories. Srikant et al. (2020) demonstrated that a broad diversity in the boardroom could present a virtuous cycle and help organisations garner positive social performance outcomes and promote greater boardroom diversity. Overall, there are many reasons why boardroom diversity should include sexual orientation diversity. Notably, there are many organisational drivers and individual benefits for promoting sexual orientation diversity in the boardroom. The following section explores what it means to have LGBT+ inclusion in the boardroom and how this manifests.

WHAT IT MEANS TO HAVE LGBT+ IN THE BOARDROOM, AND HOW LGBT+ EMERGENCE TAKES PLACE IN THE BOARDROOM

The meaning of LGBT+ inclusion in the boardroom needs to be unpacked at multiple levels. At the micro-level, as explained above, today's talent pool is more diverse than ever before in terms of sexual orientation and other diversity categories. Research shows that talented individuals are increasingly driven to find work that allows them to experience authentic self (Reis et al., 2017). However, there are some prominent examples of LGBT+ boardroom members who disclosed their sexual identities, such as *Tim Cook* (CEO of Apple) and *Beth Ford* (CEO of Lands O'Lakes) (Abadi, 2018); recent studies highlight that coming out at work remains a challenge for many individuals, especially in the process of their pursuit of leadership positions (Trau et al., 2018).

What complicates LGBT+ inclusion in the boardroom is similar to gender diversity in the boardroom: what kind of LGBT+ will be included? There are often uneven power relations among lesbians, gays, bisexuals and trans, and others. These are considered part of the LGBT+ umbrella, and varying degrees and possibilities of visibility, recognition and respectability are afforded to subgroups of LGBT+ at work and in life. Divergence of experiences among subgroups of LGBT+ means that their subjective experiences and barriers that they face en route to boardroom positions could be markedly different. For example, Dilmaghani (2018) and Buser et al. (2015) showed that lesbians display higher levels of competitiveness than gay men in their careers and that openly gay and lesbian workers would be constrained in career progression compared to their LGBT+ counterparts who pass as cis-hetero at work. Thus there remains a penalty for being out with LGBT+ identity at work.

Similar concerns are raised about what kind of women are appointed (Hillman et al., 2002) and what kind of minority ethnic and black individuals (Peterson et al., 2007) could be selected for boardroom positions through gender or ethnic quotas. Thus we need to attend to the intersectionality of the LGBT+ community. The LGBT+ acronym is an umbrella term, which brings all sexual orientation and gender identity categories together. However, this does not mean that the priorities and experiences of subgroups within the LGBT+ category are convergent. We need to acknowledge that the LGBT+ as a social movement, similar to feminist, anti-racist, postcolonial, and other movements, has a central agenda for fundamental human rights and some tensions and conflicts of interests among its subgroups and members (Kamasak et al., 2019). The most famous of such strains is between demands for acceptance of LGBT+ lives in authentically LGBT+ ways versus needs for normalisation and acceptance of LGBT+ lives as equals in a cis-gender/cis-hetero dominated world. Similar tensions exist between liberal and radical factions of feminist and post-colonial groups in terms of social movements' divergent needs for acceptance, normalisation and retention of unique and authentic identity. Therefore, it is essential to consider what dimensions of subgroups in considering how LGBT+ inclusion may mean in the boardroom as a broad-brush approach may only promote divisions and create uneven outcomes.

Huse (2011) demonstrated, in his work that used the metaphors of 'golden skirts' versus 'golden sacks', that gender quotas in Scandinavian countries have re-centred the focus of board membership from male domination to talent. This focus shift was because women were solely recruited based on their abilities. At the same time, men could make it into board positions using a more comprehensive range of mechanisms such as social and cultural ties and other unearned privileges. A similar turn needs to be achieved from the focus on LGBT+ identity and the various forms of stigmatisation and discrimination they could face to the potential contribution of LGBT+ talent to the boardroom. Research shows that LGBT+ talent substantially contributes to their organisations (Cunningham, 2011).

Although we would not like to pursue an essentialist agenda regarding specific LGBT+ talent, some studies demonstrate the unique skills that LGBT+ provide due to their different life experiences. For example, Snyder (2006) explained that LGBT+ individuals make more engaging and effective leaders due to several factors, which he terms as 'G quotient', including inclusion, adaptability, creativity, connectivity, communication, intuition and collaboration, which are specific competencies that they develop due to the challenges that they have faced in their life course. Without adopting a deterministic line of argumentation about LGBT+ talent, we would like to draw attention to some common qualities of LGBT+ individuals regarding their life experiences that prove helpful for their roles in leadership positions. Therefore, LGBT+ specific talents are conditioned by and acquired due to being and experiencing life as LGBT+ individuals. There are several other talents that LGBT+ individuals are reported to possess due to their divergent life and work experiences: First, LGBT+ individuals may develop considerable resilience over their life experiences due to the rampant and endemic nature of LGBT+ discrimination (Asakura & Craig, 2014). Such strength may present a transferable competence that helps them overcome hardship at work. Second, if an organisation provides a safe space for LGBT+ members to come out, the LGBT+ individuals may display authenticity, which is again a sought after quality in leadership positions (Webster et al., 2018). Third, LGBT+ individuals may also benefit the boardroom with their senses of empathy (Valdovinos, 2018), garnered in the process of coming out or passing, sociality and relationality, which are gained as a result of their struggles against stigmatisation, exclusion and discrimination, and adaptability, which is accrued as a result of the ambivalence that they experience across varied contexts.

While an industry or organisation may accrue the above benefits of recruiting LGBT+ talent, in the same way, they may lose such talent if they are hostile or unprepared for LGBT+ inclusion. For example, the asset management industry is the most dynamic part of the global financial services sector (Walter, 1999). However, the asset management industry leaders are alarmed that there may be a diversity drought looming in the asset management industry due to a mismatch with what the industry offers and what talented workers want (Morrissey et al., 2018). In addition, there are changing tastes in the future workforce (work–life balance, sociality at work) as they demand inclusive workplaces (Ng & Burke, 2005). There is increased competition for talented workers from other industries such as high tech and entrepreneurship. Inclusion of the LGBT+ talent, as a litmus test for all forms of inclusion, may help such sectors connect with the new normal and achieve the transformation they need in work redesign. Such inclusive leadership approaches may prepare industries and organisations to recruit, develop and retain talent from more expansive pools. If inclusion is managed well, LGBT+ talent promises new riches to the boardroom, which can help organisations to capture demographic and socio-moral changes in their environments and talent pipelines.

COMING OUT AND LGBT+ TALENT IN THE BOARDROOM

Visibility is vital for any talent to be recognised at work. Being visible also goes for LGBT+ talent in terms of symbolic, network-based, and individual visibility (McFadden & Crowley-Henry, 2018). Although organisations' discursive recognition of sexual orientation identities provides extended visibility, LGBT+ talent needs an inclusive environment and culture to be energised.

Coming out provides LGBT+ individuals with dignity and honesty at the personal level, fair and normalised relationships with colleagues (Humphrey, 1999) and a sense of belonging to the community (Toft, 2020). Therefore, processes and experiences of coming out are pivotal for LGBT+ talent to experience inclusion at work. The statement of *Jeffrey Krogh* (Managing Director, Media & Telecom Finance Team at BNP Paribas) regarding the closet experience is representative in this respect (Qvist, 2015: 1): "There's a lot of worrying, planning and energy that goes into being in the closet. That is energy that could otherwise be channelled to the job that you're there to do." As the quote suggests, coming out could provide several benefits for LGBT+ talent to unleash their potential at work.

There are three distinct parts in coming out at work for LGBT+ in the boardroom. First, there is a talent trade-off in the closet. Although progressive movements seek to provide visibility for diverse sexual orientation identities, it is still not always easy to come out at work, even in countries that protect and promote the rights of LGBT+ individuals. According to the Corporate Equality Index (CEI) report prepared by the Human Rights Campaign Foundation (HRC, 2021), even though 94 per cent of Fortune 500 companies have developed policies to prevent discrimination against gender identity, 46 per cent of LGBT+ workers across the United States remain closeted at work. HRC (2018) also revealed the prominent obstacles to coming out at work: the fear of being stereotyped, the possibility of damaging or losing relations with colleagues, the feeling of bothering other people with their concerns and the fear that colleagues would consider them as making sexual advances urge LGBT+ to stay in the closet (Özbilgin et al., 2022). However, as LGBT+ individuals move up in positions of power and influence, they may find it easier to come out with their sexual orientation and gender identities at work. In the closeted stage, instead of using the full extent of their talents, LGBT+ individuals focus on protecting themselves against discrimination and harassment, fighting hard for recognition in hostile environments, which may have homophobic, biphobic and transphobic banter and risk of involuntary outing, and achieve security in the workplace (Denier & Waite, 2019). LGBT+ individuals may trade off their gender identity with job security in such a setting. Thus, in the boardroom case, the above-cited fears could be appeased if the boardroom culture is prepared for LGBT+ inclusion, and the trade-off may be between varied forms of talent that LGBT+ individuals deploy and their performance in the boardroom.

Second, remaining in the closet wastes LGBT+ talent. In addition to stealing time and energy from productive work, being closeted is a transformative stage through which LGBT+ individuals develop cognitive and experiential skills, such as self-reflection, flexibility, originality, empathy and sociability, among others. For example, while 83 per cent of LGBT workers in the USA are in a workplace expecting them to share their social life, feeling obliged to hide their sexual orientation identity keeps them from non-work conversations and prevents them from socialising (HRC, 2014). Even though some organisations support coming out and LGBT+ rights, their culture can create a 'gay-friendly closet' by promoting the concealment of sexual orientation identity marks as required by professionalism, and hiding in the workplace turns into an acceptable practice for LGBT+ workers (Williams et al., 2009; Kelly et al., 2020). This stage of passing as cis-hetero resembles the cocoon stage in the development of the butterfly, where the LGBT+ identity remains dormant and concealed.

The third stage is coming out in the boardroom. For this to happen, LGBT+ individuals would need an LGBT+ inclusive culture. The inclusive workplace enables LGBT+ individuals to focus on their job performance and feel safe rather than concealing themselves (Lim et al., 2019). Supportive policies for coming out reportedly have the strongest correlation with the effectiveness of LGBT+ inclusion at work (Webster et al., 2018). Coming out often breaks the cocoon of LGBT+ and facilitates unleashing potential LGBT+ talent (Hewlett & Yoshino, 2016). In addition, LGBT+ supportive policies help shape the recognition and positive subjective experience of LGBT+ workers (Pichler et al., 2017).

Overall, from hostility to LGBT+ identities to their inclusion in the boardroom, there are three distinct stages of evolution. First, it is crucial to remove homophobic, biphobic and transphobic cultures and structures that render boardroom environments hostile to LGBT+ individuals. The second stage is to introduce a set of inclusive organisational behaviours in the boardroom so that the boardroom culture and practices allow room for LGBT+ identities to emerge. Third, coming out should be encouraged and made possible by rules and policies of acceptance and compatibility of LGBT+ identities with the boardroom cultures.

CONCLUSION: TOWARDS A RAINBOW AGENDA FOR PROMOTING LGBT+ INCLUSION IN THE BOARDROOM

Boardroom diversity is often framed along gender lines, focusing on equal representation of women in the main (Kakabadse et al., 2015). However, boardroom diversity has gained an intersectional character (Crenshaw, 2017) thanks to the progressive social movements, such as Pride Marches, the Black Lives Matter and the feminist movements, demanding a more inclusive agenda for boardroom diversity beyond gender. However, we also explained in the chapter that the prospects of LGBT+ inclusion meet considerable resistance in compulsory heterosexuality, which informs all aspects of social, economic and political life. In the context of compulsory heterosexuality, the inclusion of LGBT+ individuals in the boardroom is likely to happen after a long march. In this chapter, we collected evidence of the emergence of LGBT+ diversity in the boardroom, defined its parameters, identified why LGBT+ inclusion is imperative for boardroom diversity and how it would manifest. We conclude the chapter with a rainbow approach to promote LGBT+ inclusion in the boardroom. Reflecting on each colour's meaning in the rainbow flag, we propose a change agenda to promote LGBT+ inclusion.

The agenda for promoting LGBT+ inclusion in the boardroom is paved with the hurdle of heteronormativity that remains intact across many organisations. Despite these significant roadblocks, the LGBT+ movement has made tremendous progress promoting LGBT+ inclusion in the boardroom. In this section, drawing on the symbolism of the colours of the rainbow in the pride flag, we propose a change agenda for organisations to build LGBT+ inclusion in the boardroom. There are eight colours in the rainbow pride flag, which stands for many social movements, not just LGBT+ rights. Pink is for sexuality. Red signifies life. Orange is for healing. Yellow represents the sunlight. Blue is for arts. Indigo is for harmony. Violet is for the spirit.

Pink is for Sexuality

One of the challenges to LGBT+ inclusion has been the invisibility of LGBT+ individuals as they have not been traditionally counted and accounted for. Quantifiable demonstration of LGBTI+ diversity would make the boardroom more LGBT friendly. Better data and monitoring is essential to provide visibility to LGBT+ in the boardroom. Since not every LGBT+ individual may wish to come out at work due to privacy and safety concerns that are still valid today (Badgett, 2020), it is the responsibility of the boardroom to ensure the safety and inclusion of members if they are to come out. Monitoring and data collection activities often serve to legitimate and make it acceptable for LGBT+ identities to be counted and accounted for. In particular, organisations could capture LGBT+ data in the boardroom and the talent pipeline. For example, IBM was included in the list '250 LGBT+ High Potential/Top Talent Worldwide', which includes companies that monitor high potential LGBT+ staff (Workplace Pride Foundation, 2012). Subscription to such external initiatives or internal data collection and monitoring systems help the boardroom to prepare itself for representational and cultural changes.

However, in many boardroom appointments, the pooling of candidates and recruitment practices are outsourced to recruitment agencies and headhunters (Özbilgin & Tatli, 2007). Therefore, monitoring the methods of recruitment agencies and headhunters for LGBT+ friendly recruitment could ensure that LGBT+ relevant data could be collected by these agencies also.

Red is for Life

There is a lifecycle of discrimination that face LGBT+ individuals from birth to death bed (Öztürk and Özbilgin, 2014; Kamasak et al., 2019). The LGBT+ movement tackles the hegemonic order of compulsory heterosexuality across all life and work domains. This contestation requires multilevel interventions. Beyond protective legislation and company policies, it is also essential to prevent LGBT+ individuals from being hurt by workplace relationships. LGBT+ individuals often have to distance themselves from or hide their authentic selves to avoid verbal harassment, humiliating jokes and taunting at work (Meyer, 2010; Baker & Lucas, 2017). Forcing LGBT+ individuals to be out against their will is another major problem encountered at work. Organisations should not tolerate mistreatments and take precautions to support inclusive practices for LGBT+ talent. Building structures that will support the security and privacy of LGBT+ individuals against the risk of involuntary disclosure could help gain their trust (Dym et al., 2019). Research suggests that formal policies and practices could be developed to educate non-LGBT+ individuals about acceptable and unacceptable forms of behaviours and procedures regarding disclosure and privacy of LGBT+ identities (Webster et al., 2018). Organisations could prove their discourses, policies and practices against homophonic, biphobic and transphobic elements. This activity could be performed by either internal agents or external consultants who are specialised in this topic. Bias-proofing the boardroom would help it prepare for sexual orientation diversity, rendering it a safe space for LGBT+ inclusion.

Orange is for Healing

The past trauma of the history of stigmatisation, symbolic, physical and psychological discrimination and bias that LGBT+ individuals experienced in the hegemonic order of compulsory heterosexuality should be remedied. The remedy could be only possible through healing. However, we do not only propose healing of the LGBT+ community. Healing through individual- and institutional-level interventions should address the uneven nature of the heteronormative order that haunts personal relationships and institution-making practices. Healing is a shared process that should be everyone's responsibility that should take concrete form in organisational discourses, policies and procedures. There are many interventions offered by organisational psychology, such as mindfulness training, unconscious bias training, awareness-raising programmes and institutional interventions such as proofing of systemic and institutional biases and exclusionary practices against LGBT+ (Singh and O'Brien, 2020). Furthermore, organisations could use LGBT+ networks, Pride Month and LGBT+ allies and champions to cross-fertilise innovative ideas for collective healing where identity and orientation fault lines could be replaced with new forms of solidarity among staff (Maks-Solomon and Drewery, 2021).

Yellow is for Sunlight

Sunlight makes it possible to see the world as we believe it is natural and authentic. Visibility through authenticity is an excellent way through which LGBT+ individuals could flourish in the boardroom. Combating compulsory heteronormativity and allowing for expressions of authenticity for LGBT+ individuals that are true to their nature could help save considerable energy, which they need to use to behave like heterosexuals at work (Best, 2019). Furthermore, allowing atypical board members to display authenticity without losing the trust and respect of other board members could help improve board performance. Such a change would impact LGBT+ individuals and women in the boardroom positively. Women also report similar levels of discomfort with the loss of authenticity when they take up board positions (Sayce and Özbilgin, 2014).

Blue is for Arts

In this context, arts signifies how LGBT+ individuals, like artists in life, could be the outsiders within, innovators from the margins, like other atypical individuals who can join leadership positions (Samdanis and Özbilgin, 2020). The innovative potential of LGBT+ individuals could be revealed if they are allowed to enter the orthodoxy as heterodox others (Greenhalgh et al., 2021). When LGBT+ issues are considered, an immediate focus is made on sexual orientation and gender identity aspects of LGBT+ individuals. Such a narrow focus diminishes the humanity of LGBT+ individuals. Like the demands of feminist, anti-racist, disability movements, the LGBT+ movement demands more to an individual than their single demographic category alone (Özbilgin and Erbil, 2021). Recognising the innovative potential of LGBT+ individuals like other atypical newcomers to the boardroom needs to move from purism to pluralism in framing leadership talent in the boardroom. The pluralism is only possible if boardroom paradigms for evidence for talent shift from the lock-in of the traditional mindsets that suffer from heteronormativity towards interdisciplinarity and the recognition of the value of the other legitimate forms of 'being' and 'doing' in the boardroom.

Indigo is for Harmony

Much of the LGBT+ literature on workplaces relations focuses on the deficit model, that is, the exclusion, demarcation and discrimination based on gender identity and sexual orientation at work. We propose that beyond the deficit model, there is significant potential to see the harmony that effective inclusion of LGBT+ individuals could bring to the boardroom. Most LGBT+ individuals make their career and workplace choices based on the reputation and supportive structures that organisations offer for LGBT+ inclusion (McFadden, 2015). Therefore, bias-proofing the boardroom is not enough to ensure inclusion. From how board members interact to how they socialise and conduct themselves should be transformed to provide a supportive and inclusive environment for LGBT+ talent. This transformation could be possible by recognising the unique and idiosyncratic needs of the LGBT+ in the boardroom, such as recognition and legitimation of their work habits, romantic relationships and socialisation patterns (Sears et al., 2018). As most boardrooms are built on heteronormative principles (Rumens, 2011), acceptance and inclusion of the LGBT+ identity would require a deep level of cultural change at the level of fundamental and taken-for-granted assumptions of the boardroom.

Violet is for Spirit

There is a need for multilevel interventions for promoting the inclusion of LGBT+ individuals in the boardroom. At the micro-individual level, LGBT+ individuals need mentoring and training to qualify for boardroom roles. They also require boardroom-level sponsorship for their LGBT+ talent to be recognised better. There is also a significant need for LGBT+ specific leadership programmes. At the meso-organisational level, boardroom diversity should have a concrete case for sexual orientation diversity as an essential inclusion category. This kind of diversity needs buy-in from the boardroom. Furthermore, this effort should not remain at the inclusion of sexual orientation as a category alone. It should be considered part of the diversity-led boardroom transformation at multiple levels.

We argue that recognising, recruiting and retaining LGBT+ talent in the boardroom at a practical level requires multifaceted change. We outline below the kind of changes that practitioners of equality, diversity and inclusion could consider for fostering LGBT+ inclusion in the boardroom:

- *Change representation*: out LGBT+ members in the boardroom and ally role models at the board level could pioneer change of boardroom composition (Fullerton, 2013).
- *Change the cognitive frames*: organisations could define talent in the boardroom in LGBT+ inclusive ways and shape the mental structures in the boardroom in more inclusive ways through the influence and buy-in of champions and agents of change (Wright et al., 2006).
- *Change the conversation*: organisations may tackle banter and phobic discourses, focus on the positive contribution of LGBT+ in the boardroom, achieve buy-in from current members.

- *Change policies*: organisations could offer supportive coming out policies, bias and harassment proofing policies, tackle client and investor bias and deliver supportive policies to make the boardroom LGBT+ friendly.
- *Change culture*: create an LGBT+ supportive culture and climate in the boardroom and the organisational ecosystem.

REFERENCES

Abadi, M. (2018). New Land O'Lakes CEO Beth Ford just became the first openly gay woman to lead a Fortune 500 company – take a look at her career so far. https://www.businessinsider.com/beth-ford-land-o-lakes-ceo-2018-7 (accessed 13 March 2021).

Acker, J. (1990). Hierarchies, jobs, bodies: a theory of gendered organizations. *Gender & Society*, 4(2), 139–58.

Acker, J. (2012). Gendered organizations and intersectionality: problems and possibilities. *Equality, Diversity and Inclusion*, 31(3), 214–24.

Alper, A. & Shalal, A. (2021). Biden calls for expanded efforts to protect LGBTQ rights globally. https://www.reuters.com/article/us-usa-biden-lgbt-idUSKBN2A42KF (accessed 12 March 2021).

Asakura, K. & Craig, S. L. (2014). "It gets better" … but how? Exploring resilience development in the accounts of LGBTQ adults. *Journal of Human Behavior in the Social Environment*, 24(3), 253–66.

Badgett, M. V. L. (2020). Collecting LGBT+ data for diversity: initiating self-ID at IBM. https://www.umass.edu/employmentequity/collecting-lgbt-data-diversity-initiating-self-id-ibm (accessed 21 March 2021).

Baker, S. J. & Lucas, K. (2017). Is it safe to bring myself to work? Understanding LGBTQ experiences of workplace dignity. *Canadian Journal of Administrative Sciences/Revue Canadienne des Sciences de L'Administration*, 34(2), 133–48.

Best, D. (2019). The challenges of authenticity: leadership as a lesbian. In M. McIntosh, H. Nicholas & A. H. Huq (eds), *Leadership and Diversity in Psychology* (pp. 131–41). Routledge.

Bourdieu, P. (2001). *Masculine Domination*. Stanford University Press.

Bourdieu, P. & Wacquant, L. (2013). Symbolic capital and social classes. *Journal of Classical Sociology*, 13(2), 292–302.

Buser, T., Geijtenbeek, L., & Plug, E. (2015). Do gays shy away from competition? Do lesbians compete too much? IZA Discussion Papers, No. 9382, Institute for the Study of Labor (IZA), Bonn.

Byington, E. K., Tamm, G. F., & Trau, R. N. (2021). Mapping sexual orientation research in management: a review and research agenda. *Human Resource Management*, 60(1), 31–53.

Crenshaw, K. W. (2017). *On Intersectionality: Essential Writings*. The New Press.

Cunningham, G. B. (2011). The LGBT advantage: examining the relationship among sexual orientation diversity, diversity strategy, and performance. *Sport Management Review*, 14(4), 453–61.

Denier, N. & Waite, S. (2019). Sexual orientation at work: documenting and understanding wage inequality. *Sociology Compass*, 13(4), e12667.

Dilmaghani, M. (2018). Sexual orientation, labour supply and occupational sorting in Canada. *Industrial Relations Journal*, 49(4), 298–318.

Duberman, M. (1993). *Stonewall*. Dutton.

Dym, B., Brubaker, J. R., Fiesler, C., & Semaan, B. (2019). "Coming out okay": community narratives for LGBTQ identity recovery work. *Proceedings of the ACM on Human–Computer Interaction*, 3(CSCW), 1–28.

Florida, R. (2002). The economic geography of talent. *Annals of the Association of American Geographers*, 92(4), 743–55.

Florida, R., Mellander, C., & Stolarick, K. (2008). Inside the black box of regional development—human capital, the creative class and tolerance. *Journal of Economic Geography*, 8(5), 615–49.

Fric, K. (2017). Access to the labour market for gays and lesbians: research review. *Journal of Gay & Lesbian Social Services*, 29(4), 319–61.

Fullerton, M. (2013). Diversity and inclusion – LGBT inclusion means business. *Strategic HR Review*, 12(3), 121–5.

Greenhalgh, T., Özbilgin, M., & Contandriopoulos, D. (2021). Orthodoxy, *illusio*, and playing the scientific game: a Bourdieusian analysis of infection control science in the COVID-19 pandemic. *Wellcome Open Research*, 6. https://wellcomeopenresearch.org/articles/6-126.

Griffin, P. (2013). Gendering global finance: crisis, masculinity, and responsibility. *Men and Masculinities*, 16(1), 9–34.

Guynn, J. (2020). New California law, the first of its kind, requires racial diversity on corporate boards of directors. https://www.usatoday.com/story/money/2020/09/30/california-law-requires-racial-diversity-corporate-boards/5874469002/ (accessed 13 March 2021).

Harter, S. (2002). *Authenticity.* In C. R. Snyder & S. J. Lopez (eds), *Handbook of Positive Psychology* (pp. 382–94). Oxford University Press.

Hewlett, S. A. (2011). The cost of closeted employees. https://hbr.org/2011/07/the-cost-of-closeted-employees (accessed 13 March 2021).

Hewlett, S. A. & Yoshino, K. (2016). LGBT-inclusive companies are better at 3 big things. https://hbr.org/2016/02/lgbt-inclusive-companies-are-better-at-3-big-things (accessed 21 March 2021).

Hillman, A. J., Cannella Jr, A. A., & Harris, I. C. (2002). Women and racial minorities in the boardroom: how do directors differ? *Journal of Management*, 28(6), 747–63.

HRC [Human Right Campaign Foundation] (2014). The cost of the closet and the rewards of inclusion. https://assets2.hrc.org/files/assets/resources/Cost_of_the_Closet_May2014.pdf (accessed 21 March 2021).

HRC [Human Right Campaign Foundation] (2018). A workplace divided: understanding the climate for LGBTQ workers nationwide. https://assets2.hrc.org/files/assets/resources/AWorkplaceDivided-2018.pdf?_ga=2.159885373.1628497410.1616172687-1160822243.1616172687 (accessed 18 March 2021).

HRC [Human Rights Campaign Foundation] (2021). Corporate equality index 2021. https://hrc-prod-requests.s3-us-west-2.amazonaws.com/CEI-2021-revised-030121.pdf?mtime=20210304182627&focal=none (accessed 18 March 2021).

Humphrey, J. C. (1999). Organizing sexualities, organized inequalities: lesbians and gay men in public service occupations. *Gender, Work & Organization*, 6(3), 134–51.

Huse, M. (2011). The golden skirts: changes in board composition following gender quotas on corporate boards. Australian and New Zealand Academy Meeting, Wellington, NZ. https://www.anzam.org/wp-content/uploads/pdf-manager/473_ANZAM2011-148.PDF.

ILGA (2020a). Sexual orientation laws in the world. https://ilga.org/sites/default/files/downloads/ENG_ILGA_World_map_sexual_orientation_laws_dec2020.png (accessed 13 March 2020).

ILGA (2020b). Annual review of the human rights situations of lesbian, gay, bisexual, trans and intersex people in Europe and Central Asia. https://www.ilga-europe.org/sites/default/files/Annual%20Review%202020.pdf (accessed 13 March 2021).

Kakabadse, N. K., Figueira, C., Nicolopoulou, K., Hong Yang, J., Kakabadse, A. P., & Özbilgin, M. F. (2015). Gender diversity and board performance: women's experiences and perspectives. *Human Resource Management*, 54(2), 265–81.

Kamasak, R., Özbilgin, M., Baykut, S., & Yavuz, M. (2019). Moving from intersectional hostility to intersectional solidarity: insights from LGBTQ individuals in Turkey. *Journal of Organizational Change Management*, 33(3), 456–76.

Kelly, M., Carathers, J., & Kade, T. (2020). Beyond tolerance: policies, practices, and ideologies of queer-friendly workplaces. *Sexuality Research and Social Policy*, 18(4), 1–16.

Kucukaltan, B. & Özbilgin, M. F. (2019). Cosmopolitanism and entrepreneurship in Istanbul and London. In N. Mouraviev & N. K. Kakabadse (eds), *Entrepreneurship and Global Cities: Diversity, Opportunity and Cosmopolitanism*. Routledge.

Lasio, D., Serri, F., Ibba, I., & Manuel De Oliveira, J. (2019). Hegemony and heteronormativity: homonormative discourses of LGBTQ activists about lesbian and gay parenting. *Journal of Homosexuality*, 66(8), 1058–81.

Levitt, H. M. & Ippolito, M. R. (2014). Being transgender: navigating minority stressors and developing authentic self-presentation. *Psychology of Women Quarterly*, 38(1), 46–64.

Lim, F., Jones, P. A., & Paguirigan, M. (2019). A guide to fostering an LGBTQ-inclusive workplace. *Nursing Management*, 50(6), 46–53.

Maks-Solomon, C. & Drewry, J. M. (2021). Why do corporations engage in LGBT rights activism? LGBT employee groups as internal pressure groups. *Business and Politics*, 23(1), 124–52.

McFadden, C. (2015). Lesbian, gay, bisexual, and transgender careers and human resource development: a systematic literature review. *Human Resource Development Review*, 14(2), 125–62.

McFadden, C., & Crowley-Henry, M. (2018). 'My people': the potential of LGBT employee networks in reducing stigmatization and providing voice. *The International Journal of Human Resource Management*, 29(5), 1056–81.

Mergen, A. & Özbilgin, M. F. (2021). Understanding the followers of toxic leaders: toxic *illusio* and personal uncertainty. *International Journal of Management Reviews*, 23(1), 45–63.

Meyer, D. (2010). Evaluating the severity of hate-motivated violence: intersectional differences among LGBT hate crime victims. *Sociology*, 44(5), 980–95.

Morrissey, H., Terry, J., Bennett, K., Miller, L. & McCloskey, L. (2018). Understanding diversity and inclusion in the investment management industry. https://www.pwc.co.uk/financial-services/assets/pdf/pwc-diversity-project-understanding-diversity-and-inclusion.pdf (accessed 7 March 2021).

Ng, E. S. & Burke, R. J. (2005). Person–organization fit and the war for talent: does diversity management make a difference? *The International Journal of Human Resource Management*, 16(7), 1195–210.

Noga-Styron, K. E., Reasons, C. E., & Peacock, D. (2012). The last acceptable prejudice: an overview of LGBT social and criminal injustice issues within the USA. *Contemporary Justice Review*, 15(4), 369–98.

Nourafshan, A. M. (2017). From the closet to the boardroom: regulating LGBT diversity on corporate boards. *Albany Law Review*, 81, 439.

ONS (2019). Religion by sex and age group, Great Britain, January to December 2019. https://www.ons.gov.uk/peoplepopulationandcommunity/culturalidentity/religion/adhocs/12137religionbysexandagegroupgreatbritainjanuarytodecember2019 (accessed 13 March 2021).

OUTStanding.com (2020). 2020 top 100 LGBT+ executives. https://outstanding.involverolemodels.org/poll/2020-top-100-lgbt-executives/ (accessed 18 March 2021).

Özbilgin, M. (2017), Cinsellik ve emek: Butler ve Bourdieu ile kazanımların kırılganlığını ve direnişi sorgulamak. *KAOSQ+*, 5, 97–106.

Özbilgin, M. F., Erbil, C., Baykut, S., & Kamasak, R. (2022). Passing as resistance through a Goffmanian approach: normalized, defensive, strategic, and instrumental passing when LGBTQ+ individuals encounter institutions. *Gender, Work & Organization*, 1–19. https://doi.org/10.1111/gwao.12928.

Özbilgin, M. & Soytemel, E. (2020). Resistance against sexual orientation equality and the LGBTI+ movement: cis-gender privilege, heteronormative fragility and compulsory heterosexuality, *International Review of Sociology*. https://irs-blog.com/2020/07/14/resistance-against-sexual-orientation-equality-and-the-lgbti-movement-cis-gender-privilege-heteronormative-fragility-and-compulsory-heterosexuality-mustafa-f-ozbilgin-and-ebru-soyteme.

Özbilgin, M. & Tatli, A. (2007). *Opening Up Opportunities Through Private Sector Recruitment and Guidance Agencies*. Equal Opportunities Commission.

Özbilgin, M., Tatli, A., Ipek, G., & Sameer, M. (2016). Four approaches to accounting for diversity in global organisations. *Critical Perspectives on Accounting*, 35, 88–99.

Öztürk, M. B. & Özbilgin, M. (2014). From cradle to grave. In F. Colgan & N. Rumens (eds), *Sexual Orientation at Work: Contemporary Issues and Perspectives*. Routledge.

Öztürk, M. B., Rumens, N., & Tatli, A. (2020). Age, sexuality and hegemonic masculinity: exploring older gay men's masculinity practices at work. *Gender, Work & Organization*, 27(6), 1253–68.

Peterson, C. A., Philpot, J., & O'Shaughnessy, K. C. (2007). African-American diversity in the boardrooms of the US Fortune 500: director presence, expertise and committee membership. *Corporate Governance: An International Review*, 15(4), 558–75.

Pichler, S., Ruggs, E., & Trau, R. (2017). Worker outcomes of LGBT-supportive policies: a cross-level model. *Equality, Diversity and Inclusion: An International Journal*, 36(1), 17–32.

Predmore, S. (2020). Feminist and gender studies approaches to financialization. In P. Mader, D. Mertens & N. van der Zwan (eds), *The Routledge International Handbook of Financialization* (pp. 102–12). Routledge.

Qvist, B. (2015). The case for coming out at work. https://www.theguardian.com/sustainable-business/2015/jan/23/case-coming-out-lgbt-sexuality-workplace (accessed 20 March 2021).

Reis, G. G., Braga, B. M., & Trullen, J. (2017). Workplace authenticity as an attribute of employer attractiveness. *Personnel Review*, 46(8), 1962–76.

Roberson, Q., Ryan, A. M., & Ragins, B. R. (2017). The evolution and future of diversity at work. *Journal of Applied Psychology*, 102(3), 483.

Roseneil, S., Crowhurst, I., Hellesund, T., Santos, A. C., & Stoilova, M. (2013). Changing landscapes of heteronormativity: the regulation and normalization of same-sex sexualities in Europe. *Social Politics*, 20(2), 165–99.

Rumens, N. (2011). Minority support: friendship and the development of gay and lesbian managerial careers and identities. *Equality, Diversity and Inclusion: An International Journal*, 30(6), 444–62.

Saba, T., Özbilgin, M., Ng, E., & Cachat-Rosset, G. (2021). Guest editorial: ineffectiveness of diversity management: lack of knowledge, lack of interest or resistance? *Equality, Diversity and Inclusion: An International Journal*, 40(7), 765–9. https://doi.org/10.1108/EDI-09-2021-374.

SALT (2019). Diversifying your business: how an inclusive workplace boosts productivity. https://www.youtube.com/watch?v=LNWOOZ1FLUA (accessed 18 March 2021).

Samdanis, M. & Özbilgin, M. (2020). The duality of an atypical leader in diversity management: the legitimization and delegitimization of diversity beliefs in organizations. *International Journal of Management Reviews*, 22(2), 101–19.

Sanchez-Hucles, J. V. & Davis, D. D. (2010). Women of color in leadership: complexity, identity, and intersectionality. *American Psychologist*, 65(3), 171–81. https://doi.org/10.1037/a0017459.

Sayce, S. & Özbilgin, M. F. (2014). Pension trusteeship and diversity in the UK: a new boardroom recipe for change or continuity? *Economic and Industrial Democracy*, 35(1), 49–69.

Schilt, K. & Westbrook, L. (2009). Doing gender, doing heteronormativity: "gender normals", transgender people, and the social maintenance of heterosexuality. *Gender & Society*, 23(4), 440–64.

Sears, T., Terry, J., Wendel, P., Brown, J., Miller, L., Gerders, M. & Ashworth, J. (2018). Out to succeed: realising the full potential of LGBT+ talent. https://outleadership.com/wp-content//uploads/2018/05/OutNEXT-PwC-Survey-2-footers-Final-.pdf (accessed 23 March 2021).

Singh, R. S. & O'Brien, W. H. (2020). The impact of work stress on sexual minority employees: could psychological flexibility be a helpful solution? *Stress and Health*, 36(1), 59–74.

Slootmaeckers, K., Touquet, H. & Vermeersch, P. (2016). *EU Enlargement and Gay Politics*. Palgrave Macmillan.

Snyder, K. (2006). *The G Quotient: Why Gay Executives Are Excelling as Leaders ... and What Every Manager Needs to Know*. John Wiley & Sons.

Srikant, C., Pichler, S., & Shafiq, A. (2020). The virtuous cycle of diversity. *Human Resource Management*. https://doi.org/10.1002/hrm.22037.

Toft, A. (2020). Identity management and community belonging: the coming out careers of young disabled LGBT+ persons. *Sexuality & Culture*, 24(6), 1893–912.

Trau, R., O'Leary, J., & Brown, C. (2018). 7 myths about coming out at work. https://hbr.org/2018/10/7-myths-about-coming-out-at-work (accessed 13 March 2021).

Valdovinos, J. (2018). Rocky journey toward effective LGBT leadership: a qualitative case study research of the perceptions of openly gay male leaders in high-level leadership positions (doctoral dissertation, Brandman University).

Van den Bosch, R. & Taris, T. W. (2014). The authentic worker's well-being and performance: the relationship between authenticity at work, well-being, and work outcomes. *The Journal of Psychology*, 148(6), 659–81.

Walter, I. (1999). The global asset management industry: competitive structure and performance. *Financial Markets, Institutions & Instruments*, 8(1), 1–78.

Warner, M. (1991). Introduction: fear of a queer planet. *Social Text*, 29: https://doi.org/10.2307/466295.

Webster, J. R., Adams, G. A., Maranto, C. L., Sawyer, K., & Thoroughgood, C. (2018). Workplace contextual support for LGBT employees: a review, meta-analysis, and agenda for future research. *Human Resource Management*, 57(1), 193–210.

Williams, C. L., Giuffre, P. A., & Dellinger, K. (2009). The gay-friendly closet. *Sexuality Research & Social Policy*, 6(1), 29–45.

Wimberly, G. L., Wilkinson, L., & Pearson, J. (2015). LGBTQ student achievement and educational attainment. In G. L. Wimberly (ed.), *LGBTQ Issues in Education: Advancing a Research Agenda*. American Educational Research Association.

Workplace Pride Foundation (2012). Talent to change for LGBT employee research leading the way in diversity. https://workplacepride.org/download/talent-to-change-for-final-full-report-pdf/?wpdmdl=6102&refresh=605849d649e681616398806 (accessed 22 March 2021).

Wright, T., Colgan, F., Creegany, C., & McKearney, A. (2006). Lesbian, gay and bisexual workers: equality, diversity and inclusion in the workplace. *Equal Opportunities International*, 25(6), 465–70.

5. Board diversity: the impact of dynamic capabilities, absorptive capacity and ambidexterity

Carl Åberg, Hilde Fjellvær and Cathrine Seierstad

Diversity has become an increasingly important dimension in social science. Kirton and Greene (2015) describe diversity as a descriptor of the workforce or group that can refer to a wide range of differences which can be social group based, such as gender, race/ethnicity, age, religion, disability, sexual orientation, or they can be individual characteristics, which include qualifications, lifestyle, personality, interest, talents, values, experiences and many others. Diversity can also be understood as visible or invisible differences or as surface-level diversity (such as demographic differences) and deep-level differences (such as personal differences) (Harrison et al., 2002). Additionally, some aspects of diversity can be job-related (such as knowledge, experience and functional background) or less job-related (such as age, gender and race) (Webber & Donahue, 2001). Tasheva and Hillman (2019) distinguish between human capital, social capital and demographic diversity.

Within board research, gender diversity has received the most attention since the early 2010s. This is largely due to the introduction of gender quotas which has resulted in an increase of women on board (WoB) research (Kirsch, 2018). As we will demonstrate, the diversity perspective is an important dimension when discussing corporate entrepreneurship and boards. Nevertheless, we argue that it is important to have a deeper-level understanding of diversity and that different forms of diversity might be important for entrepreneurial activities. Specifically, we argue that there is a need for understanding how diversity can be used and managed to positively facilitate corporate entrepreneurship and value creation. In this chapter, we concentrate our discussions on job-related diversity attributes among board members, for instance their skills, abilities and knowledge. These attributes are of great importance when pursuing cognitive tasks related to entrepreneurship. Our unit of analysis is the board as a group, and its impact on corporate entrepreneurship. Our aim is to integrate the discussion on diversity, corporate entrepreneurship and boards. Thus, we answer the following research question: How can board job-related diversity attributes be used and managed to positively facilitate corporate entrepreneurship?

In this chapter, we extend our understanding of how diversity among board members contributes to corporate entrepreneurship, competitive advantage and value creation. We use various recent resource theories to show that board diversity in itself is not enough. It must be managed and used by organizations in successful ways in order to have a positive impact. To explain how, we apply the resource theories of dynamic capabilities perspective (Teece et al., 1997), absorptive capacity (Cohen & Levinthal, 1991) and ambidexterity (Tushman & O'Reilly, 1996). With their common foundation in the resource-based view of the firm (Barney, 1991), all three perspectives consider how resources, in terms of knowledge, information, competencies and capabilities, are built, acquired and exploited in ways that allow companies to achieve competitive advantage and value creation. Diversity in background, knowledge, information, competencies and capabilities should be considered as playing a pivotal role in meeting the resource requirements that allow firms to be innovative and entrepreneurial. The importance of diversity (and in particular different forms of job-related diversity) is therefore taken into consideration when discussing the three perspectives. This has to date largely been missing from the board and diversity debate.

In the remainder of this chapter, we first define corporate entrepreneurship and describe the characteristics of an entrepreneurial board. Following that, boards are discussed from a dynamic capabilities perspective, an absorptive capacity perspective and from ambidexterity perspectives. The three perspectives are discussed in terms of background/characteristics of the perspective, theoretical dimensions and their relation to boards and diversity. Finally, we present an integrated framework for researching and understanding entrepreneurial boards from a diversity perspective.

CORPORATE ENTREPRENEURSHIP AND THE ENTREPRENEURIAL BOARD

Corporate entrepreneurship is entrepreneurship in existing organizations. It has been defined as "the process by which individuals inside organizations pursue opportunities independent of the resources they currently control" (Hisrich & Kearney, 2011, p. 12). Corporate entrepreneurship is conducted to create outputs such as strategic renewal, internal innovation and organizational transformations, thus allowing firms to sustaining competitiveness (Guth & Ginsberg, 1990; Stevenson & Jarillo, 1990). It refers to activities that organizations undertake in order to encourage change as well as promote calculated risk-taking (Zahra et al., 2009).

Corporate entrepreneurship is a rather universal concept that can be applied to many different organizations both in the private and public sector as well as in for-profit and not-for-profit organizations. One requirement for successful corporate entrepreneurship is that it is managed and coordinated to provide value (Hisrich & Kearney, 2011). Therefore, it has been suggested that leaders in the upper echelons of organizations, including board members, need to provide continued attention to and support for corporate entrepreneurship for it to be successful (Zahra et al., 2000).

Traditionally, board members have been described as internal resources to the firm that supplement the management with experience and knowledge in order to contribute to value creation (Huse, 2007). They use this knowledge and experience for the purpose of contributing to both control and service tasks. From an entrepreneurial perspective, the essence of what the board does is to pursue opportunities leading to value creation. From this entrepreneurial perspective we define the board as a group of cognitive and dynamic individuals, interacting with numerous actors, for their contribution to strategic renewal and value creation (Aguilera & Jackson, 2010; Åberg, 2017). In what follows, this definition is explored according to its different parts.

As a group of cognitive individuals, board members make personal interpretations of their strategic situation and form actions and make decisions based on this. As such, strategic choices made by boards are said to reflect a set of "givens" that make up the cognitive base that they make their personal interpretations on and bring to the decision process (Hambrick & Mason, 1984). The cognitive base reflects board members' knowledge. In essence, knowledge built through training and experience can assist boards as they engage in processes of scanning, interpretation, attention and formulation (Carpenter et al., 2004). We suggest that diversity in knowledge enriches entrepreneurial activities.

Characterized as dynamic individuals, board members can provide valuable capabilities that contribute to competitive advantage, especially in environments of unpredictable and rapid change (Åberg & Shen, 2019). Hence, boards may use their capabilities to renew firm resources to address constantly changing environments. For example, boards renew firm resources as they may engage in complex processes concerning investments, business model design and succession. It has here been suggested that diversity enhances organizational flexibility and allows organizations to be more agile, thus being able to respond to changes in the external environment at a faster pace and lower cost (Roberson et al., 2017).

By being characterized as individuals that interact with numerous actors, boards may solve tasks by interacting and working together with a large and complex network of people (Bankewitz et al., 2016). Interaction allows board members to share information and knowledge, attain new information and knowledge and solve complex problems. In environments of constant change, board members interact not only with each other, the management team, the CEO and shareholders, but also with external stakeholders of the organization. They do this as a means of acquiring new valuable knowledge for exploiting emerging opportunities and exploring different options for corporate entrepreneurship (Zahra et al., 2009). It may be argued through social network theory that diversity in individuals' networks facilitates access to a wider variety of knowledge and information.

Finally, our understanding of an entrepreneurial board suggests that the board contributes to strategic renewal and value creation (Huse, 2005). In particular, it has been found that boards' involvement in entrepreneurial activities may lead to strategic change (Åberg & Torchia, 2019). It has also been found that boards' involvement in strategic decision-making may significantly impact strategic renewal and leads to changes in organizational performance and value creation (Golden & Zajac, 2001; Westphal & Fredrickson, 2001).

Based on this understanding of an entrepreneurial board, in the coming parts of the chapter we use entrepreneurial resource perspectives (dynamic capabilities, absorptive capacity and ambidexterity) to discuss the contribution that job-related diversity attributes may have on the entrepreneurial board and its potential consequences. Our framework for discussing diversity, corporate entrepreneurship and boards is summarized in Figure 5.1.

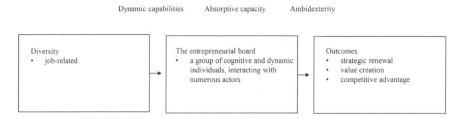

Figure 5.1   Integrated framework for discussing diversity, boards and corporate entrepreneurship

DYNAMIC CAPABILITIES

The dynamic capabilities perspective has brought new light to the resources based view (Barney, 1991) by emphasizing not only the importance of resources but also the capabilities that enhance resource configurations in dynamic markets (Teece et al., 1997). As such, the dynamic capabilities perspective has moved closer to describe how organizations evolve and sustain their competitive advantage in markets of constant change. Recent theoretical developments have provided the means of studying boards from this perspective as theoretical dimensions have been developed both on an individual and team level. Referred to as dynamic managerial capabilities, these dimensions focus on managers' capabilities in sensing and seizing opportunities, and reconfiguring assets to enhance resource configurations and adapt to changing environmental conditions. Next, we present how these relate to the board.

Board Dynamic Managerial Capabilities

Dynamic managerial capabilities are capabilities that direct attention to how managers use their resources to identify opportunities, make strategic decisions and reconfigure resources to achieve strategic change. Dynamic managerial capabilities have been defined as "the capabilities with which managers build, integrate, and reconfigure organizational resources and competences" (Adner & Helfat, 2003, p. 1012). Sensing, seizing and reconfiguring are important dynamic managerial capabilities that can be seen as processes which help explain how boards respond to changing business environments (Åberg & Torchia, 2019). Global dynamic managerial capabilities have further been found to enhance firms' global strategy and performance (Tasheva & Nielsen, 2020).

    Sensing includes a board's ability in staying alert and discovery proficiencies, which are important for recognizing opportunities as they appear as well as anticipating strategic threats. It is the initial phase in creating change and reacting to it. In most organizations, recognizing opportunities and threats is an element of the strategy process that takes place on a managerial level. Boards can in this process contribute with their judgments and often unique perspectives when the management conveys opportunities and threats to them (Huse, 2007). Anticipating and recognizing aspects that need to be taken into consideration in the strategy process require boards to scan, search and interpret information that could potentially impact the firm's ability to create value. The board's prior knowledge and experience may here influence the efficiency to which the board can create an understanding of the current situation and recognize new opportunities and trends in the industry. Without the necessary knowledge and experience, boards may misinterpret situations and fail to identify opportunities and threats in a timely manner (Kor & Misangyi, 2008). When boards anticipate change and identify opportunities, they engage in the initial phase of creating something new and they motivate their organizations in overcoming rigidity and inertia that sometimes limit change in their organizations. As such, boards' contribution to sensing is a process that often facilitates corporate entrepreneurship and strategic renewal.

The second dynamic managerial capability is that of seizing. Seizing is about applying reasoning and problem-solving skills in order to respond to opportunities and threats that have been identified in the sensing phase. In essence, problem solving is here about finding a way around an obstacle to reach a goal while reasoning is about evaluating information, opinions and thoughts to draw a conclusion (Helfat & Martin, 2015). Boards have here been described as expert problem solvers that apply these skills to strategic processes of choice, change and control (Forbes & Milliken, 1999; Rindova, 1999). Boards also use their seizing capabilities when they make decisions. Often it entails decisions about investments, committing funds and deciding on new strategies. These types of decisions are often made under complex and uncertain conditions, thus requiring them to make judgments, use their creativity and get the timing right in their responses. Here it has been suggested that boards use their knowledge and experience to make the most efficient responses and decisions (Kor & Sundaramurthy, 2009).

The last dynamic managerial capability is that of reconfiguring. The successful identification of technological and market opportunities, as well as the selection of which opportunities to scrutinize, can lead to enterprise growth and profitability. A key to sustained growth, innovation and profitability is reconfiguration capabilities. This can be defined as the ability to enhance, combine, recombine and modify the firms' resources and capabilities as the organization grows, and as technologies and markets change (Teece, 2007). It may be that the organization is forced to reconfigure its operational assets or modify the organizational structure in order to maintain evolutionary fitness. This is how well the organization is aligned to the internal and external situation. Organizations that maintain evolutionary fitness may be successful in building cumulative knowledge of how to efficiently transform the business (Sirmon et al., 2007). Boards' reconfiguring capabilities may be vital as they are in a position to mobilize resources and create strategic renewal (Åberg

& Torchia, 2019). For example, their reconfiguring capabilities are essential in the process of replacing the CEO or other executives in the management team. In these processes, boards are required to overcome organizational resistance to change. Here, boards' ability to communicate change, motivate change and perusing others to follow the lead, are factors that overcomes resistance to change. It may also be board members social skills which can foster cooperation and build trust and thus also help overcome resistance to change and inertia (Helfat & Martin, 2015).

Diversity among board members can have an impact on the three dynamic managerial capabilities. It promotes sensing as a board with diverse values, backgrounds, knowledge and expertise produce a greater variety of ideas, a broader range of perspectives and shares unique information (Post & Byron, 2015). This, in turn, can enhance organizational innovation and corporate entrepreneurship. Boards with diverse knowledge, background, experience and perspectives may also have better understanding of the marketplace where opportunities and threats are sensed. Further, it has been suggested that a board consisting of individuals with different job experiences (job-related diversity) are more likely to collect timely and relevant information (Gabaldon et al., 2018). This creates the grounds for sensing opportunities. On the other hand, homogeneous boards have a tendency to produce fewer variety of ideas and are likely to hamper the critical evaluation of different ideas, thus generating fewer innovative solutions and contributing less to sensing and the entrepreneurial process. Similarly, seizing and thus the quality of problem-solving and decision-making, is dependent on diverse mindsets. With diversity among board members, the likelihood of generating novel decisions, greater creativity and strategic innovations is higher (Kamasak et al., 2019). These arguments follow the assumption that diverse teams in terms of functional background, educational background and company tenure make high-quality and innovative decisions by collecting broader range information and generating more strategic proposals (Finkelstein et al., 2009). Additionally, research suggest that diversity can be an influential group-level factor that enhances the board's decision-making comprehensiveness, which again results in decisions of better quality and creativity (Rindova, 1999; Torchia et al., 2018). Finally, reconfiguring and especially the processes of overcoming inertia and resistance to change may be fostered through a diverse board. A board with diverse experiences can create better grounds for communication, cooperation, empathy and social interaction and thus overcome resistance to change and inertia. However, the impact that diversity may have on reconfiguring capabilities may be debated as it could be negative. Here, the problems primarily driven by interpersonal conflicts and inefficient information sharing may be less visible in homogeneous boards. In line with these arguments, Roberson et al. (2017) suggest that team diversity in knowledge and capabilities may reduce communication and cooperation, thus reducing work group functioning and potentially impacting the team's ability to reconfigure resources.

In Table 5.1, we outline a set of questions that, based on the dynamic capabilities perspective, may enhance our understanding of how boards contribute to sensing, seizing and reconfiguring and the role of diversity. Investigating these issues would also contribute to a better understanding of board processes and behaviour and therefore strengthen "black box" research on boards (Daily et al., 2003; Huse, 2005).

Table 5.1   *Research questions connecting board dynamic managerial capabilities and diversity*

Board Dynamic Managerial Capabilities	
Sensing	• How does the board identify new opportunities?
	• How does the board create new opportunities for the organization?
	• How is the board kept alert to changes in the business environment?
	• What role does diversity play here?
	• What type of diversity strengthens/weakens sensing?
Seizing	• How does the board find solutions to opportunities identified?
	• How does the board evaluate opportunities?
	• How does the board decide on new opportunities?
	• What role does diversity play here?
	• What type of diversity strengthens/weakens seizing?
Reconfiguring	• How does the board mobilize change?
	• How does the board motivate change?
	• How does the board communicate change?
	• What role does diversity play here?
	• What type of diversity strengthens/weakens reconfiguring?

ABSORPTIVE CAPACITY

The prominence of absorptive capacity has been visible across the fields of strategic management, entrepreneurship, technology management and international business (Zahra & George, 2002). Absorptive capacity adds understanding to the entrepreneurial learning process, and the concept should be seen as a set of firm abilities with the purpose to managing information and knowledge. Cohen and Levinthal (1991, p. 128) have provided a frequently used definition of absorptive capacity, describing it as "the ability of a firm to recognize the value of new, external information, assimilate it and apply it to commercial ends". Hence, they see absorptive capacity as a resource that is critical to organizations' innovative capabilities. They also argue that diversity in knowledge and expertise can facilitate innovative processes.

Boards have also been studied in terms of their absorptive capacity. In particular, it has been argued that boards' ability to recognize and assimilate external knowledge through their often extensive networks may allow them to create a knowledge bank for efficient responses to strategic and entrepreneurial decisions. By possessing absorptive capacity, boards can help identify opportunities for growth, incorporate useful information as boards make strategic and innovative decisions and make sure members of the management have the right knowledge and information when they make strategic choices. Three sequential processes are vital for an organization's ability to assimilate external knowledge (Lane et al., 2006). These three processes have also been analysed on a board level (Schønning et al., 2018) and include exploratory learning, transformative learning and exploitative learning.

Absorptive Capacity at Board Level

Exploratory learning refers to the ability to recognize and understand potentially new valuable knowledge outside the firm (Lane et al., 2006, p. 856). In essence, the boards' current stock of knowledge is not enough as strategic decisions are formed. Boards therefore establish scanning mechanisms to recognize and understand new valuable knowledge in the external environment. However, the boards' recognition and understanding of new valuable external knowledge may differ in terms of speed, effort and intensity to which new knowledge is gathered (Schønning et al., 2018). As suggested by Bankewitz et al. (2016), today's business environments require fast responses to changing strategic contexts, thus requiring boards to anticipate and comprehend drivers that constitute unpredictable changes and surprises. Thus, knowledge and information diversity could be of great benefit to the entrepreneurial process.

The second dimension of absorptive capacity, transformative learning, involves assimilating valuable external knowledge. In this context, assimilation refers to the ability to combine the acquired knowledge with existing practices (Lane et al., 2006). Boards would therefore apply transformative learning when they relate their newly acquired knowledge to what is already known. The goal with transformative learning is that knowledge is developed and maintained over time. It requires that boards combine, share and store their existing knowledge and use new knowledge to adapt their existing knowledge to emerging opportunities (Schønning et al., 2018). To foster transformative learning, it is essential that board members communicate with each other as they create the necessary social conditions for sharing information and learning. Such communication may be more formal, which takes place through interaction during board meetings, but also less formal interactions that take place between board meetings. Hence, transformative learning is likely to depend on the quality of these interactions. For example, lengthy presentations of known knowledge does not contribute to transformative learning and may actually result in less time for boards to engage in critical discussions (Machold & Farquhar, 2013). On the other hand, transformative learning in between board meetings is likely to depend on good relationships between individual board members but also between board members and the management. Such relationships can create the social conditions for balancing knowledge, open discussions and sharing of information (Garg & Eisenhardt, 2016).

Exploitative learning, the last dimension of absorptive capacity, is about applying the knowledge that has been assimilated. It means that the knowledge is applied in order to create knowledge outputs or commercial outputs (Lane et al., 2006). For the board, exploitative learning is about their ability to harvest and incorporate knowledge into its operations. It may be that the board incorporates acquired or transformed knowledge into its decision processes. Moreover, it has been suggested that exploitation of board members' knowledge has a positive impact on the efficiency of strategic decisions and boards involvement in strategy (Schønning et al., 2018).

Diversity among board members should also be seen as something that may have an impact on absorptive capacity. It would be positive for firms' absorptive capacity if board members, as boundary spanners to the external environment, possessed diverse networks of contacts. This would increase the likelihood for the board of being exposed to new information and knowledge (Lowik et al., 2017). This would positively impact the explorative learning of the board. This is in line with social network theory. The social network theory argues that diversity in individuals' network connections facilitates access to broad and different types of information and knowledge. This positively influences knowledge diffusion and assimilation. Diversity in knowledge would also be positive for transformative learning as it would enhance the extensiveness and comprehensiveness to which existing knowledge can be combined with new acquired knowledge. Additionally, it would be important for boards to have members with heterogeneous backgrounds and experiences as a homogeneous board is more likely to favour internal perspectives and more often resist external ideas which would limit their exploitative learning. Resistance to external perspectives would have a negative impact on the boards' absorptive capacity. Hence, diversity among board members could foster increased absorptive capacity. However, as discussed above, absorptive capacity requires transformative learning, where social conditions and interactions should be constructive. Here, a too diverse board in terms of background, knowledge and capabilities may create grounds for reduced communication and cooperation, thus potentially reducing their ability to develop and maintain knowledge through social interaction.

A focus on board absorptive capacity would enhance our understanding of boards' explorative learning, transformative learning and exploitative learning. To understand how boards are involved in the process of recognizing, assimilating and applying external information to commercial ends, it would be interesting to investigate the questions formulated in Table 5.2.

Table 5.2   Research questions connecting board absorptive capacity and diversity

Board Absorptive Capacity	
Exploratory learning	• How does the board identify new valuable external information in existing networks?
	• How does the board identify new valuable external information in new networks?
	• What role does diversity play here?
	• What type of diversity strengthens / weakens exploratory learning?
Transformative learning	• How does the board combine existing knowledge with newly acquired knowledge?
	• How do board members share knowledge with other board members?
	• What role does diversity play here?
	• What type of diversity strengthens/weakens transformative learning?
Exploitative learning	• How does the board apply the knowledge they possess?
	• How does the board incorporate knowledge into its operation?
	• What role does diversity play here?
	• What type of diversity strengthens/weakens explorative learning?

AMBIDEXTERITY

Ambidexterity has been defined as "the ability of an organization to both explore and exploit – to compete in mature technologies and markets where efficiency, control, and incremental improvement are prized and to also compete in new technologies and markets where flexibility, autonomy, and experimentation are needed" (O'Reilly & Tushman, 2013, p. 324). Importantly, organizations capable of pursuing exploration and exploitation simultaneously have shown to outperform other firms (O'Reilly & Tushman, 2013). However, perusing exploration and exploitation at the same time is not an easy task and may lead to conflicting goals, contradictive activities and the presence of tensions in organizations (Jansen et al., 2008).

Boards can be seen as a key governing body that influences the extent to which organizations simultaneously pursue exploration and exploitation. For example, through their involvement in strategy, board members play an important role in initiating and deciding on whether organizations are balancing high levels of both exploration and exploitation or avoiding being ambidextrous (Oehmichen et al., 2016). Furthermore, board members may, through their participation in advisory tasks, encourage and support senior leaders in the achievement of ambidexterity. This may be of particular relevance as the pursuit of ambidexterity may create considerable challenges for senior executives as they are forced to deal with contradictory strategic agendas and paradoxes in decision-making (Jansen et al., 2008). Boards may therefore be beneficial to solving these situations by providing cognitive abilities and diversity in knowledge (Rejeb et al., 2019).

Ambidexterity at Board Level

Considering ambidexterity from the board level, exploitation and exploration should be seen as two distinct organizational learning strategies that determine how an organization develops and renews its resource base. Exploitation strategies are supported by incremental fine tuning, focusing, efficiency-seeking plans and refinement of knowledge. The aim is to make minor improvements to product and processes through enhancement of knowledge and competencies that serves existing markets and customers. Exploration, on the other hand, is about strategies supported by risk taking, innovation, experimentation and divergent thinking. Exploration aims to make radical changes to products, services or processes by meeting the needs of emerging markets and customers (Oehmichen et al., 2016; Rejeb et al., 2019). Roberson et al. (2017) suggest that job-related diversity, as, for example, in industry experience, network ties and functional background enhances organizational flexibility and allows organizations to be more agile. In regard to exploration and exploration, this could allow for a more efficient and simultaneous conduct of both these activities, thus fostering entrepreneurship.

Most evidently, boards influence exploitation strategies as they perform financial, operational and strategic controls. These tasks concern the control and evaluation of financial performance, resources allocations, management effectiveness, operational activities and strategy implementation. A strong focus on control and evaluation activities performed by the board may have negative impact on risk taking, innovation and experimentation and be more concerned with assuring the achievement of short-term financial and efficiency goals (Rejeb et al., 2019). In most cases, this would lead to an imbalance in ambidexterity as a result of focusing on exploitation at the expense of exploration. Board members with diverse job-related backgrounds and experiences could unsettle this imbalance and create simultaneous pursuit of exploration and exploitation. On the other hand, service tasks may be about providing advice, counselling and assistance by drawing on their human, social and relational capital (Zahra & Pearce, 1989). The service the board members provide can lead to both radical developments that meet emerging markets, but also incremental improvements that enhance the short-term position, thus contributing to both exploitation and exploration. Board members with a background in innovation and marketing may pay more attention to exploration, while board members with a background in finance and production may pay more attention to exploitation (García-Granero et al., 2018). Thus, board members having job-related diversity would help nurture the simultaneous achievement of both exploration and exploitation. Additionally, one could argue that diversity in experience and functional backgrounds of board members would enhance their strategic flexibility. That strategic flexibility would allow the board to pay attention to both exploration and exploitation. However, this diversity could also lead to conflicts and disagreements as diversity may lead to the forming of sub-groups and consequently the formation of intra-group biases that negatively impacts decision-making (Gabaldon et al., 2018). This may create an inability of the board to reach a consensus of how to simultaneously carry out exploration and exploitation.

Finally, to better understand whether and how boards encourage the simultaneous pursuit of exploration and exploitation, several interesting avenues are open for investigation, as shown in Table 5.3.

Table 5.3   *Research questions connecting board ambidexterity and diversity*

Board Ambidexterity	
Exploration & exploitation	• To what extent is the board encouraging risk taking, innovation and experimentation?
	• To what extent is the board encouraging incremental improvements, fine-tuning and efficiency seeking?
	• How does the board handle the paradox of short-term vs. long-term achievement of goals?
	• How does the board handle the paradox of radical vs. incremental change?
	• How does the board handle the paradox of serving existing vs. emerging markets?
	• What role does diversity play in exploration and exploitation?
	• What type of diversity strengthens/weakens simultaneous conduct of exploration and exploitation?

AN INTEGRATED BOARD ENTREPRENEURIAL FRAMEWORK

Three different entrepreneurial perspectives have been discussed to provide an understanding of how job-related diversity attributes of boards contribute to strategic renewal and value creation. In doing so, we have moved beyond the usual theoretical perspectives that have commonly been applied to the study of boards. Specifically, we have looked at the dynamic processes that boards engage in as they respond to constantly changing business environments, new technology advancements, intensified competition and greater requirements to innovate. At the same time, we have used the three theoretical perspectives to emphasize the importance of board diversity and its relationship to corporate entrepreneurship and value creation. Table 5.4 combines these perspectives to illustrate the consequences of different types of job-related diversity attributes and the impact they have on our three theoretical perspectives. As seen in the table, the consequences of different types of job-related diversity attributes have both positive and negative impact on the different types of dynamic capabilities, absorptive capacity and ambidexterity. The job-related diversity attributes that we propose future research into have been defined in a note to the table. As illustrated in Table 5.4, we argue, for example, that the job-related diversity attribute of *task-related knowledge* (defined as, level of knowledge that pertains to the work) has the consequences of *better understanding of the marketplace* which then has a positive impact on the board dynamic managerial capability of *sensing* (+) and so on. The table and our previous discussions highlight that the journey to develop a comprehensive understanding of these relationships has just begun. We therefore hope that the framework presented in the table can inspire and facilitate future research on diversity, boards and corporate entrepreneurship.

Table 5.4   *A board entrepreneurial and diversity framework*

Type of Job-related Diversity Attributes*	Consequences	Impact on Board Dynamic Managerial Capabilities
Task-related knowledge, functional background and industry background	Better understanding of marketplace	Sensing (+)
Functional background, task-related knowledge	Produce a greater variety of ideas and a broader range of perspectives	Sensing (+)
Functional background and industry background	More likely to collect timely and relevant information	Sensing (+)
Functional background, educational background and company tenure	Higher likelihood of innovation and decision-making with diverse mindsets	Seizing (+)
Functional background and industry background	More likely to overcome inertia and resistance to change	Reconfiguring (+)
Task-related knowledge	Diversity may reduce communication and cooperation	Sensing (−), Seizing (−) and Reconfiguring (−)

Type of Diversity	Consequences	Impact on Absorptive Capacity
Network ties	More boundary spanning information and knowledge recognition	Explorative learning (+)
Networks ties and task-related knowledge	Potential for higher knowledge diffusion and transfer	Transformative learning (+)
Task-related knowledge and functional background	Confronting ideas leading to higher reflection and refining of ideas	Exploitative learning (+)
Task-related knowledge and functional background	Reduced communication and cooperation	Explorative learning (−), transformative learning (−), exploitative learning (−)
Type of Diversity	*Consequences*	*Impact on Ambidexterity*
Industry background, network ties and functional background	Enhances organizational flexibility and allows organizations to be more agile	Ambidexterity (+)
Industry background and functional background	Simultaneous achievement of different priorities	Ambidexterity (+)
Functional background and industry background	Formation of intra group biases	Ambidexterity (−)

Note: *The job-related diversity attributes are defined as follows: *Task-related knowledge*, level of knowledge that pertains to the work (Pelled et al., 1999); *Functional background*, level of exposure to different functional areas (Pelled et al., 1999); *Industry background*, level of exposure to different industries (Pelled et al., 1999); *Educational background*, level and specialization of education (Pelled, 1996); *Company tenure*, number of years having worked for the company (Pelled, 1996); *Network ties*, level of connections to facilitate access to different types of knowledge and information (Roberson et al., 2017).

CONCLUSION

Recent resource theories contribute to show that it is not enough to have diversity on a board. The diversity must also be used. These theories show how job-related diversity can be applied to achieve corporate entrepreneurship and value creation. We have shown in this chapter that different attributes of job-related diversity among board members can be of great importance to organizations pursuing corporate entrepreneurship and value creation. The understanding of job-related diversity, and how to use it, is timely and relevant. The importance should be emphasized in a time when teams in the upper echelons of organizations are becoming more diverse and requirements on entrepreneurship and innovation are of growing importance (Narayan et al., 2020). Through the application of three resource theories, we make interesting and innovative contributions to the important topic of boards and diversity. We have demonstrated how organizations can actually manage and use board job-related diversity. We therefore hope that the discussions and analysis presented in this chapter will provide boards with principles and practices that foster the use of the positive attributes of board diversity. We promote the use of the recent resource theories as dynamic capabilities, absorptive capacity and ambidexterity in future research about boards and diversity.

REFERENCES

Åberg, C. (2017). *Dynamic managerial capabilities and boards of directors*. Witten/Herdecke University.

Åberg, C., & Shen, W. (2019). Can board leadership contribute to board dynamic managerial capabilities? An empirical exploration among Norwegian firms. *Journal of Management and Governance, 24*(1), 169–97. https://doi.org/10.1007/s10997-019-09460-6.

Åberg, C., & Torchia, M. (2019). Do boards of directors foster strategic change? A dynamic managerial capabilities perspective. *Journal of Management and Governance, 24*(3), 655–84. https://doi.org/10.1007/s10997-019-09462-4.

Adner, R., & Helfat, C. E. (2003). Corporate effects and dynamic managerial capabilities. *Strategic Management Journal, 24*, 1011–25. https://doi.org/10.1002/smj.331.

Aguilera, R. V., & Jackson, G. (2010). Comparative and international corporate governance. *Academy of Management Annals, 4*(1), 485–556. https://doi.org/10.1080/19416520.2010.495525.

Bankewitz, M., Aberg, C., & Teuchert, C. (2016). Digitalization and boards of directors: a new era of corporate governance? *Business and Management Research, 5*(2). https://doi.org/10.5430/bmr.v5n2p58.

Barney, J. (1991). Firm resources and sustained competitive advantage. *Journal of Management, 17*(1), 99–120.

Carpenter, M. A., Geletkanycz, M. A., & Sanders, W. M. G. (2004). Upper echelons research revisited: antecedents, elements, and consequences of top management team composition. *Journal of Management, 30*(6), 749–78. https://doi.org/10.1016/j.jm.2004.06.001.

Cohen, W. M., & Levinthal, D. A. (1991). Absorptive capacity: a new perspective on learning and innovation. *Administrative Science Quarterly, 35*(1), 128–52.

Daily, C. M., Dalton, D. R., & Cannella, A. A. (2003). Corporate governance: decades of dialogue and data. *Academy of Management Review, 8*(3), 371–82.

Finkelstein, S., Hambrick, D. C., & Cannella, A. A. (2009). *Strategic leadership: theory and research on executives, top management teams, and boards*. Oxford University Press. https://doi.org/10.1093/acprof:oso/9780195162073.001.0001.

Forbes, D. P., & Milliken, F. J. (1999). Cognition and corporate governance: understanding boards of directors as strategic decision-making groups. *Academy of Management Review, 24*(3), 489–505. https://doi.org/10.5465/AMR.1999.2202133.

Gabaldon, P., Kanadlı, S. B., & Bankewitz, M. (2018). How does job-related diversity affect boards' strategic participation? An information-processing approach. *Long Range Planning, 51*(6), 937–52.

García-Granero, A., Fernández-Mesa, A., Jansen, J. J. P., & Vega-Jurado, J. (2018). Top management team diversity and ambidexterity: the contingent role of shared responsibility and CEO cognitive trust. *Long Range Planning, 51*(6), 881–93. https://doi.org/10.1016/j.lrp.2017.11.001.

Garg, S., & Eisenhardt, K. M. (2016). Unpacking the CEO-board relationship: how strategy-making happens in entrepreneurial firms. *Academy of Management Journal, 60*(5), 1828–58. https://ssrn.com/abstract=2840068.

Golden, B. R., & Zajac, E. J. (2001). When will boards influence strategy? Inclination × power = strategic change. *Strategic Management Journal, 22*(12), 1087–111. https://doi.org/10.1002/smj.202.

Guth, W. D., & Ginsberg, A. (1990). Guest editors' introduction: corporate entrepreneurship. *Strategic Management Journal, 11*, 5–15.

Hambrick, D. C., & Mason, P. A. (1984). Upper echelons: the organization as a reflection of its top managers. *Academy of Management Journal, 9*(2), 193–206.

Harrison, D. A., Price, K. H., Gavin, J. H., & Florey, A. T. (2002). Time, teams, and task performance: changing effects of surface-and deep-level diversity on group functioning. *Academy of Management Journal, 45*(5), 1029–45.

Helfat, C. E., & Martin, J. A. (2015). Dynamic managerial capabilities: a perspective on the relationship between managers, creativity, and innovation. In C. Shalley (ed.), *The Oxford handbook of creativity, innovation, and entrepreneurship* (pp. 421–30). Oxford University Press.

Hisrich, R., & Kearney, C. (2011). *Corporate entrepreneurship: how to create a thriving entrepreneurial spirit throughout your company.* McGraw Hill Professional.

Huse, M. (2005). Accountability and creating accountability: a framework for exploring behavioural perspectives of corporate governance. *British Journal of Management, 16*(s1), S65–S79. https://doi.org/10.1111/j.1467-8551.2005.00448.x.

Huse, M. (2007). *Boards, governance and value creation: the human side of corporate governance.* Cambridge University Press.

Jansen, J. J., George, G., Van den Bosch, F. A., & Volberda, H. W. (2008). Senior team attributes and organizational ambidexterity: the moderating role of transformational leadership. *Journal of Management Studies, 45*(5), 982–1007.

Kamasak, R., Özbilgin, M., Kucukaltan, B., & Yavuz, M. (2019). Regendering of dynamic managerial capabilities in the context of binary perspectives on gender diversity. *Gender in Management: An International Journal, 35*(1), 19–36. https://doi.org/10.1108/gm-05-2019-0063.

Kirsch, A. (2018). The gender composition of corporate boards: a review and research agenda. *The Leadership Quarterly, 29*(2), 346–64.

Kirton, G., & Greene, A. M. (2015). *The dynamics of managing diversity: a critical approach.* Routledge.

Kor, Y. Y., & Misangyi, V. F. (2008). Outside directors' industry-specific experience and firms' liability of newness. *Strategic Management Journal, 29*(12), 1345–55. https://doi.org/10.1002/smj.709.

Kor, Y. Y., & Sundaramurthy, C. (2009). Experience-based human capital and social capital of outside directors. *Journal of Management, 35*(4), 981–1006. https://doi.org/10.1177/0149206308321551.

Lane, P. J., Koka, B. R., & Pathak, S. (2006). The reification of absorptive capacity: a critical review and rejuvenation of the construct. *Academy of Management Review, 31*(4), 833–63.

Lowik, S., Kraaijenbrink, J., & Groen, A. J. (2017). Antecedents and effects of individual absorptive capacity: a micro-foundational perspective on open innovation. *Journal of Knowledge Management, 21*(6), 1319–41. https://doi.org/10.1108/jkm-09-2016-0410.

Machold, S., & Farquhar, S. (2013). Board task evolution: a longitudinal field study in the UK. *Corporate Governance: An International Review, 21*(2), 147–64. https://doi.org/10.1111/corg.12017.

Narayan, S., Sidhu, J. S., & Volberda, H. W. (2020). From attention to action: the influence of cognitive and ideological diversity in top management teams on business model innovation. *Journal of Management Studies, 58*(8), 2082–110.

O'Reilly, C., & Tushman, M. L. (2013). Organizational ambidexterity: past, present, and future. *Academy of Management Perspectives, 27*(4), 324–38. https://doi.org/10.2139/ssrn.978493.

Oehmichen, J., Heyden, M. L. M., Georgakakis, D., & Volberda, H. W. (2016). Boards of directors and organizational ambidexterity in knowledge-intensive firms. *The International Journal of Human Resource Management, 28*(2), 283–306. https://doi.org/10.1080/09585192.2016.1244904.

Pelled, L. H. (1996). Demographic diversity, conflict, and work group outcomes: an intervening process theory. *Organization Science, 7*(6), 615–31.

Pelled, L. H., Eisenhardt, K. M., & Xin, K. R. (1999). Exploring the black box: an analysis of work group diversity, conflict and performance. *Administrative Science Quarterly*, *44*(1), 1–28.

Post, C., & Byron, K. (2015). Women on boards and firm financial performance: a meta-analysis. *The Academy of Management Journal*, *58*(5), 1546–71.

Rejeb, W. Ben, Berraies, S., & Talbi, D. (2019). The contribution of board of directors' roles to ambidextrous innovation. *European Journal of Innovation Management*, *23*(1), 40–66. https://doi.org/10.1108/ejim-06-2018-0110.

Rindova, V. (1999). What corporate boards have to do with strategy: a cognative perspective. *Journal of Management Studies*, *36*(7). https://doi.org/10.1111/1467-6486.00165.

Roberson, Q., Holmes IV, O., & Perry, J. L. (2017). Transforming research on diversity and firm performance: a dynamic capabilities perspective. *Academy of Management Annals*, *11*(1), 189–216.

Schønning, A., Walther, A., Machold, S., & Huse, M. (2018). The effects of directors' exploratory, transformative and exploitative learning on boards' strategic involvement: an absorptive capacity perspective. *European Management Review*, *16*(3), 683–98. https://doi.org/10.1111/emre.12186.

Sirmon, D. G., Hitt, M. A., & Ireland, R. D. (2007). Managing firm resources in dynamic environments to create value: looking inside the black box. *The Academy of Management Review*, *32*(1), 273–92.

Stevenson, H. H., & Jarillo, J. C. (1990). A paradigm of entrepreneurship: entrepreneurial management. *Strategic Management Journal*, *11*, 17–27.

Tasheva, S., & Hillman, A. J. (2019). Integrating diversity at different levels: multilevel human capital, social capital, and demographic diversity and their implications for team effectiveness. *Academy of Management Review*, 44(4), 746–65.

Tasheva, S., & Nielsen, B. B. (2020). The role of global dynamic managerial capability in the pursuit of international strategy and superior performance. *Journal of International Business Studies*, 1–20. https://doi.org/10.1057/s41267-020-00336-8.

Teece, D. J. (2007). Explicating dynamic capabilities: the nature and microfoundations of (sustainable) enterprise performance. *Strategic Management Journal*, *28*(13), 1319–50. https://doi.org/10.1002/smj.640.

Teece, D. J., Pisano, G., & Shuen, A. (1997). Dynamic capabilities and strategic management. *Strategic Management Journal*, *18*(7), 509–33. https://doi.org/10.1002/(SICI)1097 -0266(199708)18:7<509::AID-SMJ882>3.0.CO;2-Z.

Torchia, M., Calabrò, A., Gabaldon, P., & Kanadli, S. B. (2018). Women directors' contribution to organizational innovation: a behavioral approach. *Scandinavian Journal of Management*, *34*(2), 215–24. https://doi.org/10.1016/j.scaman.2018.02.001.

Tushman, M. L., & O'Reilly, C. (1996). Ambidextrous organizations: managing evolutionary and revolutionary change. *California Management Review*, *38*(4), 8–30. https://doi.org/10 .2307/41165852.

Webber, S. S., & Donahue, L. M. (2001). Impact of highly and less job-related diversity on work group cohesion and performance: a meta-analysis. *Journal of Management*, *27*(2), 141–62.

Westphal, J. D., & Fredrickson, J. W. (2001). Who directs strategic change? Director experience, the selection of new CEOs, and change in corporate strategy. *Strategic Management Journal*, *22*(12), 1113–37. https://doi.org/10.1002/smj.205.

Zahra, S. A., Filatotchev, I., & Wright, M. (2009). How do threshold firms sustain corporate entrepreneurship? The role of boards and absorptive capacity. *Journal of Business Venturing*, *24*(3), 248–60. https://doi.org/10.1016/j.jbusvent.2008.09.001.

Zahra, S., & George, G. (2002). Absorptive capacity: a review, reconceptualization and extension. *Academy of Management Review*, *27*(2), 185–203.

Zahra, S., Neubaum, D., & Huse, M. (2000). Entrepreneurship in medium-size companies: Exploring the effects of ownership and governance systems. *Journal of Management*, *26*(5), 947–976.

Zahra, S., & Pearce, J. A. (1989). Boards of directors and corporate financial performance: a review and integrative model. *Journal of Management*, *15*(2), 291–334.

6. Board of director international experience and CSR engagement in Asian emerging economies

Abdullah Al-Mamun, Michael Seamer, Jeremy Galbreath and Mariano L.M. Heyden

To what extent do firms in emerging economies engage in corporate social responsibility (CSR)? CSR engagement entails activities and practices that further the social good, by going beyond legal or regulatory requirements to balance a firm's economic goals with those of broader stakeholders (Barnett, 2007). In the context of emerging economies, some suggest that firms face lower pressures for CSR than their counterparts in developed countries and therefore tend to demonstrate less engagement (Khan et al., 2013; Young et al., 2008). In part, this is believed to be due to lower local pressures from stakeholders, such as regulators or advocacy groups, who are often weakly organized or lack sufficient societal backing. Yet, studies suggest emerging economy firms are not entirely devoid of CSR engagement.

Welford (2004) identified that, with respect to CSR, while firms in emerging economies tend to lag firms in developed economies, they nonetheless demonstrate some level of engagement and that "there is great scope for [firms in both types of economies] to learn from each other" (p. 31). Baskin (2006), in turn, found that after strict screening of criteria of the Dow Jones Sustainability Index (a global barometer of CSR engagement), a small, but still significant 7.8 percent were from emerging-market firms. More recently, Yin (2017) indicates that the number of firms reporting on engagement in CSR practices in the emerging economy phase of China increased from 32 in 2006 to 1,705 by 2012, a nearly 94 percent compound annual growth rate. While such studies are important in recognizing the increasing prevalence of CSR engagement in emerging economies, what remains largely understudied are the *drivers* of firm-level CSR engagement in these economies.

In our study, we take the perspective that while there is evidence to suggest that some firms in emerging economies are engaging in CSR, weakly organized government and stakeholder influence around a firm's broader social responsibilities—and even societal indifference to the extent to which firms demonstrate engagement in CSR—remains (Khan et al., 2013; Young et al., 2008). In this sense, the decision of firms in emerging economies to engage in CSR is likely to be highly discretionary. Here, internal factors are believed to be important (Yin, 2017). We propose that one key internal factor is the board of directors (Masulis & Mobbs, 2011). Boards of directors enact a key governance role by drawing on their knowledge and experience to shape the scope of stakeholder concerns, including concerns related to CSR, in firm strategy decisions (Hillman & Dalziel, 2003; Katmon et al., 2019). However, an unexamined plausibility is that the extent to which boards of firms in emerging economies engage with CSR may be influenced by their experience accumulated with firms in developed economies (Lee & Roberts, 2015). As such, the 'internationalization' of boards takes on importance (Oxelheim et al., 2013); namely, the level of international experience of the highest decision-making authority in the firm—the board of directors.

We make a few key contributions to the literature. First, we distinguish between different types of international experience of board members from emerging economies. While we can expect that international experience matters more generally, we distinguish between different types of international experience of board members (i.e., international experience accumulated in other emerging economies; international experience accumulated in developed economies). In doing so, we argue that experience accrued by directors in different foreign economic contexts may help explain variation in local CSR engagement in emerging economies.

Second, we conceptualize boards as a conduit for cross-national learning of corporate conduct, exemplified here in terms of CSR engagement. To do so, we draw on resource dependence theory (RDT) (Pfeffer & Salancik, 1978). RDT largely focuses on the interdependencies of firms with the external environment. In our case, we focus on the directors of firms in emerging economies and the extent to which they provide knowledge gained through developed economy experiences (Heyden et al., 2015). Given the increasing recognition by emerging economies that they can learn from norms and standards (e.g., CSR) prevalent in the larger global environment, the context of international experience of directors in emerging economies becomes an important attribute (Chapple & Moon, 2005; Mishra & Suar, 2010).

Third, drawing on RDT, we hypothesize along two core mechanisms through which a board's international experience may influence CSR engagement in firms in emerging economies (Lee & Roberts, 2015; Miletkov et al., 2017). The first is the *diverse experience accumulation* within international environments that reinforces or expands the worldview of directors to alternative business practices, standards, and stakeholder awareness. The second is through the *reverse knowledge transfer* (Colakoglu et al., 2014; Dhanaraj et al., 2004; Lazarova & Tarique, 2005), where emerging economy firms' strategies can be informed by the international learnings of their directors. Thus, the reverse knowledge transfer of directors can provide the firm with global views and international learnings that can assist in fostering CSR engagement. As such, we highlight cross-border effects of boards and make an important contribution to the paucity of theory on why emerging economy firms differ in CSR engagement. Together, we advance the concept of board international experience as an important attribute that can help explain CSR engagement in emerging economy firms.

CONCEPTUAL BACKGROUND AND HYPOTHESES

The experience of boards is important for understanding why firms vary in their strategic choices (Hearn, 2015; Heyden et al., 2015; Singh & Delios, 2017), especially as pertaining to CSR engagement (Katmon et al., 2019). The international business and strategy literature has acknowledged the role of boards and the importance of international experience of domestic directors as an emerging focal topic of research (Daily et al., 2000; Filatotchev et al., 2019; Lee & Roberts, 2015). Although studies have looked at how and why boards internationalize the experiences of their directors (Beji et al., 2020; Oxelheim et al., 2013), and have shown that director' international experience matters (Lee & Roberts, 2015), not all international experience may matter in the same way (Miletkov et al., 2017). As such, the context of international director experience could, for instance, underpin the institutional standards of CSR engagement that they have been subjected to, their experience in consolidating varied stakeholder needs, and broader expectations of the corporation's role in society. Yet, despite increasing research on emerging economies (Meyer, 2004; Meyer et al., 2009; Wright et al., 2005), little is known about how the context of accumulated international experience (developed or emerging) of local directors' influences variation in CSR engagement across firms in emerging economies.

Local Experience

According to Fredrickson (1986, p. 281), "[c]ontext within which decisions are made and implemented—may motivate or impede strategic activity." Directors on the board, who are limited to experience accumulated within their local context (Estrin et al., 2018), may restrict their scope of strategic activity. This is because they are likely to have a limited view of uncertainties faced by the firm and the resources that need to be acquired to reduce complexity and constraints (Maitland & Sammartino, 2015). More directly, the internationalization of markets is creating an environment where resource dependencies are affected and have changed (e.g., dependence on low-cost countries for manufacturing and production processes, increased access to information and knowledge) (Ghemawat, 2007, 2017). However, if directors on boards only operate within local contexts, they may be limited in their understanding of the broader global environment and how foreign learnings can improve local policies.

With respect to social responsibility, although global expectations for engagement are growing, evidence suggests that firms in developing economies tend to face weaker pressures to adopt CSR and have lower sanctions for being socially irresponsible as standards and norms tend to be lower in this area (Khan et al., 2013; Young et al., 2008). Further, in relation to firm ethical behavior, CSR is generally lower and more dispersed in emerging economies (Khan et al., 2013; Young et al., 2008). Hence, when directors of emerging economy firms have only accumulated local context experience and resources, we argue that they are unlikely to readily reduce uncertainties related to the potential consequences of not engaging in CSR.

We therefore posit:

HYPOTHESIS 1 (H₁): Boards of directors in emerging economy firms with a greater degree of director experience accumulated in the local context will be associated with lower levels of CSR engagement.

International Experience from Similar Context

Following RDT, researchers have established that directors, based on their unique set of experiences, bring a number of resources to the board including knowledge, information, specialized expertise, and an understanding of policies and standards (Heneman III & Milanowski, 2011). Some of these resources are attained through serving on the boards of firms in other countries and are effective mechanisms for minimizing external uncertainties firms face from the environment (Hillman et al., 2000). In particular, directors who accumulate cross-border experiences are likely to encourage new behaviors and/or strategies (Le & Kroll, 2017) which are perpetuated from diverse perspectives and contemporary thinking beyond local contexts. However, context is likely the critical feature here.

   Directors on boards in emerging economy firms who have accumulated experience and resources by serving on boards of firms in other *emerging* economies may not produce the required levels of reverse knowledge transfer (Dhanaraj et al., 2004; Yang et al., 2008). This is because attributes of a country shape expectations of, and pressures on, companies and institutions. When cross-national contexts are similar, differences from which directors can learn are less likely to become salient (Pankaj, 2001). While cross-border exposure may heighten directors' experience and resources acquired, operating in similar contexts is unlikely to result in strategically differential and diverse outcomes, particularly with respect to CSR engagement. Hence:

HYPOTHESIS 2 (H₂): Boards of directors in emerging economy firms with a greater degree of director international experience accumulated in other emerging economies, will be associated with lower levels of CSR engagement.

International Experience from Developed Country Firms

Matten and Moon (2008) argue that acceptance of CSR as a business practice has spread, particularly among developed economies, although emerging economies are not altogether removed (Baskin, 2006; Welford, 2004). The difference is that developed economies tend to have more robust national business systems (NBS) (Matten & Moon, 2008; Whitley, 1998) than do emerging economies. The robust NBS of developed economies demonstrate sound political systems that encourage (if not hold to account) firms to engage in CSR. In some cases, law requires socially responsible practices, such as pollution control, of firms operating in developed countries; which can make them more commonplace topics in broader strategy discussions. Robust NBS are believed to lead to greater engagement with CSR by firms located in developed economies (Campbell, 2007; Matten & Moon, 2008).

While the pressure across emerging economy firms to engage in CSR may be less readily present than firms operating in developed economies, we argue that they may be undermining future opportunities, reputation, and legitimacy. To better grasp opportunities from CSR and to better manage or reduce potential uncertainties from *not* engaging in socially responsible practices, we put forth that directors with international experience accumulated from firms headquartered in developed countries are vital because of regulatory accountability for environmental issues (e.g., carbon emissions and pollution reporting; Galbreath, 2012), 'soft laws' or quasi-legal instruments (e.g., Global Reporting Initiative and the Dow Jones Sustainability Index; Baskin, 2006), and cultural or normative expectations (e.g., philanthropy; Matten & Moon, 2008). Post the global financial crisis (GFC), higher education institutions further emphasized business programs focused on business ethics, CSR, and sustainability (Evans & Weiss, 2008). The view is that such programs 'spill over' knowledge of and expectations for CSR of the firms operating in these economies (Marano et al., 2017).

Given such a focus on CSR, directors on boards of emerging economy firms that accumulate international experience from firms headquartered in developed countries are more likely to bring varied ideas, skills, and perspectives related to social responsibility to decision-making. This accumulated experience and knowledge can also be (re)combined in new ways to enable boards to explore novel ways in which to engage in CSR. Further, directors with international experience from firms headquartered in developed countries are exposed to geocentric attitudes and mindsets that value ideas independent of their developed economy perspectives (Nielsen & Nielsen, 2010).

Taken together, directors on boards of emerging economy firms who have accumulated international experience from firms in developed countries will be more likely to adopt best practices learned from their foreign experience (Dhanaraj et al., 2004; Yang et al., 2008). Such directors avail firms with a number of resources including: (1) international quality of advice and counsel (Dhanaraj et al., 2004; Yang et al., 2008); (2) international networks and/or professional ties (Aggarwal, 2020); and (3) insight into and understanding of national business systems, regulatory, and cultural institutions (Pfeffer & Salancik, 1978). The directors, by virtue of their international experience from developed countries, may introduce some of these rationales at home, acknowledging untapped potential benefits of CSR engagements, such as legitimacy, reputation, and customer loyalty. Hence:

HYPOTHESIS 3 (H_3): Boards of directors in emerging economy firms with a greater degree of director international experience accumulated from firms headquartered in developed economies, will be associated with higher levels of CSR engagement.

DATA AND METHODS

Given a paucity of empirical research on CSR engagement across Asian emerging economy firms, this study focuses on Malaysia, Pakistan, and the Philippines as some fast-emerging exemplars of the region. These three countries also provide us with an interesting context for the research (Abdullah et al., 2016; Ramdani & Witteloostuijn, 2010) with their recent pledge to stakeholders to improve corporate governance principle implementation and to initiate policies and procedures consistent with those adopted in developed economies since the Sarbanes–Oxley Act. These countries are also suitable emerging economies in which to conduct our study because of having comparable institutional realities, regulatory frameworks, and cultural values, as evident from the partial similarity table summarized in Table 6.1.

Sampling

We initially targeted the largest 300 listed companies from the selected economies (100 largest companies from each stock exchange). However, due to resource and time constraints, our final sample yielded 238 companies, comprising 10,608 director profiles of publicly listed companies from the three relevant stock exchanges: Bursa Malaysia, Pakistan Stock Exchange, and the Philippines Stock Exchange over five consecutive years from 2010 through 2014. Analysis of director profiles was gathered from relevant company annual reports, which were retrieved either from the appropriate stock exchange or company websites. DataStream was accessed in order to extract financial data for each company. CSR engagement data was acquired from the CSRHub database.

Dependent Variable

We employ the CSR engagement of the focal Asian emerging economy firms as the dependent variable. We relied on the CSRHub database that rates companies from 144 countries and provides access to CSR and sustainability ratings of emerging economy firms using four categories: community engagement, employee welfare, environmental sustainability, and corporate governance (Al-Mamun & Seamer, 2021). This study uses all four ratings for the five consecutive years 2010 to 2014, with quarterly scores averaged for each year to generate a yearly score for each company.

Independent Variables

This study is concerned with three main predictive variables: domestic directors with experience confined to the home country (H_1), domestic directors with accumulated international experience from other emerging economies (H_2), and directors with accumulated international experience from firms headquartered in developed countries (H_3). Domestic director local experience is measured as the number of directors

Table 6.1   Partial similarity of Asian economies compared to selected Asian emerging economies

Country	Economic			Regulatory		Cultural and Social		
	Economic[1] GDP (b)	GDP per capita[b]	FDI inflows[c] (m)	Regulatory[d] (Quality)	Legal System	Cultural[1]	Population[f]	Religious Ethnicity
Malaysia	255.02	6,319.0	9,060.0	70.81	Common Law	100	28.11	Islam
Pakistan	177.41	748.0	2,022.0	30.62	Common Law	55	170.6	Islam
Philippines	199.59	1,403.4	1,298.1	44.98	Common Law & Civil Law	94	93.73	Christianity & Islam
China	6,100.62	2,891.1	114,734.0	44.50	Socialist legal system	80	1,348.54	Taoism, Buddhism, Islam, Protestantism & Catholicism
India	1,656.62	1,031.6	27,417.1	39.23	Common Law	77	1,231.21	Hinduism, Buddhism, Jainism & Sikhism
Singapore	236.42	34,758.4	55,075.8	98.09	Common Law	74	5.08	Buddhism, Islam, Hinduism & Christianity
S. Korea	1,094.50	22,086.9	9,497.4	78.95	Judicial system	60	49.55	Christianity
Japan	4,648.47	36,296.3	−1,251.8	81.82	Civil Law & Common Law	54	128.1	Shinto & Buddhism
Indonesia	377.90	1,570.2	13,770.6	37.80	Civil Law	78	242.5	Islam
Thailand	210.09	3,163.9	14,555.0	56.46	Civil Law & Common Law	64	67.21	Buddhism

Note: [a] Figures in billion US$, 2010 values retrieved from World Bank Data Bank World Development indicators: http://data.worldbank.org/data-catalog/world-development-indicators. [b] Figures in US$, retrieved from World Bank Data Bank World Development indicators: http://data.worldbank.org/data-catalog/world-development-indicators. [c] Figures in million US$, 2010 values retrieved from United Nations Conference on Trade and Development (UNCTAD): http://unctad.org/en/Pages/DIAE/World%20Investment%20Report/Annex-Tables.aspx. [d] Figures produced by World Bank yearly and the values are as of 2010. They show the effectiveness of regulatory system of the country: http://data.worldbank.org/data-catalog/world-development-indicators. [e] Figures represent Power Distance of Hofstade Cultural Dimensions. [f] Figures presented in millions as retrieved from World Bank Data Bank World Development indicators: http://data.worldbank.org/data-catalog/world-development-indicators.

appointed to the board with accumulated experience from local companies only, divided by total board size. Similarly, directors with accumulated experience from other emerging economies and from firms headquartered in developed economies are measured as the proportion of these directors to total board size using hand-collected data from board member profiles contained in the relevant firm's annual report.

Control Variables

We control for several variables of theoretical merit in our case, such as board size, board meeting frequency, board member age, board members' tenure, board education qualifications, board gender diversity, board independence, board members from developed countries, CEO–chair duality, CEO tenure, CEO age, CEO gender, CEO education qualifications, foreign ownership, and firm size. We also controlled for country and year to be consistent with extant studies (see e.g., Su et al., 2016).

ANALYSIS AND RESULTS

The Generalized Estimating Equations (GEE) approach is used to analyze the data, which is increasingly extolled as best practice in strategy and management research (Echambadi et al., 2006). We assessed the model fit based on the level and significance of the Wald's Chi-square statistic (Ballinger, 2004). The descriptive statistics and correlation matrix results are presented in Tables 6.2a and 6.2b. Table 6.3 presents the results of the application GEE to estimate the influence the board's accumulated international experience on CSR engagement among emerging economy firms. We also test for the presence of multicollinearity, using a two-tailed test, and address endogeneity concerns with the analysis of lagged independent variables (results available on request) and find that correlation coefficients and variance inflation factor (VIF) results suggest multicollinearity is not an issue with this study (Hill & Adkins, 2007).

Table 6.2a   Means, descriptive statistics, and correlations of board international experiences and other controlling variables of emerging economy firms

	Mean	SD	1	2	3	4	5	6	7	8	9	10
CSR	1.667	0.123	1									
Board members with no international experience	0.454	0.193	-.113**	1								
Board members international experience from other emerging economies	0.114	0.129	.107**	-.162**	1							
Board members accumulated international experiences in developed countries	0.256	0.118	.076**	-.714**	-0.019	1						
Board size	0.947	0.104	.058*	-.235**	.221**	.279**	1					
Board tenure	8.934	4.171	-.078**	0.009	-.061*	0.023	-.105**	1				
Board age	58.709	5.902	-.085**	0.037	-0.019	-0.026	-0.056	.174**	1			
Board advanced degree	0.493	0.250	-.096**	-0.019	-.335**	.168**	-.141**	0.048	.086**	1		
Board gender diversity	0.085	0.102	.090**	-0.018	.156**	-0.016	.130**	-0.052	-.191**	-.225**	1	
Board outsiders	0.525	0.225	-.133**	-0.023	-.181**	.083*	-.063*	-.072*	.268**	.360**	-.369**	1
Developed country board member	0.177	0.098	.062*	-.616**	.126**	.174**	0.009	-0.019	0.045	-0.006	0.022	.061*

	Mean	SD	1	2	3	4	5	6	7	8	9	10
CEO duality	0.797	0.402	0.020	-.100**	.067*	.081**	.145**	-0.043	.079**	0.047	-0.034	.117**
CEO tenure	7.725	6.482	-0.048	0.036	0.042	-.082**	-0.004	.563**	.163**	-.201**	0.036	-.151**
CEO age	55.497	7.484	-0.025	0.054	0.021	-.064*	0.045	.151**	.643**	-0.048	-.091**	.067*
CEO gender	0.042	0.201	0.046	0.033	-0.034	0.005	0.011	0.027	-0.026	-.104**	.123**	-0.057
CEO advanced degree	0.516	0.500	.123**	-.063*	-0.002	.061*	.102**	.072*	-0.013	.096**	-0.028	-.100**
Firm sales	4.851	0.963	.146**	0.015	.252**	-.096**	.101**	-.122**	-.150**	-.278**	.083**	-.271**
Foreign ownership	0.165	0.156	0.055	-.098**	0.002	.123**	0.038	-0.045	0.001	0.029	-0.025	0.014
Malaysia	0.429	0.495	.098**	.078**	.358**	-.302**	-0.009	-.293**	0.042	-.583**	.153**	-.267**
Philippines	0.163	0.370	.094**	-.099**	.154**	.112**	.170**	.354**	-.342**	-.124**	.117**	-.356**
Pakistan	0.408	0.492	-.169**	-0.005	-.477**	.220**	-.119**	0.029	.215**	.675**	-.242**	.537**

Note: * p < .05; ** p < .01; *** p < .001. Analytics included year dummies [2010 = Dummy year, 2010; 2011 = Dummy year, 2011; 2012 = Dummy year, 2012; 2013 = Dummy year, 2013; 2014 = Dummy year, 2014] which are not presented here due to resource constraints; however, available on request.

Table 6.2b   *Means, descriptive statistics and correlations of board international experiences and other controlling variables of emerging economy firms*

	11	12	13	14	15	16	17	18	19	20	21
Developed country board member	1										
CEO-duality	.079**	1									
CEO tenure	−0.014	−0.030	1								
CEO age	−0.015	−.122**	.300**	1							
CEO gender	−0.043	−0.001	−0.045	−0.040	1						
CEO advanced degree	−0.042	−0.040	−0.004	0.009	−0.045	1					
Firm sales	−0.025	.067*	0.023	−0.040	.099**	0.016	1				
Foreign ownership	−0.007	0.057	−.120**	−0.043	0.046	.061*	−0.011	1			
Malaysia	.090**	0.023	.126**	.073*	0.026	−.232**	.369**	−.077**	1		
Philippines	−.155**	−.165**	.112**	−.088**	0.023	.242**	.147**	0.037	−.383**	1	
Pakistan	0.026	.101**	−.211**	−0.007	−0.043	0.052	−.483**	0.049	−.719**	−.366**	1

Note: * p < .05; ** p < .01; *** p < .001. Analytics included year dummies [2010 = Dummy year, 2010; 2011; 2011; 2012 = Dummy year, 2012; 2013; 2014 = Dummy year, 2013; 2014 = Dummy year, 2014] which are not presented here due to resource constraints; however, available on request.

Table 6.3 *GEE results of board international experience of emerging economy firms*

	Model 1	Model 2	Model 3	Model 4	Model 5
	Control	No Int Exp	Eme Eco Exp	Dev Con Exp	All Var
Intercept	1.742***	1.832***	1.747***	.113***	1.741***
	(.000)	(.000)	(.000)	(.000)	(.000)
Pakistan	.015	.006	.015	.018	.006
	(.409)	(.747)	(.412)	(.778)	(.731)
Philippines	−.008	−.010	−.005	.020	−.017
	(.694)	(.639)	(.830)	(.362)	(.447)
	(.000)	(.000)	(.000)	(.000)	(.000)
Sales	.014**	.014*	.014**	.007**	.014**
	(.035)	(.034)	(.036)	(.036)	(.037)
Foreign ownership	−.003	−.008	−.004	−.034	−.013
	(.924)	(.814)	(.909)	(.715)	(.699)
Board size	−.034	−.062	−.037	.059	−.084
	(.556)	(.288)	(.517)	(.169)	(.158)
Board tenure	−.004**	−.004**	−.004**	−.002**	−.004**
	(.019)	(.025)	(.019)	(.018)	(.016)
Board age	−.002	−.003*	−.002	.001*	−.003*
	(.119)	(.099)	(.114)	(.090)	(.086)
Board advanced degree	−.015	−.017	−.015	.037	−.018
	(.681)	(.648)	(.678)	(.625)	(.623)
Board gender diversity	−.033	−.031	−.035	−.062	−.034
	(.596)	(.614)	(.576)	(.611)	(.588)
Board outsiders	−.042	−.044	−.043	.035	−.040
	(.238)	(.206)	(.224)	(.256)	(.255)
Developed country board member	.114***	.013	.111***	.033**	.102**
	(.001)	(.772)	(.001)	(.017)	(.045)
CEO duality	.005	.004	.004	.004	.004
	(.723)	(.789)	(.752)	(.752)	(.765)
CEO tenure	.000	.000	.000	.001	.000
	(.723)	(.691)	(.739)	(.710)	(.732)
CEO age	.001	.001	.001	.001	.001
	(.513)	(.413)	(.505)	(.371)	(.369)
CEO gender	.016	.017	.017	.032	.015
	(.620)	(.609)	(.601)	(.641)	(.629)
CEO advanced degree	.025*	.024*	.025*	.013**	.027**
	(.057)	(.063)	(.059)	(.041)	(.042)
H_1: Proportion board members with no international experience		−.080***			.024
		(.003)			(.580)
H_2: Proportion board members international experience from other emerging economies			.022		.021
			(.622)		(.637)
H_3: Proportion board members accumulated international experiences from firms in developed countries				.033***	.173***
				(.001)	(.001)
Wald Chi-square	454.338	471.518	449.331	504.578	479.032

	Model 1	Model 2	Model 3	Model 4	Model 5
	Control	No Int Exp	Eme Eco Exp	Dev Con Exp	All Var
DF	21	22	22	22	22
QIC	125.256	127.768	129.853	126.634	134.252
QICC	52.455	54.327	54.449	54.2	58.191

Note: $n = 1049$. * $p < 0.05$; ** $p < 0.01$; *** $p < 0.001$. Year dummies included but omitted here due to space constraints.

Results

Hypothesis 1 predicts that domestic directors with experiences restricted to sitting on boards of emerging economy firms will have a negative or no influence on firm CSR engagement practices. Our results from Table 6.3 show a negative and statistically significant value (beta = $-.80$, $p < .01$) in model 2, and no influence in the full model (5) (beta = $.024$, $p > .10$). We relied on [full] model 5 to draw conclusions on hypothesis support. We hence have lack of evidence to support H_1. Hypothesis 2 predicts that domestic directors with accumulated international experience from similar contexts in other emerging economies will have either a negative impact or no influence on the CSR engagement practices of emerging economy firms. Our results show that domestic directors with international experience in other emerging economy firms do not have a statistically significant association with CSR engagement practices in emerging economy firms with model 3 and 5, showing beta = $.02$, $p > .10$ and beta = $.02$, $p > .10$, respectively. Hypothesis 3 proposes that board members with developed country experience would positively affect CSR engagement practices among emerging economy firms. In model 4 and 5 we estimate the impact of board members' accumulated international experience from firms headquartered in developed countries on CSR engagement practices of emerging economy firms, (beta = $.03$, $p < .01$) and (beta = $.17$, $p < .01$), providing empirical supports for the theoretical arguments developed for H_3. Based on results presented in Table 6.3, H_3 is supported.

Endogeneity

Apart from model estimation using GEE, we take further consideration of potential the endogeneity issues related to the nature of our data. This is because many of the focal governance mechanisms such as board context experience, CEO characteristics, board independence, and gender diversity may not be random, rather reflecting a self-selection bias that coincides with other firm governance mechanisms (e.g., CEO characteristics, outsiders, board tenure, education, and age; Sidhu et al., 2020). Consistent with extant studies, we accept that it is often difficult to completely eliminate endogeneity issues with this type of data (see Ali et al., 2018). However, we are confident that the statistical analytics, particularly those based on lagged independent variables, should provide a degree of comfort that even if endogeneity due to reverse-causality is considered, our key findings concerning board international experience and CSR engagement remain reliable based on lagged independent variables (results available on request).

The overall finding of the study is that international experience accumulated from firms headquartered in developed countries can effectively influence firm CSR engagement across Asian emerging economies. This finding is consistent with our theoretical assumption that the knowledge resources imported by these directors are utilized to mitigate the external uncertainties those firms are exposed to. Overall, these results bolster empirical evidence that suggests that emerging economy firms view CSR engagement as an operating expense (see e.g., Khan et al., 2013) and see CSR engagement as a developed country phenomenon (Chapple & Moon, 2005). These findings also show that CSR is not homogeneous across different types of firms (see e.g., Al-Mamun et al., 2016a) and that the international experience–CSR engagement nexus results from an important resource acquisition/transfer from developed to emerging economies.

DISCUSSION

Drawing on RDT, we have argued that the knowledge and experience resources imported by board members with international experience encourage the formulation of positive strategies for CSR engagement. We further argued that boards with international experience accumulated from firms headquartered in developed countries will encourage CSR engagement due to their exposure to international best practices and recognition of the importance of a wider group of stakeholders for the firm (Chapple & Moon, 2005). The results suggest that board members with international experience have a positive effect on the CSR engagement of emerging economy firms but do not offer any evidence of a similar effect for board international experience accumulated by domestic directors from similar contexts in other emerging economies. To the best of our knowledge, this is the first study to examine the relationship between board local/emerging economy experience vs international experience and CSR engagement across Asian emerging economy firms.

Implications for Theory

This study makes an important contribution to both the CSR and corporate governance literature by investigating the impact of board member imported knowledge resources (Aggarwal, 2020; Hillman et al., 2000) accumulated through international experiences (Le & Kroll, 2017) from firms headquartered in developed countries and CSR engagement strategies in emerging economy firms. We also investigate for a similar effect for domestic directors with international experience gained in other emerging economy firms. Our empirical evidence of a positive association between board member international experience accumulated from firms headquartered in developed countries and CSR builds on RDT by suggesting that access to resources from developed country domains are important in encouraging CSR engagement among emerging economies. This aligns with the internationalization of emerging country firms to developed countries through importing the experiences and adopting the best practices from developed countries. This is because companies from emerging economies are highly dependent on foreign product and capital markets (Oxelheim et al., 2013), particularly the developed country ones. Early literature on firms' internationalization suggests that emerging economy firms' internationalization is achieved through deepening their commitment and investment (Tsai & Eisingerich, 2010); our results from this study shows at the firm level they make similar reference to board of directors experience from the foreign market, especially the developed country ones.

We also contribute to the literature regarding reverse knowledge transfer (Colakoglu et al., 2014; Dhanaraj et al., 2004; Lazarova & Tarique, 2005) as our study reveals that the appointment of members with accumulated international experience from developed country firms matters for increased CSR engagement among emerging economy firms. The findings of no relationship between domestic directors with international experience from other emerging economies and CSR suggests that international experience accumulated from similar contexts may not positively impact CSR engagement in emerging economy firms. This finding is consistent with the notion of reverse knowledge transfer (Dhanaraj et al., 2004; Yang et al., 2008) which assumes that reverse knowledge transfer accrues either from developed to emerging economies or emerging to developed economies, not from similar context. This is further consistent with our assumption and argument that the context of director experience matters (Husted et al., 2016).

Emerging economies are important focus due to their divergent institutional characteristics (Al-Mamun et al., 2017; Al-Mamun & Seamer, 2021), varied uncertainties, and less diverse family-dominated ownership of firms (Perkins et al., 2014; Wilkinson et al., 2014). This factor may compromise resource utilizations and the concentration of power resources may restrict CSR engagement (Oh et al., 2018). However, board members that accumulate international experience from firms headquartered in developed countries are unlikely to be influenced by these variations and will strive to contribute their distinctively collated resources (Carpenter et al., 2001; Hillman et al., 2000). Even though the markets are competitive (Wilkinson et al., 2014) and local stakeholders may not always view CSR engagement as a priority (Khan et al., 2013), board members with international experience from firms headquartered in a developed country possess cognitive resources that have a significant positive influence on CSR engagement among Asian emerging economy firms. These directors are also more likely to be exposed to international policies and standards relating to ethical business conduct such as UN SDGs,[1] ISO,[2] GRI,[3] CSR in EU policy,[4] ASEAN,[5] and SAARC[6] (Dhanaraj et al., 2004; Yang et al., 2008).

The assumption that board members with accumulated international experience from developed country firms are more likely to have and value international professional ties is also consistent with our findings. In order to sustain the trust, contacts, and reputations gained through international professional ties, directors with international experience are more likely to promote CSR engagement among emerging economy firms with which they are involved. Importantly then, our study raises a call to examine other aspects of director international experience, such as the length of international assignments and/or (mixed) nationality issues. We suggest, based on the finding in this study, that experience and knowledge accessed through experience working with firms headquartered in developed countries is an important channel through which CSR engagement in emerging economy firms is fostered.

Limitations and Future Research

Our findings and conclusions should be considered within the limitations of the study. First, we have accounted for board members' international experience accumulated from developed countries and controlled for board members' origin from developed countries. It maybe that domestic directors with developed economy international experience and directors with origins in developed economies have differing impacts on CSR engagement in emerging economy firms; as well as influencing different topics related more broadly to CSR that we have not covered here (e.g., Al-Mamun et al., 2016b). Future studies could examine the relationship between experience contexts of developed country board and non-board managers (e.g., COO, CFO) and CSR engagement of emerging economy firms as well as the scale of CSR engagement and the level of change over the period of developed country member appointment (Georgakakis et al., 2019).

Second, we were unable to measure the impact of the length of experience domestic board members had from employment with other emerging economy or developed economy firms. Future studies may also focus on continuity of appointment and the role engaged individuals held in the emerging and developed economy firms. A lengthy gap between employment with other emerging economy firm and appointment to a local firm board may negate the impact of any exposure to ethical business practices and standards gained from cross-border firms because of the differences in cultural attributes and institutional distance between the countries (Pankaj, 2001). Finally, we encourage studies including firms from other emerging economy regions such as South America, Africa, and Eastern Europe. Unpacking country-level variation through multi-level examinations can further add explanatory power to the core ideas advanced here.

NOTES

1.　United Nations Sustainable Development Goals.
2.　International Organization for Standardization.
3.　Global Reporting Initiatives.
4.　European Commission Strategy on CSR.
5.　Association for Southeast Asian Nations.
6.　South Asian Association for Regional Cooperation.

REFERENCES

Abdullah, S. N., Ismail, K. N. I. K., & Nachum, L. (2016). Does having women on boards create value? The impact of societal perceptions and corporate governance in emerging markets. *Strategic Management Journal, 37*, 466–76.

Aggarwal, V. A. (2020). Resource congestion in alliance networks: how a firm's partners' influence the benefits of collaboration. *Strategic Management Journal, 41*, 627–55.

Al-Mamun, A., Heyden, M. L., & Seamer, M. (2016a). Corporate social action in developing economies. In R. Manos and I. Drori (Eds.), *Corporate Responsibility* (pp. 38–72). Springer.

Al-Mamun, A., Rafique, Q., & Heyden, M. L. (2016b). Transgender individuals in Asian Islamic countries: an overview of workplace diversity and inclusion issues in Pakistan, Bangladesh, and Malaysia. In T. Köllen (Ed.), *Sexual Orientation and Transgender Issues in Organizations – Global Perspectives on LGBT Workforce Diversity* (pp. 167–80). Springer.

Al-Mamun, A. & Seamer, M. (2021). Board of director attributes and CSR engagement in emerging economy firms: evidence from across Asia. *Emerging Markets Review, 46*, 100749.

Al-Mamun, A., Yasser, Q. R., Seamer, M., & Heyden, M. L. (2017). Women on corporate boards and financial performance in fast-emerging markets: insights from Malaysia. In N. Muenjohn & A. McMurray (Eds.), *The Palgrave Handbook of Leadership in Transforming Asia* (pp. 349–64). Springer.

Ali, S., Liu, B., & Su, J. J. (2018). Does corporate governance quality affect default risk? The role of growth opportunities and stock liquidity. *International Review of Economics & Finance, 58*, 422–48.

Ballinger, G. A. (2004). Using generalized estimating equations for longitudinal data analysis. *Organizational Research Methods, 7*, 127–50.

Barnett, M. L. (2007). Stakeholder influence capacity and the variability of financial returns to corporate social responsibility. *Academy of Management Review, 32*, 794–816.

Baskin, J. (2006). Corporate responsibility in emerging markets. *Journal of Corporate Citizenship, 24*, 29–47.

Beji, R., Yousfi, O., Loukil, N., & Omri, A. (2020). Board diversity and corporate social responsibility: empirical evidence from France. *Journal of Business Ethics, 173*(6), 1–23.

Campbell, J. L. (2007). Why would corporations behave in socially responsible ways? An institutional theory of corporate social responsibility. *Academy of Management Review, 32*, 946–67.

Carpenter, M. A., Sanders, W. G., & Gregersen, H. B. (2001). Bundling human capital with organizational context: the impact of international assignment experience on multinational firm performance and CEO pay. *Academy of Management Journal, 44*, 493–511.

Chapple, W., & Moon, J. (2005). Corporate social responsibility (CSR) in Asia: a seven-country study of CSR web site reporting. *Business & Society, 44*, 415–41.

Colakoglu, S., Yamao, S., & Lepak, D. P. (2014). Knowledge creation capability in MNC subsidiaries: examining the roles of global and local knowledge inflows and subsidiary knowledge stocks. *International Business Review, 23*, 91–101.

Daily, C. M., Certo, S. T., & Dalton, D. R. (2000). International experience in the executive suite: the path to prosperity? *Strategic Management Journal, 21*, 515–23.

Dhanaraj, C., Lyles, M. A., Steensma, H. K., & Tihanyi, L. (2004). Managing tacit and explicit knowledge transfer in IJVs: the role of relational embeddedness and the impact on performance. *Journal of International Business Studies, 35*, 428–42.

Echambadi, R., Campbell, B., & Agarwal, R. (2006). Encouraging best practice in quantitative management research: an incomplete list of opportunities. *Journal of Management Studies, 43*, 1801–20.

Estrin, S., Meyer, K. E., & Pelletier, A. (2018). Emerging economy MNEs: how does home country munificence matter? *Journal of World Business*, *53*(4), 514–28.

Evans, F. J., & Weiss, E. J. (2008). Views on the importance of ethics in business education. *Advancing Business Ethics Education*, *10*, 43–66.

Fredrickson, J. W. (1986). The strategic decision process and organizational structure. *Academy of Management Review*, *11*, 280–97.

Filatotchev, I., Poulsen, A., & Bell, R. G. (2019). Corporate governance of a multinational enterprise: firm, industry and institutional perspectives. *Journal of Corporate Finance*, *57*, 1–8.

Galbreath, J. (2012). Are boards on board? A model of corporate board influence on sustainability performance. *Journal of Management & Organization*, *18*, 445–60.

Georgakakis, D., Heyden, M. L., Oehmichen, J. D., & Ekanayake, U. I. (2019). Four decades of CEO–TMT interface research: a review inspired by role theory. *The Leadership Quarterly*. https://doi.org/10.1016/j.leaqua.2019.101354.

Ghemawat, P. (2007). Managing differences: the central challenge of global strategy. *Harvard Business Review*, *85*, 58–68, 140.

Ghemawat, P. (2017). *The Laws of Globalization and Business Applications*. Cambridge University Press.

Hearn, B. (2015). Institutional influences on board composition of international joint venture firms listing on emerging stock exchanges: evidence from Africa. *Journal of World Business*, *50*, 205–19.

Heneman III, H. G., & Milanowski, A. T. (2011). Assessing human resource practices alignment: a case study. *Human Resource Management*, *50*, 45–64.

Heyden, M. L., Oehmichen, J., Nichting, S., & Volberda, H. W. (2015). Board background heterogeneity and exploration–exploitation: the role of the institutionally adopted board model. *Global Strategy Journal*, *5*, 154–76.

Hill, R., & Adkins, L. (2007). Collinearity. In B. H. Baltagi (Ed.), *A Companion to Theoretical Econometrics* (pp. 256–78). Blackwell Publishing.

Hillman, A. J., Cannella, A. A., & Paetzold, R. L. (2000). The resource dependence role of corporate directors: strategic adaptation of board composition in response to environmental change. *Journal of Management Studies*, *37*, 235–56.

Hillman, A. J., & Dalziel, T. (2003). Boards of directors and firm performance: integrating agency and resource dependence perspectives. *Academy of Management Review*, *28*, 383–96.

Husted, B. W., Montiel, I., & Christmann, P. (2016). Effects of local legitimacy on certification decisions to global and national CSR standards by multinational subsidiaries and domestic firms. *Journal of International Business Studies*, *47*, 382–97.

Katmon, N., Mohamad, Z. Z., Norwani, N. M., & Al Farooque, O. (2019). Comprehensive board diversity and quality of corporate social responsibility disclosure: evidence from an emerging market. *Journal of Business Ethics*, *157*(2), 1–35.

Khan, A., Muttakin, M. B., & Siddiqui, J. (2013). Corporate governance and corporate social responsibility disclosures: evidence from an emerging economy. *Journal of Business Ethics*, *114*, 207–23.

Lazarova, M., & Tarique, I. (2005). Knowledge transfer upon repatriation. *Journal of World Business*, *40*, 361–73.

Le, S., & Kroll, M. (2017). CEO international experience: effects on strategic change and firm performance. *Journal of International Business Studies*, *48*, 573–95.

Lee, J.-H., & Roberts, M. J. (2015). International returnees as outside directors: a catalyst for strategic adaptation under institutional pressure. *International Business Review*, *24*, 594–604.

Maitland, E., & Sammartino, A. (2015). Decision making and uncertainty: the role of heuristics and experience in assessing a politically hazardous environment. *Strategic Management Journal*, *36*(10), 1554–78.

Marano, V., Tashman, P., & Kostova, T. (2017). Escaping the iron cage: liabilities of origin and CSR reporting of emerging market multinational enterprises. *Journal of International Business Studies*, *48*(3), 386–408.

Masulis, R. W., & Mobbs, S. (2011). Are all inside directors the same? Evidence from the external directorship market. *The Journal of Finance*, *66*(3), 823–72.

Matten, D., & Moon, J. (2008). "Implicit" and "explicit" CSR: a conceptual framework for a comparative understanding of corporate social responsibility. *Academy of Management Review*, *33*, 404–24.

Meyer, K. E. (2004). Perspectives on multinational enterprises in emerging economies. *Journal of International Business Studies*, *35*(4), 259–76.

Meyer, K. E., Estrin, S., Bhaumik, S. K., & Peng, M. W. (2009). Institutions, resources, and entry strategies in emerging economies. *Strategic Management Journal*, *30*(1), 61–80.

Miletkov, M., Poulsen, A., & Wintoki, M. B. (2017). Foreign independent directors and the quality of legal institutions. *Journal of International Business Studies*, *48*, 267–92.

Mishra, S., & Suar, D. (2010). Does corporate social responsibility influence firm performance of Indian companies? *Journal of Business Ethics*, *95*, 571–601.

Nielsen, S., & Nielsen, B. B. (2010). Why do firms employ foreigners on their top management team? An exploration of strategic fit, human capital and attraction-selection-attrition perspectives. *International Journal of Cross Cultural Management*, *10*, 195–209.

Oh, W.-Y., Chang, Y. K., & Kim, T.-Y. J. J. o. M. (2018). Complementary or substitutive effects? Corporate governance mechanisms and corporate social responsibility. *Journal of Management*, *44*, 2716–39.

Oxelheim, L., Gregorič, A., Randøy, T., & Thomsen, S. (2013). On the internationalization of corporate boards: the case of Nordic firms. *Journal of International Business Studies*, *44*, 173–94.

Pankaj, G. (2001). Distance still matters: the hard reality of global expansion. *Harvard Business Review*, *79*(8), 137–47.

Perkins, S., Morck, R., & Yeung, B. (2014). Innocents abroad: the hazards of international joint ventures with pyramidal group firms. *Global Strategy Journal*, *4*, 310–30.

Pfeffer, J., & Salancik, G. (1978). *The External Control of Organizations: A Resource-Dependence Perspective*. Harper & Row.

Ramdani, D., & Witteloostuijn, A. v. (2010). The impact of board independence and CEO duality on firm performance: a quantile regression analysis for Indonesia, Malaysia, South Korea and Thailand. *British Journal of Management*, *21*, 607–27.

Sidhu, J. S., Heyden, M. L., Volberda, H. W., & Van Den Bosch, F. A. (2020). Experience maketh the mind? Top management teams' experiential background and cognitive search for adaptive solutions. *Industrial and Corporate Change*, *29*, 333–50.

Singh, D., & Delios, A. (2017). Corporate governance, board networks and growth in domestic and international markets: evidence from India. *Journal of World Business*, *52*, 615–27.

Su, W., Peng, M. W., Tan, W., & Cheung, Y.-L. (2016). The signaling effect of corporate social responsibility in emerging economies. *Journal of Business Ethics*, *134*, 479–91.

Tsai, H. T., & Eisingerich, A. B. (2010). Internationalization strategies of emerging markets' firms. *California Management Review*, *53*(1), 114–35.

Welford, R. (2004). Corporate social responsibility in Europe and Asia. *Journal of Corporate Citizenship*, 31–47. https://doi.org/10.9774/GLEAF.4700.2005.SP.00007.

Whitley, R. (1998). Internationalization and varieties of capitalism: the limited effects of cross-national coordination of economic activities on the nature of business systems. *Review of International Political Economy*, *5*, 445–81.

Wilkinson, A., Wood, G., & Demirbag, M. J. H. R. M. (2014). Guest editors' introduction: people management and emerging market multinationals. *Human Resource Management, 53*, 835–49.

Wright, M., Filatotchev, I., Hoskisson, R. E., & Peng, M. W. (2005). Strategy research in emerging economies: challenging the conventional wisdom. *Journal of Management Studies, 42*(1), 1–33. https://doi.org/10.1111/j.1467-6486.2005.00487.x.

Yang, Q., Mudambi, R., & Meyer, K. E. (2008). Conventional and reverse knowledge flows in multinational corporations. *Journal of Management, 34*, 882–902.

Yin, J. (2017). Institutional drivers for corporate social responsibility in an emerging economy: a mixed-method study of Chinese business executives. *Business & Society, 56*, 672–704.

Young, M. N., Peng, M. W., Ahlstrom, D., Bruton, G. D., & Jiang, Y. (2008). Corporate governance in emerging economies: a review of the principal–principal perspective. *Journal of Management Studies, 45*, 196–220.

7. Directors' digital expertise and board diversity: empirical evidence from Dutch boards

Jana Oehmichen, Michelle Weck and Hans van Ees

Firms are exposed to the digitalization of their environment. That leads to increasing strategic relevance of "digital". Assets, products, and markets become digital. This digitalization involves threats, but also offers opportunities (Sebastian et al., 2017). The major threat is the emergence of new digital competitors. Since they come from very different industries, they have not been on firms' competitive radar before. A prominent example of consequences of these new competitors is, for instance, Amazon's acquisition of WholeFoods. Opportunities can be realized through, for example, new data-driven business models and artificial intelligence (see, e.g., Sorescu, 2017; Zapadka, Hanelt, Firk, & Oehmichen, 2020).

Adding digital expertise to the board can help firms to handle these threats and opportunities of the digital transformation. Several institutions, such as the Dutch national register, suggest that supervisory boards become more digital (Nationaalregister.nl, 2019). However, this change in the board composition can also have consequences for the overall board diversity. Specifically, it may be that digital skills increase age diversity within the boardroom, because one would assume that digital directors are on average younger. Therefore, we want to investigate whether Dutch firms have already responded to this call for more digital expertise in the boardroom, and if yes, what consequences this has for board diversity. More specifically, we ask (1), whether firms add digital experts to their boards, (2) whether these experts differ from non-digital board members with respect to non-job-related and job-related diversity dimensions and hence increase boards' overall diversity, and (3) whether different kinds of digital experts differ with respect to these diversity dimensions. We answer these research questions with a descriptive analysis of the supervisory boards of the 25 largest Dutch firms listed in the AEX on December 31, 2019. This analysis is explorative and based on a rather small sample. However, it might provide interesting first insights to spark interest in future research about digital directors in more competitive samples.

Drawing on literature about board tasks (e.g., Forbes & Milliken, 1999; Minichilli, Zattoni, & Zona, 2009) and board capabilities (Klarner, Yoshikawa, & Hitt, 2021), we argue that digitalization might have significant effects on traditional board tasks such as spotting and appointing management talents as well as bargaining competitive and effective compensation contracts. We then integrate a diversity lens (e.g., Tasheva & Hillman, 2019; Wiersema & Bantel, 1993) and explain why adding digital experts to the board could also be a nice opportunity to increase overall board diversity and how such diversity could help reduce inertia, promote strategic change, and, hence, manage the digital transformation even better. Nevertheless, increased diversity related to additions of digital experts can also have disadvantages, such as tokenism (compare, e.g., Farh et al., 2020; Torchia, Calabrò, & Huse, 2011). In the conceptual part of this article, we discuss these two sides of the coin of digital expertise and diversity in boards.

To provide some first empirical insights into the relationship of digital expertise and diversity in boards, we look at a cross-section of Dutch firms. Our empirical results indicate that Dutch firms are on average doing well with respect to digital expertise in their supervisory boards. However, we also observe that adding digital experts to the board does not increase board diversity. In a last step, we distinguish different modes of digital expertise, to explore whether especially entrepreneurial digital experts increase diversity. But also for this idea, we only find limited support.

LITERATURE AND THEORY

Traditional Board Tasks in the Digital Era

Board research summarizes board tasks to the following two tasks: giving strategic advice and monitoring their firms' managers (Forbes & Milliken, 1999; Veltrop, Molleman, Hooghiemstra, & van Ees, 2018). The expertise that directors bring to the board room plays a major role in the boards' ability to successfully fulfill these tasks (e.g., Faleye, Hoitash, & Hoitash, 2018; Lungeanu & Zajac, 2019; Oehmichen, Schrapp, & Wolff, 2017). For the advice task, research has shown, for instance, that sustainability-related expertise of boards improves environmental performance (Homroy & Slechten, 2019), that board industry expertise increases the success of internationalization strategies (Chen, Kor, Mahoney, & Tan, 2017), and that expertise in mergers and acquisitions of board members improves the quality of acquisition decisions (Field & Mkrtchyan, 2017; Oehmichen, Firk, Wolff, & Haas, 2021). From previous research about monitoring tasks, we know that board members, board and management expertise help in bargaining for more efficient executive compensation packages (Sun & Cahan, 2009), that financial expertise on boards reduces the likelihood of earnings management (Badolato, Donelson, & Ege, 2014), and that the external network of board members in the nomination committee improves CEO appointment decisions (Zhang, 2008).

How do we expect these board tasks to change with digitalization? Strategic advice, which is needed in the digital era, changes since companies face new challenges: Platform firms from other industries can represent a new competitive threat. These businesses follow a winner-takes-all strategy, "typically argued via the logics of network externalities, natural monopolies, and first-mover advantages" (Wareham, Fox, & Cano Giner, 2014: 1210). At the same time, new opportunities can be realized through, for example, data-driven business models (Sorescu, 2017) and AI strategies (Zapadka et al., 2020). For many firms this requires a radical strategic transformation and an adjustment of organizational structures. Board members who experienced these dynamics in other firms before can help in this situation. This expertise is specifically developed when directors had digital management positions before (either management positions in digital firms or digital positions in the management of rather traditional firms).

Furthermore, as many disruptors' organizations are still benefitting from the early years garage settings (compare, e.g., the beginning of Apple and HP), traditional companies may want to create organizational structures that are also able to capture technological disruptions. Firms need to learn how to build such "garages" internally and how to integrate them properly. Board members who experienced garage atmospheres during their previous positions may be more able to increase acceptance for the new digital organizational particularities. For example, agile processes and a higher failure tolerance can feel quite different from traditional management approaches. In addition, the traditional company car may not serve as a carrot anymore to attract and hold digital talent, which may seek instead to participate in the firms' successes via employee stock ownership programs. Board members who collected digital experience in an entrepreneurial context can be helpful to handle these challenges. Based on experiences about agile work and new incentives, they can provide advice about how to successfully navigate through the digital transformation.

New challenges for boards will also arise with respect to their monitoring responsibilities. Firms increasingly appoint Chief Digital Officers (CDOs) (compare, e.g., René Steenvoorden who is CDO at Randstad since 2016; for detailed numbers see, e.g., Firk, Hanelt, Oehmichen, & Wolff, 2021) or are actively searching for CEOs with digital expertise nowadays. In consequence, the nomination committee of a board that is responsible for spotting new talents (see, e.g., Zhang, 2008: 862 for more details about the nomination committees' role in executive selections) must be able to reach candidates with such a digital skillset. While filling the funnel may still work via traditional ways of using specialized recruiters, boards need their relationship-building capabilities (Klarner et al., 2021) to win these digital natives. Having a common background (e.g., by already having managed a digital transformation or having ties to digital scaleups) may become essential for board members to convince the job candidates that they can become successful in their new position. It also helps to monitor their activities later.

Furthermore, digital strategies require changes in executive compensation structures. Classical compensation contracts condition the compensation on established financial figures. Although these figures are increasingly future looking, for instance through vesting periods (see, e.g., McGuire, Oehmichen, Wolff, & Hilgers, 2019), they might not be future looking enough to incentivize a digital transformation of the entire business model. Turning a digital transformation into success can last longer than the typical CEO tenure and requires a certain tolerance for experimentation and failures. Therefore, additional strategic goals directing CEOs towards digital transformations could complete CEO compensation arrangements. Defining such goals requires the board to understand the uniqueness of digital transformations.

In summary, digital expertise can enable directors to improve advice and monitoring in times of the digital transformation. For different challenges in the digital transformation, different sources of digital expertise matter. We specifically distinguish managerial and entrepreneurial digital expertise and want to answer this first research question empirically:

RQ1: Do Dutch firms appoint directors with managerial digital and entrepreneurial digital expertise to their boards?

Digital Directors and Diversity

Appointing directors with digital expertise could also result in an increase in the overall diversity of their boards. Increasing board diversity could have significant benefits for a successful digital transformation, but can also be associated with some costs. In the following paragraphs, we will first theorize about potential effects of board diversity on digital transformation and then develop arguments about how adding digital expertise to the board might also increase board diversity.

Diversity research distinguishes between job-related and non-job-related demographic diversity dimensions (e.g., Pelled, Eisenhardt, & Xin, 1999). Job-related differences are more often related to positive outcomes such as increased information processing and the consideration of more diverse viewpoints. Those differences may provide a larger pool of knowledge resources that are helpful in dealing with non-routine problems (van Knippenberg & Schippers, 2007), ultimately leading to more creativity and innovation because it improves information sharing and information elaboration (Hinsz, Vollrath, & Tindale, 1997). Additionally, previous research indicates that diversity improves performance in complex tasks (Ellemers & Rink, 2016), the quality of financial reporting (Huang, Huang, & Lee, 2014), and group problem-solving (Homan et al., 2008).

Contrastingly, diversity also leads to more social categorization stereotyping and dysfunctional conflicts (van Knippenberg, De Dreu, & Homan, 2004). Thus, diversity can also cause conflict, miscommunication, and discrimination, resulting in in-group preferences, decreased trust for out-group members, and decreased communication between different groups (van Knippenberg & Schippers, 2007). Previous research has pointed out that positive effects of diversity stem from task conflicts (Jehn, Northcraft, & Neale, 1999; Pelled et al., 1999), while negative effects of diversity tend to the disruption of the status quo, the threat created by the change, and the increased social categorizing can foster or increase dysfunctional conflict (Pelled et al., 1999). Overall, negative consequences of diversity are more related to non-job-related differences. This suggests that homogeneous groups can outperform diverse ones (Hofhuis, Van Der Zee, & Otten, 2012). Previous board diversity research confirms the importance of diversity costs and benefits (Hillman, 2015). From previous studies, we know that diversity within the board can foster more creative and innovative discussions (Wiersema & Bantel, 1993), makes firms more attractive to a diverse set of employees (Hillman, Shropshire, & Cannella, 2007) and fosters a larger set of essential resources via ties with different external constituencies (Adams & Funk, 2012; Nielsen & Huse, 2010). Nevertheless, board diversity may constrain the implementation of strategic changes or lead to inefficiencies (Adams & Ferreira, 2007, 2009) and tokenism (Torchia et al., 2011).

With respect to effects on strategic outcomes, previous research has shown effects of board diversity performance (Miller & Triana, 2009), ambidexterity (Oehmichen, Heyden, Georgakakis, & Volberda, 2017), entrepreneurial orientation (Tuggle, Schnatterly, & Johnson, 2010), and strategic change (Triana, Miller, & Trzebiatowski, 2014).

Digital transformation nowadays means that board diversity in dimensions beyond the additional digital expertise could be beneficial in handling new challenges in monitoring and advice tasks. This can help break with old and, for digital transformation inefficient compensation contracts, attract new talent, and mitigate inertia and induce the strategic change, which is needed for the digital transformation. Therefore, appointing digital experts to the board might represent an opportunity to also increase board diversity in other job-related and non-job-related dimensions. Previous research has shown that boards have the tendency to appoint new members who are comparable to themselves (e.g., Gould, Kulik, & Sardeshmukh, 2018). This behavior is called homophily (McPherson, Smith-Lovin, & Cook, 2001). We propose that appointing digital experts triggers boards to break with such homophilious behavior and hence create space for more diversity also in other dimensions. This leads us to our second and third research questions:

RQ2: Do digital experts differ from non-digital board members with respect to non-job-related and job-related diversity dimension and hence increase boards' overall diversity?

RQ3: Do different kinds of digital experts differ with respect to these diversity dimensions?

DATA

Sample and Data Sources

The goal of the empirical part of this study is to investigate whether digital directors are already represented on Dutch supervisory board, and to learn whether digital board members affect board diversity. Therefore, we construct the following database.

Our sample includes all 25 firms that were listed at the AEX on December 31, 2019. We collected information about all non-executive board members of these firms from BoardEx. Our sample encompasses 190 director positions (if a director is on the board of more than one AEX board, he/she is included in the analysis more than once. Examples are Ben Noteboom who is sitting on four AEX boards or Ben van der Veer sitting on three AEX boards). BoardEx provides us the names of the directors, their current role (e.g., the information, which director is the chairperson of the board) and details about demographics such as age, gender, nationality, and tenure. Subsequently, to identify the digital board members, we collected additional information via an intensive press research of the CVs of these directors. We manually reviewed each board member based on several categories of digital expertise, such as digital management expertise, functional digital expertise, educational digital expertise, entrepreneurial digital expertise, and digital achievement and awards. This last category also included media coverage for having successfully managed a digital transformation. A director who collected experience in at least one of these five categories was coded as digital director.

Board Diversity

To capture board diversity, we looked at the non-job-related diversity dimensions gender, age, and nationality and the job-related diversity dimension tenure. Furthermore, we calculated the overall diversity of the group of non-digital and the group of digital board members. This measure is calculated as the sum of the Blau-Index of gender, the Blau-Index of nationality, the coefficient of variation of age, and the coefficient of variation of tenure.

RESULTS

RQ1: Digital Experts on Dutch Boards

First, we want to give an overview of how AEX-listed firms are generally positioned with respect to digital board expertise. Therefore, we show firm-level results about whether AEX-listed firms have digital expertise on their boards. Our data show the following:

- 92 percent of the firms (23 firms) have at least one digital director.
- Only 40 percent of the firms (10 firms) have a chairman with digital expertise.
- 22 percent of the AEX directors (41 of 190) have digital expertise.
- 17 percent of the digital experts on boards (7 of 41) have entrepreneurial digital expertise.

In summary, AEX firms are generally doing not too badly when it comes to digital expertise. Overall, this expertise at the very top of the organization may indicate that the listed Dutch firms may be well equipped to handle digitalization and have a great openness towards adopting or developing new digital technologies. For example, the Covid-19 crisis has increased the speed of digitalization by years and is likely to stick around. One can expect that the AEX firms, which are generally well equipped with digital experts also at the upper echelons, may have an easier time to adapt to those changes, as those at the very top of the firm will be less likely to resist changes and are more likely to initiate digitalization as demanded by the situation.

RQ2: Digital Board Expertise and Overall Board Diversity

In this second step of the analysis, we want to investigate whether digital and non-digital board members differ with respect to non-job-related and job-related demographic diversity dimensions. Surprisingly we find the following results (also Table 7.1):

- Digital expertise does not increase board gender diversity. We find more female directors among non-digital board members (37 percent) than among digital board members (33 percent). Moreover, the standard deviation is higher among non-digital directors.
- There is no relationship between digital expertise and directors' age. Non-digital directors are on average 61.6 years old and digital directors 61.9. However, there is a bit more variation in the age of digital board members (SD = 7.25).
- The percentage of international board members is higher among non-digital board members (63 percent) than among digital board members (53 percent).
- Interestingly, we find the most striking difference between non-digital and digital board members in tenure. The average tenure of non-digital board members is 4.3 years, whereas digital board members are only 3.7 years in office.
- In a final step, we compare the overall diversity of the group of non-digital board members and of digital board members in our sample. Contrary to our initial expectations, the overall diversity of non-digital board members is higher (2.39) than the overall diversity of digital board members (2.15).

Table 7.1   *Comparison between digital (N= 45) and non-digital (N= 145) board members with respect to non-job-related and job-related demographic diversity dimensions*

	Mean	SD	Frequency
Age (not digital director)	61.57	6.64	145
Age (digital director)	61.89	7.25	45
Gender (not digital director)	.37	.49	145
Gender (digital director)	.33	.47	45
Nationality (i.e., Dutch vs International) (not digital director)	.37	.48	145
Nationality (i.e., Dutch vs International) (digital director)	.47	.51	45
Tenure (not digital director)	4.33	3.92	138*
Tenure (digital director)	3.70	2.64	41

Note: *One firm was not available on BoardEx; thus, the sample is reduced for tenures.

In summary, contrary to our expectations, the non-digital board members seem to be more diverse than digital board members. This means that firms do not yet seem to make use of digital board members as a novel "diversity channel" for their boards. Furthermore, it is interesting to see that digital board members have a lower tenure than non-digital board members. This can have several consequences. On the one hand, this could mean that digital board members have fresher views on the firms and hence help to break with inertia. On the other hand, they might be perceived as outsider who has difficulties in having a say in the boardroom. Finally, the findings contradict the notion that boards will use open board seats to fulfill multiple diversity requirements at once. It may be interesting to research this further (e.g., within the U.S. context where the topic of diversity is much more prominent and the external pressure for board diversity stronger).

Another interesting avenue is to explore the nature of the supply of diverse digital experts. Both digital expertise and board position seem to be highly associated with male dominance. Therewith, there might be a short supply of female directors with digital expertise. At this point in time, it may be that ethnically diverse males can benefit most from joining the boards as digital experts. We did not consider this dimension because ethnical diversity is very limited in boards in the Netherlands.

RQ3: Diversity Differences between Entrepreneurial and Non-entrepreneurial Digital Board Members

As mentioned previously, digital expertise can come through very different channels. The channel that is probably most exotic to previous board compositions is entrepreneurial expertise. After having found that digital board members are actually less diverse than non-digital board members, we are now excited to see whether at least this subgroup of digital board members, the entrepreneurial digital board members, helps to increase board diversity. Hence, we compare entrepreneurial and non-entrepreneurial digital board members (for a summary, Table 7.2):

- Gender diversity does not increase with entrepreneurial digital board members. Only 14 percent of entrepreneurial digital board members are female whereas 37 percent of non-entrepreneurial digital board members are female.
- However, international diversity increases with entrepreneurial digital board members: 72 percent of entrepreneurial digital board members are international whereas only 50 percent of non-entrepreneurial digital board members are international.
- Furthermore, entrepreneurial digital experts have effects on diversity in age and tenure, since entrepreneurial digital board members are younger (58.7 years compared to 62.5 years of non-entrepreneurial digital board members) and have lower tenures (2.3 years compared to 4 years of non-entrepreneurial digital board members).

Table 7.2   *Comparison between digital board members (N= 45) with entrepreneurial (N= 7) and non-entrepreneurial (N=38) digital expertise*

	Mean	SD	Frequency
Age (not digital director)	62.47	7.12	38
Age (digital director)	58.71	7.65	7
Gender (not digital director)	.37	.49	38
Gender (digital director)	.14	.38	7
Nationality (i.e., Dutch vs International) (not digital director)	.50	.51	38
Nationality (i.e., Dutch vs International) (digital director)	.28	.49	7
Tenure (not digital director)	3.98	2.76	38
Tenure (digital director)	2.34	1.50	7

In summary, we see that, in some dimensions such as nationality, age, and tenure, appointing a "new kind" of digital expert (entrepreneurial digital expert) increases the diversity. However, the effects are not very large. Hence, we see potential for more diversity through this channel. The fact that entrepreneurial experience has an even lower percentage of women is not entirely surprising. Previous research has revealed that there is still a large gender gap in entrepreneurship (Guzman & Kacperczyk, 2019). Causes range from disparities in early investment, which indicates that women are less likely to obtain external funding to greater risk aversion and to gendered preferences of investors (ibid., 2019). Overall, analysis indicates that this "new kind" of digital expert will not increase gender diversity within the boardroom in the short term.

In taking all of those results together, the results indicate that, although digital experts bring fresh perspectives to the boardroom in the Netherlands, they are not yet a driver of non-task-related diversity.

DISCUSSION AND CONCLUSION

In this study, we showed that 92 percent of the AEX-listed firms had at least one digital expert on their board in 2019. This large proportion of firms with digital experts on boards in the Netherlands is quite astonishing as, for example, the SEC data for the U.S. suggests a much lower percentage of digital expertise for boards of S&P500 firms. This difference clearly indicates that the Netherlands is ahead of the curve when it comes to digitalization of their boards. This might be to the advantage for the Dutch firms because those at the very top of the organization are usually tasked with initiating strategic change and thus digitalization. Interestingly, these digital directors do not seem to differ much from non-digital directors with respect to gender, age, and nationality. However, digital board members have a lower tenure compared to non-digital board members. Additionally, when looking at an overall diversity measure based on gender, age, tenure, and nationality, the results show that the group of non-digital directors is more diverse than the group of digital directors. When looking at the sources of digital expertise, we found out that only 16 percent of digital board members have some entrepreneurial digital expertise. These entrepreneurial digital board members differ slightly from non-entrepreneurial digital board members in any diversity dimension. They are slightly more international, younger, and have lower tenures. However, the percentage of women among these entrepreneurial digital board members is lower. This indicates that, despite different backgrounds, boards still seem to look for a quite comparable blueprint of directors, thereby possibly overseeing interesting pools of new-generation board candidates. There are several potential explanations for this matter. First of all, introducing digital expertise may seem daunting for the board and to keep disruptions minimal, they look for the typical director blueprint. Specifically, it may be that when directors with radically new skills enter the board, a situation emerges that is similar to that described in the classical socialization model. This model shows that newcomers interrupt group processes, which is generally not appreciated by the incumbents. Thus, to avoid such situations there might be a preference for digital directors that are as similar to the existing group as possible. Another perspective that cannot be neglected is that much of the recruitment of new directors hinges upon the "old-boys club". The lack of access to such networks makes it difficult for women and other minorities and younger generations to gain access to board positions. Accordingly, creating a formal national system for the recruitment could help to reduce the bias that those currently in power simply rely on their network which is very homogeneous from a socio-economic perspective to fill the need for new expertise within the boardroom. The third major reason for the observed phenomenon may be that there is little supply of diverse directors with digital expertise at this moment. In the long run, it is necessary to create specific programs that encourage girls and women to gain digital expertise to reduce the supply problem. With regard to nationality diversity, practical concerns may also play a role. In each country, digitalization has its unique features and international digital expertise may not translate easily to the Dutch context. Contrastingly, there are many digital features in the Netherlands which international board members are not familiar with. Taken together, this may create a preference for national digital experts.

Without doubt, our study is explorative in nature and is based on a rather small sample, which limits generalizability and does not allow for more sophisticated quantitative methods. Nevertheless, we are confident that this study opens up several avenues for interesting future research. First, future research could dive deeper into the relationship of digital expertise and board tenure. On the one hand, the fact that digital experts have lower board tenures is quite intuitive since their expertise is also only of matter since recent times. On the other hand, it could be very interesting to understand which side-effects this low tenure has. From previous research we know that status differences on boards matter (He & Huang, 2011), that status is not necessarily attributed to those with the highest expertise (Veltrop, Molleman, Hooghiemstra, & van Ees, 2017), and that social biases can impact status within the board (Sidhu, Feng, Volberda, & Van Den Bosch, 2020). Oldtimers (high-tenured group members) often block or discredit the input of newcomers (low-tenured group members) (Rink, Kane, Ellemers, & van der Vegt, 2013) and thus attribute a lower status (Bunderson, 2003). Given that the digital experts on the boards on our sample have shorter tenure, it leads to the question as to what extent their knowledge is actually used. Future research may investigate to what extent the knowledge of digital experts is actually used. Second, the observed homogeneity between non-digital and digital experts suggests that pressures for conformance may continue to drive the recruitment and nomination of board members. This then leads to the question as to what extent the introduction of digital expertise will be supportive of the radical business transformation that may be called for. To put it differently, to what extent is it feasible or likely that boards may serve as a catalyst of structural change? Recent preliminary research about this suggests the opposite (Hoppmann, Naegele, & Girod, 2019) and it may be interesting to explore the (non)diversity origins of such inertia in more detail. Third, qualitative research could explore in more detail which sources firms use to appoint digital directors and whether the use of alternative sources such as active recruitment from digital start-ups provides more chances to increase both the percentage of entrepreneurial digital board members and overall board diversity.

REFERENCES

Adams, R. B., & Ferreira, D. 2007. A theory of friendly boards. *The Journal of Finance*, 62(1): 217–50.

Adams, R. B., & Ferreira, D. 2009. Women in the boardroom and their impact on governance and performance. *Journal of Financial Economics*, 94(2): 291–309.

Adams, R. B., & Funk, P. 2012. Beyond the glass ceiling: does gender matter? *Management Science*, 58(2): 219–35.

Badolato, P. G., Donelson, D. C., & Ege, M. 2014. Audit committee financial expertise and earnings management: the role of status. *Journal of Accounting and Economics*, 58(2–3): 208–30.

Bunderson, J. S. 2003. Recognizing and utilizing expertise in work groups: a status characteristics perspective. *Administrative Science Quarterly*, 48(4). https://doi.org/10.2307/3556637.

Chen, P. L., Kor, Y., Mahoney, J. T., & Tan, D. 2017. Pre-market entry experience and post-market entry learning of the board of directors: implications for post-entry performance. *Strategic Entrepreneurship Journal*, 11(4): 441–63.

Ellemers, N., & Rink, F. 2016. Diversity in work groups. *Current Opinion in Psychology*, 11: 49–53.

Faleye, O., Hoitash, R., & Hoitash, U. 2018. Industry expertise on corporate boards. *Review of Quantitative Finance and Accounting*, 50(2): 441–79.

Farh, C. I. C., Oh, J. K., Hollenbeck, J. R., Yu, A., Lee, S. M., et al. 2020. Token female voice enactment in traditionally male-dominated teams: facilitating conditions and consequences for performance. *Academy of Management Journal*, 63(3): 832–56.

Field, L. C., & Mkrtchyan, A. 2017. The effect of director experience on acquisition performance. *Journal of Financial Economics*, 123(3): 488–511.

Firk, S., Hanelt, A., Oehmichen, J., & Wolff, M. 2021. Chief digital officers : an analysis of the presence of a centralized digital transformation responsibility. *Journal of Management Studies*. https://doi.org/10.1111/joms.12718.

Forbes, D. P., & Milliken, F. J. 1999. Cognition and corporate governance: understanding boards of directors as strategic decision-making groups. *Academy of Management Review*, 24(3): 489–505.

Gould, J. A., Kulik, C. T., & Sardeshmukh, S. R. 2018. Trickle-down effect: the impact of female board members on executive gender diversity. *Human Resource Management*, 57(4): 931–45.

Guzman, J., & Kacperczyk, A. O. 2019. Gender gap in entrepreneurship. *Research Policy*, 48(7): 1666–80.

He, J., & Huang, Z. H. 2011. Board informal hierarchy and firm financial performance: exploring a tacit structure guiding boardroom interactions. *Academy of Management Journal*, 54(6): 1119–39.

Hillman, A. J. 2015. Board diversity: beginning to unpeel the onion. *Corporate Governance: An International Review*, 23(2): 104–7.

Hillman, A. J., Shropshire, C., & Cannella, A. A. 2007. Organizational predictors of women on corporate boards. *Academy of Management Journal*, 50(4): 941–52.

Hinsz, V. B., Vollrath, D. A., & Tindale, R. S. 1997. The emerging conceptualization of groups as information processors. *Psychological Bulletin*, 121(1): 43–64.

Hofhuis, J., Van Der Zee, K. I., & Otten, S. 2012. Social identity patterns in culturally diverse organizations: the role of diversity climate. *Journal of Applied Social Psychology*, 42(4): 964–89.

Homan, A. C., Hollenbeck, J. R., Humphrey, S. E., Van Knippenberg, D., Ilgen, D. R., et al. 2008. Facing differences with an open mind: openness to experience, salience of intragroup differences, and performance of diverse work groups. *Academy of Management Journal*, 51(6): 1204–22.

Homroy, S., & Slechten, A. 2019. Do board expertise and networked boards affect environmental performance? *Journal of Business Ethics*, 158(1): 269–92.

Hoppmann, J., Naegele, F., & Girod, B. 2019. Boards as a source of inertia: examining the internal challenges and dynamics of boards of directors in times of environmental discontinuities. *Academy of Management Journal*, 62(2): 437–68.

Huang, T. C., Huang, H. W., & Lee, C. C. 2014. Corporate executive's gender and audit fees. *Managerial Auditing Journal*, 29(6): 527–47.

Jehn, K. A., Northcraft, G. B., & Neale, M. A. 1999. Why differences make a difference: a field study of diversity, conflict, and performance in workgroups. *Administrative Science Quarterly*, 44(4): 741–63.

Klarner, P., Yoshikawa, T., & Hitt, M. A. 2021. A capability-based view of boards: a new conceptual framework for board governance. *Academy of Management Perspectives*, 35(1): 123–41.

Lungeanu, R., & Zajac, E. J. 2019. Thinking broad and deep: why some directors exert an outsized influence on strategic change. *Organization Science*. https://doi.org/10.2139/ssrn.3243557.

McGuire, J., Oehmichen, J., Wolff, M., & Hilgers, R. 2019. Do contracts make them care? The impact of CEO compensation design on corporate social performance. *Journal of Business Ethics*, 157(2): 375–90.

McPherson, M., Smith-Lovin, L., & Cook, J. M. 2001. Birds of a feather: homophily in social networks. *Annual Review of Sociology*, 27(1): 415–44.

Miller, T. L., & Triana, M. del C. 2009. Demographic diversity in the boardroom: mediators of the board diversity–firm performance relationship. *Journal of Management Studies*, 46(5): 755–86.

Minichilli, A., Zattoni, A., & Zona, F. 2009. Making boards effective: an empirical examination of board task performance. *British Journal of Management*, 20(1): 55–74.

Nationaalregister.nl. 2019. *Commissarissen overschatten hun kennis over digitalisering.* https://www.nationaalregister.nl/kennisbank/commissarissen-overschatten-hun-kennis -over-digitalisering.

Nielsen, S., & Huse, M. 2010. Women directors' contribution to board decision-making and strategic involvement: the role of equality perception. *European Management Review*, 7(1): 16–29.

Oehmichen, J., Firk, S., Wolff, M., & Haas, V. 2021. Board experience and value creation in cross-border acquisitions: the role of acquirer and target country institutions. *International Business Review.* https://doi.org/10.1016/j.ibusrev.2021.101966.

Oehmichen, J., Heyden, M. L. M., Georgakakis, D., & Volberda, H. W. 2017. Boards of directors and organizational ambidexterity in knowledge-intensive firms. *The International Journal of Human Resource Management*, 28(2): 283–306.

Oehmichen, J., Schrapp, S., & Wolff, M. 2017. Who needs experts most? Board industry expertise and strategic change—a contingency perspective. *Strategic Management Journal*, 38(3): 645–56.

Pelled, L. H., Eisenhardt, K. M., & Xin, K. R. 1999. Exploring the black box: an analysis of work group diversity, conflict, and performance. *Administrative Science Quarterly*, 44(1): 1–28.

Rink, F., Kane, A. A., Ellemers, N., & van der Vegt, G. 2013. Team receptivity to newcomers: five decades of evidence and future research themes. *Academy of Management Annals*, 7(1): 247–93.

Sebastian, I. M., Ross, J. W., Beath, C., Mocker, M., Moloney, K. G., et al. 2017. How big old companies navigate digital transformation. *MIS Quarterly Executive*, 16(3): 197–213.

Sidhu, J. S., Feng, Y., Volberda, H. W., & Van Den Bosch, F. A. J. 2020. In the shadow of social stereotypes: gender diversity on corporate boards, board chair's gender and strategic change. *Organization Studies.* https://doi.org/10.1177/0170840620944560.

Sorescu, A. 2017. Data-driven business model innovation. *Journal of Product Innovation Management*, 34(5): 691–6.

Sun, J., & Cahan, S. 2009. The effect of compensation committee quality on the association between CEO cash compensation and accounting performance. *Corporate Governance: An International Review*, 17(2): 193–207.

Tasheva, S., & Hillman, A. J. 2019. Artikel diversiteit. *Academy of Management Review*, 44(4): 746–65.

Torchia, M., Calabrò, A., & Huse, M. 2011. Women directors on corporate boards: from tokenism to critical mass. *Journal of Business Ethics*, 102(2): 299–317.

Triana, C., Miller, T. L., & Trzebiatowski, T. M. 2014. The double-edged nature of board gender diversity: diversity, firm performance, and the power of women directors as predictors of strategic change. *Organization Science*, 25(2): 609–32.

Tuggle, C. S., Schnatterly, K., & Johnson, R. A. 2010. Attention patterns in the boardroom: how board composition and processes affect discussion of entrepreneurial issues. *Academy of Management Journal*, 53(3): 550–71.

van Knippenberg, D., De Dreu, C. K. W., & Homan, A. C. 2004. Work group diversity and group performance: an integrative model and research agenda. *Journal of Applied Psychology*, 89(6): 1008–22.

van Knippenberg, D., & Schippers, M. C. 2007. Work group diversity. *Annual Review of Psychology*, 58: 515–41.

Veltrop, D. B., Molleman, E., Hooghiemstra, R. B. H., & van Ees, H. 2017. Who's the boss at the top? A micro-level analysis of director expertise, status and conformity within boards. *Journal of Management Studies*, 54(7): 1079–110.

Veltrop, D. B., Molleman, E., Hooghiemstra, R. B. H., & van Ees, H. 2018. The relationship between tenure and outside director task involvement: a social identity perspective. *Journal of Management*, 44(2): 445–69.

Wareham, J. D., Fox, P., & Cano Giner, J. L. 2014. Technology ecosystem governance. *Organization Science*, 25(4): 1195–215.

Wiersema, M. F., & Bantel, K. A. 1993. Top management team turnover as an adaptation mechanism: the role of the environment. *Strategic Management Journal*, 14(7): 485–504.

Zapadka, P., Hanelt, A., Firk, S., & Oehmichen, J. 2020. Leveraging "AI-as-a-Service" – antecedents and consequences of using artificial intelligence boundary resources. International Conference on Information Systems, ICIS 2020.

Zhang, Y. 2008. Information asymmetry and the dismissal of newly appointed CEOs: an empirical investigation. *Strategic Management Journal*, 29(8): 859–72.

8. Do nomination committees encourage corporate board diversity?

Hildur Magnúsdóttir, Throstur Olaf Sigurjonsson, Audur Arna Arnardottir and Patricia Gabaldón

In the foreword to the third edition of the *Icelandic Corporate Governance Guidelines*, published in 2009 by the Icelandic Chamber of Commerce, Business Iceland, and Icelandic Stock Exchange (NASDAQ Iceland), the whole Icelandic business community was severely criticized and urged to apply a new set of values to increase transparency and build trust. This urging came in the wake of the financial crisis in 2008, where Iceland was severely affected.

> The setbacks suffered over recent months have raised many questions concerning the infrastructure of Iceland's business sector, its focus, and responsibilities. There have been calls for a revised approach involving a new set of values. This demand is both reasonable and necessary. Distrust towards companies and the business sector bears witness to many things that might have been done differently, and it is evident that action must be taken to reclaim lost goodwill and to build credibility in the business sector. (*Corporate Governance Guidelines*, 3rd edition, 2009, p. 7)

The financial crisis created a major shift in the thinking at a societal level, from the closed-doors, mostly male boards to a new era of "open governance" that requires individuals to operate in a climate of transparency, trust, and improved decision-making (Bryant et al., 2014). Policymakers and the business elite were forced to consider more than ever "alternative ways" to govern business, even at the highest organizational level, the corporate board (Special Investigation Commission Report, 2010).

In the 3rd edition of the *Icelandic Corporate Governance* guidelines, emphasis was, for the first time, put on the importance of both gender diversity and overall board diversity. Special attention was given to the combined knowledge, skills, and competencies residing within the whole board. It was further argued that having a strong selection process could potentially be secured by a Nomination Committee (NC), populated by a minimum of three members, the majority of whom need to be independent of the board and firm management.

Iceland was amongst the first nations to pass a law on gender quota for corporate boards (Terjesen & Sealy, 2016). Icelandic law no. 13/2010 states that 40 percent of each gender must be represented on corporate boards of directors in all state-owned enterprises (SEOs), publicly traded firms (PTFs), and all private limited companies (PLCs) with 50 or more employees. The effects of this legislation have been monitored. Consequent studies have shown maturing local reflection on the concept of board diversity in the wake of the gender quota (Arnardottir & Sigurjonsson, 2017; KPMG, 2014), where general discussions about what board diversity truly entails is becoming more prominent among various business stakeholders. The board gender quota also brought about extensive re-structuring of the selection processes in many Icelandic companies, but the approaches and outcomes of that are still being debated locally (Arnardottir & Sigurjonsson, 2017).

In 2014, an NC was first embodied in a corporate governance structure of a listed company on the Iceland Stock Exchange; the majority of listed companies have since done the same. According to Icelandic legislation, a company's responsibility and liability are divided between the shareholders as represented at Annual General Meeting (AGM), the board of directors, and executive management (Law on Limited Liability Corporations, no. 2, 1995). Although shareholder authority is limited to the AGM, between AGM meetings the board has a role to ensure that a company's operations and organization are in proper order (Iceland Chamber of Commerce et al., 2021). Within this structure, the selection of new board members is one of NCs most critical role, as board composition is vital for sound corporate governance. The research question hence remains how investors, board members, and NC members view the changes entailed by the recent addition of NCs to board members' selection and whether this new governance body has led to enhanced board diversity.

NCs seek to ensure a professional selection process of board members. Board composition and board selection processes are usually described in corporate governance codes, indicating when and how new board members should be selected. However, this varies between different governance structures and countries. Agency theory frames the significant role of board members to governance of corporations (Fama & Jensen, 1983). To keep the board independent, and decrease agency conflicts, board composition becomes a weighty decision (Zahra & Pearce, 1989).

The NCs' role can be key for a board's successful functioning, as NCs oversee the board members' selection processes and can potentially affect the board's outcomes. Adequate board selection processes are essential for safeguarding the functioning of boards as monitors and resource providers (Hillman & Dalziel, 2003). Selection practices can further lead to board diversity (Terjesen & Sealy, 2016) at the individual and group level (Tasheva & Hillman, 2019). With this diversity goal in mind, selection processes and outcomes are also impacted when the board is already diverse (Gould et al., 2018). As scholars and practitioners have previously argued, integrating diversity at board level remains a debated topic (Tasheva & Hillman, 2019), with several types of diversity affecting team outcomes (Nielsen & Nielsen, 2013). NCs' members should hence be aware of the benefits and challenges of board diversity and try to attract both fitting and diverse talent. If implemented successfully, board diversity can enhance capacity for creative discussion and innovation at the board table, increase accurate and valuable advice-giving, and strengthen effective monitoring (Adams & Ferreira, 2009; Forbes & Milliken, 1999). It can also promote broader stakeholder engagement (Adams et al., 2015) and better monitoring and strategic decision-making (Huse et al., 2009).

The impact of NCs and how they can influence board members' selection process indicate at least a twofold impact on diversity at the board level. On the one hand, NCs should ensure the incorporation of more sociodemographic diversity on the boards (Mans-Kemp & Viviers, 2019; Ruigrok et al., 2006). This diversity effort, focused on gender or nationality, can be considered as superficial (Hillman et al., 2002). On the other hand, one of NCs main roles is promoting diversity of background and experience (Mans-Kemp & Viviers, 2019) as a tool to promote innovation and diverse thinking at the board level (Kanadli et al., 2018).

Corporate governance guidelines commonly published within the Nordic countries are not explicit on how NCs should be structured or how they should operate. Recent guidelines empower NCs to ensure transparent and efficient selection processes of board members (Lekvall, 2017). Hence, NCs have been established in accordance with corporate governance guidelines and given an advisory role overseeing director candidates' selection, amongst others, attempting to ensure adequate diversity amongst board members.

Iceland is an example of a country that has only recently included NCs in the governance structure of listed companies. With the introduction of NCs in Iceland, various stakeholders raised concerns regarding the committees' importance (e.g., how they should be structured, what to consider when appointing NCs members themselves, and what role NCs should take when promoting diversity in boards) (Fridriksson, 2019; Halldorsson, 2019). These concerns create the backbone of this study. The aim is to recognize NCs' potential contribution to the selection and nomination process of board members and whether and how board diversity is promoted and understood by an NC operating in a country where a board gender diversity quota is already in effect.

THE ROLE OF NOMINATION COMMITTEES

NCs are entrusted with an important role. They should establish adequate working procedures and clear selection criterion for board members' nomination (Hutchinson et al., 2015). Also included in NCs role is to carry out the evaluation process of new board members and the nomination itself (Carson, 2002; Eminet & Guedri, 2010; Ruigrok et al., 2006). Ruigrok et al (2006) argue that NCs are formed to optimize the selection decisions for new board members and professionalize the members' selection process. NCs are expected to professionalize the selection process by developing profiles of board members, interview candidates, and even use professional search firms (Ruigrok et al., 2006). NCs with recognized working procedures can be crucial institutional mechanisms in overcoming board selection process limitations (Hutchinson et al., 2015; Ruigrok et al., 2006). They should also nominate candidates that are suitable and diverse, for shareholders' approval (Mans-Kemp & Viviers, 2019). Proximity to sizable reservoirs of talent can be a key factor in choosing independent board members. For example, Mans-Kemp and Viviers (2019), citing research on NCs in South Africa, concluded that a limited talent pool could explain the under-representation of diverse candidates.

Kaczmarek et al. (2012) found that the appointment of diverse board members, regarding gender and nationality, is more likely to be supported within companies that have established an NC, particularly when the committee focuses on proposing suitable candidates reflecting the firm's characteristics and needs. The board members should also seek to ensure that the board composition aligns with external expectations (Ruigrok et al., 2006).

The NC also defines the board members' selection process, which needs to be transparent. The process should incorporate the best candidates for the board, given their individual characteristics, and the board's needs (Committee on Corporate Governance, 2019; Iceland Chamber of Commerce et al., 2021; Mans-Kemp & Viviers, 2019; NCGB, 2018; Securities Market Association, 2020; Swedish Corporate Governance Board, 2020). More transparency can enable shareholders to make more informed decisions on candidates and support boards' diversity.

According to agency theory (Fama & Jensen, 1983), shareholders, as principals, expect board members, as agents, to make decisions that will maximize the value of their investments. Therefore, the board's prime mission is governing a company's management. However, influential CEOs and board members can enhance control over boards by appointing new members like themselves (Westphal, 1994). When new members join a board, they bring with them a wide repertoire of biographic categories (e.g., gender, nationality, ethnicity). These categories would determine part of the selection process (Thatcher & Patel, 2012). According to social identity theory (Tajfel & Turner, 1986), individuals tend to select profiles having the same or similar beliefs, attitudes, or backgrounds, as they consider them easier to work with and more likable. The selection of board members may be subject to biases (i.e., the similarity-attraction paradigm) (Byrne, 1997). The appointment of new board members, and the diversity achieved afterwards affects board dynamics (Nielsen & Huse, 2010), as different sub-groups might emerge, based on salient characteristics of the group members (Markoczy et al., 2020).

Without coherent selection rules and transparency in the board member selection processes, key actors on the boards could be tempted to look for alike candidates, to favor homophily and/or similarity. Although this resemblance might make the selection easier, it has been suggested that hiring similar profiles results eventually in groupthink, harming innovation (Tajfel & Turner, 1986). Therefore, NCs as independent bodies can contribute to reducing similarity-attraction in group members' selection processes. Instead, boards would be looking for the best fit for the board by being rigorously procedural and transparent, surveying the board's needs in terms of diversity, and avoiding conformity and groupthink.

According to Icelandic legislation, companies that have more than 50 employees shall make sure that women are members of their corporate boards. In 2010, gender quota on boards was made a requirement and if the board has more than three members, it shall be ensured that the proportion of each sex is not lower than 40 percent (Law on Limited Liability Corporations, no. 2, 1995). According to Rigolini and Huse (2021), coercive pressure, like gender quotas, works better then normative and mimetic pressure only to increase diversity among women getting multiple board membership. Their findings further suggest that legal quotas may increase the diversity of women that are appointed as board members. To foster board diversity, NCs themselves also need to be diverse in composition (Mans-Kemp & Viviers, 2019; Ruigrok et al., 2006). The rainbow of profiles and ideas that need to be incorporated on boards are more easily found when NC members are distinctive, even while being synchronized in seeking the same outcome. Furthermore, when NCs are composed of diverse profiles, access to information, networks, and candidates might be made richer and smarter (Mans-Kemp & Viviers, 2019).

Although it is not the focus of this chapter, it is important to consider the network and status of NCs members as their standing/status can be considered also significant and affect a selection outcome. A committee member's network can be important, as knowledge of and access to a diverse range of candidates is essential in recruitment situations (Sjöstrand et al., 2016). To multiply the NC's network, they can use head-hunters, employment agencies, or consultants (Mans-Kemp & Viviers, 2019; Sjöstrand et al., 2016). These assets can, in addition to providing a larger network (Mans-Kemp & Viviers, 2019), also assist in facilitating the committee's work. It can also be useful for NC members to have specialist competence or experience in a company's operations or business context. The social competencies of individual members of the committee, their experience, and know-how are also factors that can be beneficial for NCs. Some experts assess that NCs members' key competencies are to be familiar with the company's operations and the company itself so they can better understand the dependencies and most relevant circumstances (Sjöstrand et al., 2016). This consideration can become important when considering NCs and how they can best promote diversity in proposing new board members.

CORPORATE GOVERNANCE GUIDELINES FOR NOMINATION COMMITTEES IN ICELAND

According to corporate governance rules in Iceland, NCs should propose potential candidates for boards of directors. They should also assess potential board members' qualifications, experience, and knowledge, while considering the board's size, composition, and diversity. In addition, they should consider performance assessments regarding the composition of the board and competence(s) of each board member (Iceland Chamber of Commerce et al., 2021).

The Iceland Chamber of Commerce, Nasdaq Iceland, and SA Business Iceland published the Icelandic Corporate Governance Codes. According to these guidelines, NCs shall ensure that the proposed board candidates collectively possess adequate experience and knowledge to best perform their duties. Furthermore, the committee should promote all shareholders' interests, acting as an advisory body in proposing and selecting candidates to be elected by the shareholders at the AGM. According to the codes, the committee also establishes criteria for ensuring proper diversity of the board (Iceland Chamber of Commerce et al., 2021).

Establishing an NC should offer clear arrangements for the nomination of members to the board and form a foundation for the shareholders to make informed decisions. This action also increases the likelihood that the company's board will possess breadth and diversity in knowledge, capabilities, and experience. NCs should consider these aspects when preparing board members' nominations. NCs in Iceland can decide to hire consultants while executing their duties, if they are independent of the company and its management (Iceland Chamber of Commerce et al., 2021).

This study aims to answer whether, and how, investors, board members, and NC members view the changes entailed by the recent addition of NCs to board members' selection and if NCs have led to enhanced board diversity.

RESEARCH METHODS

For this study, qualitative data was collected to gain insight into how NCs members, shareholders, and board members interpret their experience on NCs. We conducted 13 semi-structured interviews. The interview guide was based on the questionnaire proposed by Clune et al. (2014) – situational adjustments were made, and the questionnaire was pre-tested through discussion with various Icelandic stakeholders. The discussion provided insights into what topics needed to be further addressed concerning NCs in Iceland.

The questionnaire was divided into three parts. Part one included questions about the participants. Part two included questions on the role and structure of NCs and the pros and cons of having a NC. The third part included questions on NC processes. Two versions of the guide were constructed, one for NC members and one for other participants. Participants were selected after a meeting hosted by the Icelandic Chamber of Commerce about NCs in January 2020. Other interviewees were selected based on their experience on NCs or their input in public discussions.

The participants chosen for this study needed to be a board member of a listed firm, have current or previous experience as a member of an NC, or be a shareholder of a listed company in Iceland. Also, a consultant that had studied NCs in Iceland was interviewed. A list of participants is shown in Table 8.1. The participants were given a number and a reference to his/her role (e.g., participant one, an NC member, is "1.N". Participants that are both NC members and board members of the same company are referenced as "N-B" (e.g., participant number eight is referred to as 8.N-B). Investors are given an "I" and consultants are marked with a "C".

Table 8.1   *List of participants*

Participants	Gender	Role	Relevance for this study
1.N	Female	NC Member	NC member and chair of the committee. Has recruitment experience.
2.N	Female	NC Member	NC member. Has previous experience as a board member and as a managing director of a listed company.
3.N	Female	NC Member	NC member and chair of the committee. Has recruitment experience.
4.N	Female	NC Member	NC member and chair of the committee. Has previous experience as a board member of a listed company.
5.N	Male	NC Member	NC member. Has previous experience as a board member and managing director.
6.N	Female	NC Member	NC member and chair of the committee. Has recruitment experience.
7.N	Female	NC Member, Board Member, Consultant	Previous experience as a NC member and board member of listed company. Has experience as a consultant.
8.N-B	Male	NC Member, Board Member	NC member and a board member of a listed company. Has been chair of an NC. Experience as a managing director.
9.N-B	Male	NC Member, Board Member	NC member and a board member of a listed company. Experience as a managing director.
10.B	Male	Board member	Board member of a listed company.
11.I	Female	Institutional investor	Has experience of communication with the NC and suggesting board members in addition to experience as a managing director and board member.
12.I	Male	Institutional investor	Has experience of communication with the NC and suggesting board members in addition to experience as a managing director and board member.
13.C	Male	Consultant	Has experience as a consultant for NCs.

After the data was collected, interviews were transcribed (see the process described by Merriam, 2016). Afterwards, grounded theory was used to systematically analyze the data and develop a theory based on the data (Strauss & Corbin, 1998). The transcribed interviews were coded, with coding used to assign shorthand designations to distinct aspects of the data, so the researchers could quickly access specific data items. Open coding was used (Merriam, 2016).

This study is supported by qualitative analysis. As such, one limitation is that the researchers' perspectives might have affected the interpretation of the interviews. This was kept in mind both during the interviews and while analyzing the data, to not influence data interpretation.

The authors draw to the readers' attention to another potential limitation: in Iceland, there is a gender quota for board members (i.e., legal requirements that ensure that women have a seat on each board). Therefore, this study could be considered most relevant in countries that have similar gender quotas. This research can also apply to countries that have similar corporate governance structure as Iceland's, and to countries where NCs are underutilized in the board nomination process.

RESULTS

The aim of this study was to investigate investors', board members', and NC members' opinions on how recent NC selection processes compare to previous board nomination and selection process. We also wanted to find out if and how NCs increase diversity within corporate boards. The results are addressed under two main sub-themes: the establishment of NCs in Iceland and whether NCs promote stronger assessment processes, broader individual assessment, and wider diversity on boards in Iceland.

Establishment of NCs in Iceland

The first sub-category defined for this chapter derives from the analyses of interviewees comments regarding *"Establishment of NCs in Iceland"*. Some of our interviewees recognized that the Icelandic system prior to the establishment of NCs lacked transparency and formality. When international investment funds entered the local market, this systemic problem became more evident.

Participant 5.N said that foreign investors did not understand how the procedures for selecting board members worked in Iceland and complained that they could not participate in that process. Participant 11.I similarly mentioned: "I think they were used to the formality that NCs should bring and the systematic review of board candidates with sufficient diversity of a team in mind (...) [T]hey lacked the platform, so initially they got this ball rolling in Iceland."

Participant 12.I also argued that NCs were established mainly due to institutional investors' requirements: "They are in a different position than private investors because they must keep in mind that the public, and pensioners, require that the process be professional and transparent." Participant 4.N mentioned that there was a need for NCs to level the playing field, as the pension funds are significant investors in the Icelandic market. That could have a deterrent effect on private investors, as the pension funds could vote their representatives on the board.

The interviews supported the finding that foreign corporate governance models significantly influenced the gestation of Iceland's NCs, coupled with financial pressure to conform to more transparent, structured, and professional processes. The interviewees notably cited foreign investment funds calls for more professionalism and better procedures for appointing board members, especially to form a diverse group of board members who could support positive board dynamics.

Need for NCs to Promote Diversity on Boards in Iceland

The second sub-category defined for this chapter was "*The need for NCs to promote diversity on boards in Iceland.*" According to the interviewees, the process applied by various NCs are quite different from the traditional Icelandic method of nominating board members. In summary, the interviewees described the pre-existing system as overly informal and opaque, both when it came to finding and selecting board nominees and by not taking diverse board composition into consideration. They stressed that the more formal and professional approach by NCs more clearly defined how board members are identified and by whom, that sufficient time is given to the task, and that assessment and selection criteria are more clearly defined, both for individual assessment and board diversity enhancement.

The importance of the professional and transparent selection process was widely referenced by interviewees, with the notion that this would lead to increased trust among investors and more positive image in the eyes of the public. Participant 12.I, for example, said that the boards' selection process, if professionally performed, would improve public opinion of Icelandic business institutions. He further hoped that the pension funds would sense that the boards are as well-appointed as possible and that they have access to transparent information on how board members were selected. In this context, participant 6.N added: "This process entails a more professional process, as you are no longer just asked to become board members just because someone likes you so much or wants you to have a seat on this board. Then they just have to hope that you are qualified."

The informality of the traditional Icelandic process was also critiqued, as participant 10.B said: "The process was more informal, and the chair of the board had more responsibility, since both large shareholders and those who want to become board members frequently call him." He added: "The process was built on informal chats between shareholders ... [T]he processes was less structured and was carried out by phone calls." Various participants had experienced these informal chats and phone calls. Participant 11.I reported that she had often been asked to provide names of potential board members over the phone. Participant 5.N admitted that although it had often worked in the past to use his network to recruit board members, he would not recommend this approach today, as it was not professional.

Choosing board members under the prior system also occurred with noticeably short notice, often just before AGM's. Participant 5.N stated that the process took place at the last minute. He recounted that a board chairperson of a listed company had resigned only a few days before the AGM. Consequently, there was extremely limited time to find a replacement. Participant 7.N also said: "Before NCs, the board could be appointed in the last two hours before the deadline ... the pension funds and the investors were calling each other and trying to create a board because no one wanted to go through the trouble of voting a board at the AGM." She further commented that this process had adverse consequences: "This kind of work method just does not provide sufficient professional review of the board members, their knowledge and experience."

Various comments made by interviewees supported the notion that thorough assessment of a candidate's knowledge, skills, and competencies was often lacking; limited analysis of the overall board composition was conducted. Participant 6.N acknowledged that she had received phone calls when she was asked to become a board member for a company to which she did not feel that she would bring any added value. She had not been told how she would add to the diversity of the board and how she would contribute. Participant 12.I added:

> [T]he shareholders were off their guard and therefore the board and employees of the company needed to find people, and you can only blame the shareholders as they had all the resources and time to provide names so that [they] could choose this board. They hardly considered the board as a team and did certainly not think of the value of a diverse team.

According to the interviewees, the prior system entailed that those shareholders were sometimes picking their acquaintances for the board. However, that system can be problematic when there is a large group of shareholders, as participant 12.I pointed out: "(W)hen forty shareholders want to appoint their person on the board, it is worth the effort to have an NC to evaluate what is the best diverse team out of all these forty suggestions." Participant 11.I also admitted that when she was asked to produce names of potential female board members, she automatically always thought about the same women. She felt that it was the same with the males, that is, that they would like to work with those they recognize and therefore the more professional process applied by NCs could potentially increase the pool of people to be considered as board members.

Interviewees commented that when selecting board members under the traditional selection process, there was also more focus on choosing individuals instead of looking at the needs of the board as a whole and ensuring its diversity. Participant 9.N-B said that, in his experience: "(T)here was a lack of oversight of the group as a whole and individuals were chosen quite randomly ... [I]t was just a coincidence how the board was combined." Participant 8.N-B furthermore stated that with NCs, there is more focus on how the group is arranged, establishing the necessary criteria for candidates, and defining the skill-set, instead of just focusing on the candidates' names.

Participant 2.N also argued that the process with NCs entailed that the board be created as a team. According to her, there was not previously enough oversight of the board, and individuals were chosen independently of each other. Many participants compared the process of choosing board members to forming a balanced unit, or team. Participant 8.N-B stated that if each shareholder appointed one board member, it was as if the national football team was composed of each local squad supplying a player, without considering what position they play. Therefore, you could end up without a decent goalkeeper. In the corporate world, the board could have many persons with nearly identical knowledge and experience. Participant 2.N also argued that, with the old system, the board could end up being too homogeneous and lacking the necessary diversity; hence the best interests of the companies were not kept in mind. Participants 4.N and 11.I both indicated that the boards were often too alike. 4.N said: "I looked through the boards of listed companies and found that they all had the same profile." Participant 11.I stated: "[W]e have struggled with that in Iceland that the boards have been too homogeneous." Accordingly, participant 9.N-B told us about a listed company where four out of the five board members had the same education. He further argued that the prior system was more based on who managed to convince enough shareholders to back him as a board member, while the new system was based on the company's needs.

According to the findings, there are several important advantages of having established NCs. The key findings are summarized in Table 8.2. The table shows that the main findings can be divided into five categories. The first one is that institutional investors required NCs as they required a more professional selection process. The process with NCs becomes more transparent than the prior method for selecting board members. There is also more focus on diversity and choosing a team instead of individuals when NCs have been established.

Table 8.2   Main findings

Sub-themes	Main findings	Interview analysis
Establishment of NCs in Iceland	Required by international investors	● Prior to NC: Problematic system for foreign investors ● Requirements from institutional investors
Establishment of NCs in Iceland	Requiring more professional selection process	● Financial pressure to have more transparent, structured, and professional process ● Prior system lacked transparency and formality
Need for NCs to promote diversity on boards in Iceland	More professional and transparent process with NCs	● More professional and transparent process with NCs ● Prior process entailed informal discussions between shareholders ● Choosing board members sometimes used to be done at the last minute before the AGM ● Insufficient evaluation and professional review of board members with the prior system ● Shareholders sometimes selected their acquaintance instead of critically focusing on their knowledge and experience
Need for NCs to promote diversity on boards in Iceland	Focus on board diversity with NCs	● More clearly defined selection criteria, both for individual assessment and board diversity enhancement ● NC increases the pool of potential candidates instead of individuals often appoint the same person for multiple boards ● Prior to NC there was more focus on choosing individuals instead of looking at the needs of the board as a whole and ensuring its diversity ● People automatically provide the same names of potential board members when asked about candidates (prior to NCs) ● More risk of homogeneous board prior to NCs
Need for NCs to promote diversity on boards in Iceland	NCs focus on selecting a team instead of individuals	● Prior to NCs shareholders each appointed individuals and there was limited focus on evaluating the board as a team ● NCs entailed that the board be created as a team

DISCUSSION

In recent years, most companies listed in the Icelandic stock exchange have established NCs within their corporate governance structure. NCs have taken on the key role of proposing, evaluating, and selecting board members. They are relatively new entities in Iceland and hence not well researched. According to the Icelandic corporate governance guidelines, NCs should nominate potential board candidates by assessing potential board members' qualifications, experience, and knowledge, while considering the board's size, composition, and diversity. In addition, they should consider performance assessments regarding the composition of the board and the competence(s) of each board member (Iceland Chamber of Commerce et al., 2021).

Our study aims at assessing the extent to which different stakeholders, NCs members, shareholders, and board members of listed firms felt NCs enhance increased board diversity, given the previous less-structured nomination and selection processes. Our main findings feature the benefits of having NCs overseeing boards' selection in Icelandic listed companies. The benefits are increased transparency and a more orderly board member selection approach. The overall experience of both investors and board members participating in the research is that NCs generally apply improved professionalism and stricter methods for nominating, assessing, and selecting board members.

Furthermore, the process by which NCs operate is more likely to focus on selecting competent individuals and generating an overall stronger and diverse board. Hence, the boards' overall composition and board members' experience and knowledge are more likely to be well-considered using the NCs' selection approach. Prior research suggests that one of the key roles of NCs is to ensure board diversity (Kaczmarek et al., 2012; Mans-Kemp & Viviers, 2019; Ruigrok et al., 2006). Our research further contributes to that as we found that NCs can increase diversity. The diverse knowledge and experience of board members are more likely to be ensured. Regarding gender diversity, it is important to consider that there is a gender quota for board members that should ensure that at least 40 percent of board members should be women in Iceland. This can be a valuable insight as Rigolini and Huse (2021) found that gender quota may increase the diversity of women appointed as board members.

The approach applied for appointing board members prior to NCs arriving in Iceland has been described as more informal by our interviewees, as Sjöstrand et al. (2016) previously described. The findings from this research support that literature and conclude that establishing NCs is in accordance with current corporate governance principles (Thomsen & Conyon, 2019). That is also in accordance with the pertinent OECD (2015) guidelines. However, good corporate governance also shows that companies should be allowed to find tailor-made solutions (Thomsen & Conyon, 2019; OECD, 2015). There can also be circumstances where good corporate governance practice would be not to establish NCs, particularly when shareholders do not consider NCs beneficial. Despite this notion, this study shows that the process for selecting board members is more transparent and professional when NCs exist.

According to Byrne (1997), the selection of board members may be subject to biases (i.e., the similarity-attraction paradigm). Furthermore, according to social identity theory (Tajfel & Turner, 1986), individuals tend to select profiles having the same or similar beliefs, attitudes, or backgrounds, as they consider them easier to work with and more likable. Our findings suggest that prior to NCs, there was more focus on choosing individuals when choosing board members instead of looking at the board's needs as a whole and ensuring its diversity. That can result in the board appointed being too homogeneous, as all members have similar knowledge and experience. Through more professional selection processes, the selection of independent and competent board members strengthens internal corporate governance mechanisms. From the agency theory perspective, these independent board members counter the benefits of control from other relevant actors and promote more effective board supervision and performance.

The overall findings suggest that having NCs in Iceland can increase board diversity while also providing a more professional, transparent, and structured process for shareholders and other stakeholders.

CONCLUSION

This study explores the effect of NCs in Iceland and how they can encourage board diversity compared to prior methods for selecting board members. It has addressed how having NCs can ensure more diverse boards in Icelandic-listed companies. Our work also shows that NCs might increase professionalism and transparency. There are distinct advantages for companies to establish a NC vs. the traditional Icelandic system. According to various stakeholders, the boards' selection processes become more structured, transparent, and professional. The choice of individual board members becomes better considered and enhanced emphasis is placed on overall team composition.

Iceland is a valuable setting for researching NCs, as they are a relatively new development within corporate governance structures of Icelandic companies. As Iceland's business world is compact, the researchers were able to map all the pertinent committees and follow developments closely. In addition, as previously mentioned, there is a gender quota in Iceland for corporate boards that shall ensure gender diversity. Therefore, NCs will ensure that the gender quota is being fulfilled while also focusing on diversity concerning the knowledge and experience of board members.

However, many questions remain concerning NCs. Future research could compare the diversity of Icelandic board members nominated by NCs to that in other countries. The process of NCs, how their work is structured, and how they affect diversity could also be researched further.

REFERENCES

Adams, R. B., & Ferreira, D. (2009). Women in the boardroom and their impact on governance and performance. *Journal of Financial Economics, 94*(2), 291–309.

Adams, R. B., de Haan, J., Terjesen, S., & van Ees, H. (2015). Board diversity: moving the field forward. *Corporate Governance: An International Review, 23*(2), 77–82.

Arnardottir, A. A., & Sigurjonsson, Th. O. (2017). Gender diversity on boards in Iceland: pathway to gender quota law following a financial crisis. In H. Mensi-Klarbach, P. Gabaldon, & C. Seierstad (Eds.), *Gender Diversity in the Boardroom: European Perspectives on Increasing Female Representation.* Palgrave Macmillan. https://www.palgrave.com/gp/book/9783319561417.

Bryant, M., Sigurjonsson, Th. O., & Mixa, M. W. (2014). Restoring trust in public institutions and the financial system: the case of Iceland 2008 to 2012. Paper presented at 2014 International Conference of Critical Accounting (ICCA), New York, NY. Accessed December 8, 2016 at: http://www.ecgi.org/codes/code.php?code_id=261.

Byrne, D. (1997). An overview (and under view) of research and theory within the attraction paradigm. *Journal of Social and Personal Relationships, 14*(3), 417–31.

Carson, E. (2002). Factors associated with the development of board subcommittees. *Corporate Governance: An International Review, 10*(1), 4–18.

Clune, R., Hermanson, D. R., Tompkins, J. G., & Ye, Z. (2014). The nominating committee process: a qualitative examination of board independence and formalization. *Contemporary Accounting Research, 31*(3), 748–86.

Committee on Corporate Governance (2019). *Recommendations on Corporate Governance* (Version 4). Available at: https://corporategovernance.dk/sites/default/files/190911_recommendations_version_260819.pdf.

Eminet, A., & Guedri, Z. (2010). The role of nominating committees and director reputation in shaping the labor market for directors: an empirical assessment. *Corporate Governance: An International Review, 18*(6), 557–74.

Fama, E. F., & Jensen, M. C. (1983). Agency problems and residual claims. *The Journal of Law and Economics, 26*(2), 327–49.

Forbes, D. P., & Milliken, F. J. (1999). Cognition and corporate governance: understanding boards of directors as strategic decision-making groups. *Academy of Management Review, 24*(3), 489–505.

Fridriksson, F. (2019). Nomination committees in listed firms [*Tilnefningarnefndir í hlutafélögum*]. Available at: https://www.visir.is/g/2019190329055.

Gould, J. A., Kulik, C. T., & Sardeshmukh, S. R. (2018). Trickle-down effect: the impact of female board members on executive gender diversity. *Human Resource Management, 57*(4), 931–45.

Halldorsson, Th. F. (2019). The committees travel at light speed [*Nefndirnar fara eins og eldur í sinu um Kauphöllina*]. Available at: https://www.visir.is/g/2019190139962.

Hillman, A. J., Cannella Jr, A. A., & Harris, I. C. (2002). Women and racial minorities in the boardroom: how do directors differ? *Journal of Management, 28*(6), 747–63.

Hillman, A. J., & Dalziel, T. (2003). Boards of directors and firm performance: integrating agency and resource dependence perspectives. *Academy of Management Review, 28*(3), 383–96.

Huse, M., Nielsen, S. T., & Hagen, I. M. (2009). Women and employee-elected board members, and their contributions to board control tasks. *Journal of Business Ethics, 89*(4), 581–97.

Hutchinson, M., Mack, J., & Plastow, K. (2015). Who selects the 'right' directors? An examination of the association between board selection, gender diversity and outcomes. *Accounting & Finance, 55*(4), 1071–103.

Iceland Chamber of Commerce, Nasdaq Iceland hf., & SA Business Iceland (2021). Stjórnarhættir fyrirtækja (6th edition). Available at: https://leidbeiningar.is/wp-content/uploads/2021/06/Stjornarhaettir_fyrirtaekja_A5_IS_Vefur.pdf.

Iceland Chamber of Commerce, Nasdaq OMX Iceland hf., & SA Business Iceland (2009). *Stjórnarhættir fyrirtækja* (3rd edition). Available at: https://www.vi.is/files/cg3lokaweb_886826181.pdf.

Kaczmarek, S., Kimino, S., & Pye, A. (2012). Antecedents of board composition: the role of nomination committees. *Corporate Governance: An International Review, 20*(5), 474–89.

Kanadli, S. B., Torchia, M., & Gabaldon, P. (2018). Increasing women's contribution on board decision making: the importance of chairperson leadership efficacy and board openness. *European Management Journal, 36*(1), 91–104.

KPMG (2014). *Könnun meðal stjórnarmanna 2013* [Report among board members 2013]. Accessed December 15, 2016 at: http://www.kpmg.com/IS/is/utgefidefni/greinar-og-utgefid/skyrslur/Documents/Konnun-stjornarmanna-2013-KPMG.pdf.

Law on Limited Liability Corporations, no. 2. (1995). Available at: https://www.althingi.is/lagas/nuna/1994138.html.

Lekvall, P. (2017). The Nordic way of corporate governance. *NJB, 67*(3–4) (Autumn/Winter 2018). Available at: http://njb.fi/wp-content/uploads/2019/02/NJB_2019_3-4_Lekvall.pdf.

Mans-Kemp, N., & Viviers, S. (2019). The role of nomination committees in diversifying boards in an emerging market context. *Corporate Governance: The International Journal of Business in Society, 19*(4), 648–68.

Markoczy, L., Sun, S. L., & Zhu, J. (2020). Few women on boards: what's identity got to do with it? *Journal of Business Ethics, 165*(2), 311–27.

Merriam, S. B. (2016). *Qualitative Research: A Guide to Design and Implementation* (2nd edition). Jossey-Bass.

NCGB [Norwegian Corporate Governance Board] (2018). *The Norwegian Code of Practice for Corporate Governance* (9th edition). Available at: https://nues.no/wp-content/uploads/2018/10/NUES_eng_web_okt2018_2.pdf.

Nielsen, B. B., & Nielsen, S. (2013). Top management team nationality diversity and firm performance: a multilevel study. *Strategic Management Journal, 34*, 373–82.

Nielsen, S., & Huse, M. (2010). The contribution of women on boards of directors: going beyond the surface. *Corporate Governance: An International Review, 18*(2), 136–48.

OECD (2015). *G20/OECD Principles of Corporate Governance.* OECD Publishing.

Rigolini, A., & Huse, M. (2021). Women and multiple board memberships: social capital and institutional pressure. *Journal of Business Ethics, 169*(3), 443–59.

Ruigrok, W., Peck, S., Tacheva, S., Greve, P., & Hu, Y. (2006). The determinants and effects of board nomination committees. *Journal of Management & Governance, 10*(2), 119–48.

Securities Market Association (2020). *Finnish Corporate Governance Code 2020.* Available at: https://ecgi.global/sites/default/files/codes/documents/corporate-governance-code-2020.pdf.

Sjöstrand, S.-E., Berglund, T., Grönberg, L., Kallifatides, M., Poulfelt, F., Pöyry, S., & Sigurjonsson, O. (2016). *Nordic Corporate Governance: An Extensive In-Depth Study of Corporate Governance and Board Practices in 36 Large Companies.* Stockholm School of Economics, Institute for Research.

Special Investigation Commission Report (2010). *Skýrsla rannsóknarnefndar Alþingis* [Report of the Special Investigation Commission]. Accessed December 12, 2016 at: http://sic.althingi.is/.

Strauss, A. L., & Corbin, J. M. (1998). *Basics of Qualitative Research: Grounded Theory Procedures and Techniques* (2nd edition). Sage Publications.

Swedish Corporate Governance Board (2020). The Swedish Corporate Governance Code. Available at: http://www.bolagsstyrning.se/UserFiles/Koden/The_Swedish_Corporate_Governance_Code_1_January_2020.pdf.

Tajfel, H., & Turner, J. C. (1986). The social identity theory of intergroup behaviour. In W. G. Worchel, & S. Austin (Eds.), *Psychology of Intergroup Relations* (pp. 7–24). Nelson-Hall.

Tasheva, S., & Hillman, A. J. (2019). Integrating diversity at different levels: multilevel human capital, social capital, and demographic diversity and their implications for team effectiveness. *Academy of Management Review, 44*(4), 746–65.

Terjesen, S., & Sealy, R. (2016). Board gender quotas: exploring ethical tensions from a multi-theoretical perspective. *Business Ethics Quarterly, 26*(1), 23–65.

Thatcher, S. M., & Patel, P. C. (2012). Group fault lines: a review, integration, and guide to future research. *Journal of Management, 38*(4), 969–1009.

Thomsen, S., & Conyon, M. (2019). *Corporate Governance and Board Decisions.* Djøf Publishing.

Westphal, J. D. (1994). Who shall govern? The role of demographic similarity in new director selection. *Academy of Management Proceedings, 1*, 223–7. Available at: https://doi.org/10.5465/ambpp.1994.10344276.

Zahra, S. A., & Pearce, J. A. (1989). Boards of directors and corporate financial performance: a review and integrative model. *Journal of Management, 15*(2), 291–334.

PART III

ADVANCES IN INTERSECTIONALITY

9. Diversity on corporate boards and shareholder activism: an intersectionality approach

Sarosh Asad and Dimitrios Georgakakis

Shareholder activism has become an integral element of the modern corporate governance system. It is the use of ownership position by shareholders to influence corporate practices actively, achieve greater managerial accountability, and mitigate agency costs (Denes, Karpoff, and McWilliams, 2017; Goranova and Ryan, 2014). When discontent with the governance practices of the firm, shareholders may exit the firm by choosing to sell their shares, or use their voice (i.e., engage in activism to influence top management) (Black, 1998). While shareholder activism can be exerted through various approaches (e.g., private negotiations with management or engaging in a proxy contest), filing resolutions is the most efficient and cost-effective way for shareholders to present their concerns to the firm (Lee, Gupta, and Hambrick, 2020).

When shareholders file a resolution against a firm, it is often with the purpose of demanding reforms in corporate governance practices (Gillan and Starks, 2000; Karpoff, Malatesta, and Walkling, 1996). According to the Institutional Shareholder Services (ISS) database, the number of governance-related shareholder resolutions has constantly exceeded the number of non-governance (social policy) related resolutions over the period 2010–19 (Figure 9.1) – highlighting that corporate governance aspects are usually the reasons of why shareholders exercise their "voice" and raise complaints about corporate leadership. Examples of corporate governance resolutions include aspects surrounding executive compensation, dismissal of directors and executives, corporate disclosures, and independence of the board of directors (Goranova, Abouk, Nystrom, and Soofi, 2017). Ignoring such resolutions may have severe consequences for the targeted firm and the board of directors. For example, Greenwood and Schor (2009) analyzed a sample of 13D filings by investors from 1993 to 2006 and found that when activists targeted firms due to corporate governance issues, the final result was a takeover in 15.7 percent of the incidents. Similarly, Ertimur, Ferri, and Stubben (2010) argued that directors who fail to respond to shareholder resolutions are much more likely to incur reputational penalties in the labor market. Shareholder activism can also cost the firm indirectly as valuable employees tend to leave the firm post incidents of activism in order to reduce the potential negative career outcomes (Chen, Meyer-Doyle, and Shi, 2021).

Another corporate governance aspect that increasingly concerns shareholders is diversity in corporate boardrooms. Shareholders typically have restricted information about the firm and rely on board composition as a relevant cue of a firm's ability to

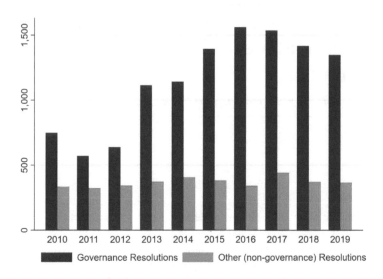

Figure 9.1   *Number of shareholder resolutions, 2010–19*

generate shareholder value (Bansal and Thenmozhi, 2019; Hillman et al., 2011). In addition, the boards of directors are directly responsible for protecting shareholders' interests by monitoring and providing resources to the management (Hillman and Dalziel, 2003). Governance failures can directly lead to lower profitability and loss of shareholder value, instigating shareholder activism. Therefore, board composition is an important aspect that shareholders consider when they attempt to establish a reciprocal relationship with the firm (Cannella and Georgakakis, 2017; Connelly, Shi, and Zyung, 2017; Georgakakis, Heyden, Oehmichen, and Ekanayake, 2019).

Shareholders may prefer diverse boards because they can be more effective in serving the interests of shareholders (Ljungqvist and Raff, 2021). Diverse boards have greater information processing capacity and, thus, are often better at serving their monitoring and resource provisioning roles to increase shareholder value (Carter, Simkins, and Simpson, 2003; Nielsen and Huse, 2010; Oehmichen, Heyden, Georgakakis, and Volberda, 2017). Earlier research rooted in agency theory (Fama and Jensen, 1983) has shown that gender and ethnic diverse boards tend to be more independent and have better attendance records in board meetings (Adams and Ferreira, 2009; Terjesen, Sealy, and Singh, 2009), which can lead to better monitoring of the management and reduces the risks of managerial opportunism (Guest, 2019). They tend to question the top management team on questionable governance prac- tices (Tee and Rassiah, 2020). Based on the notion of resource-based theory, some argue that female and ethnic minority directors provide high levels of human capital, unique resources, and network connections, leading to better governance and organ- izational effectiveness (Ibarra, 1993; Kirsch, 2018; Singh, 2007). Further, whereas an all-male board can receive criticism for selection biases grounded in homophilous demographics, a diverse board signals a path towards competency-based hiring practices. Thus, shareholders may place greater trust in diverse boards to perform directorial functions with the prospect that board diversity will, in turn, increase shareholder value (Perrault, 2015).

However, much of the existing research on the subject adopts a unidimensional approach to understanding and evaluating how shareholders perceive diversity on corporate boards, often emphasizing gender as the only critical attribute in such evaluations. However, diversity is a multidimensional construct, given that a female minority director can also be a member of another minority status group (e.g., minority in ethnicity). The multidimensional notion of board diversity links to the concept of intersectionality (Crenshaw, 1989), defined as dual or multiple minority status memberships. For example, some boards may be gender diverse and homogenous in other demographic categories (e.g., ethnicity, nationality, age), while others may embrace diversity along several dimensions. Considering diversity as a multidimensional construct can allow us to adequately appreciate how board composition impacts shareholder activism and the rise of shareholder resolutions for corporate governance issues. This line of inquiry is important because it avoids simplistic overgeneralizations across a single diversity dimension and instead allows a nuanced understanding of the experiences across intersections of diversity dimensions. For that reason, this chapter aims to highlight and emphasize an intersectional approach to understanding the diversity on corporate boards and ensuing shareholder activism.

AN OVERVIEW OF RESEARCH ON BOARD DIVERSITY AND SHAREHOLDER ACTIVISM

Shareholder activism in the U.S. dates back to the Securities and Exchange Commission Act of 1934 (section 14A-8), according to which the management of a publicly traded company is liable to allow shareholders with ownership of at least $2,000 or 1 percent of shares outstanding to submit resolutions for corporate reforms and enhance accountability (Buchanan, Netter, Poulsen, and Yang, 2012; Gillan and Starks, 2009; Shleifer and Vishny, 1986). Once submitted, these resolutions are voted on at the next annual general meeting of the corporation, or they are withdrawn by mutual consent of the shareholders submitting the resolution and the respondent managers (Rastad and Dobson, 2020). These resolutions are advisory in nature, that is, the management is not legally bound to implement the resolution even if shareholders manage to achieve majority support (Buchanan et al., 2012). However, filing resolutions is considered the first step toward initiating change, whereby shareholders draw the management's attention to issues that need to be reconsidered (Rehbein, Waddock, and Graves, 2004). Directors can also incur substantial reputational damage and may face more aggravated shareholder activism in the form of "just vote no" campaigns during directorial elections if they remain unresponsive to the shareholder demands (Del Guercio, Seery, and Woidtke, 2008; Ertimur et al., 2010).

A small but noteworthy set of studies has underscored the importance of shareholder resolutions in influencing board diversity (Table 9.1). Perrault (2015) argued that shareholders are increasingly submitting resolutions to deinstitutionalize homogenous, that is, all-male boards that lack legitimacy regarding the firm's provision of equal opportunities and may thus compromise shareholders' trust. Based on a sample of U.S. S&P 1500 firms from 1997 to 2011, Marquardt and Wiedman (2016) found that firms with gender-homogenous boards are more likely to be targeted by shareholder resolutions regarding gender diversity. Berns and Williams (2021) confirmed the findings of Marquardt and Wiedman (2016) with the same sample of firms from the period 2010 to 2017. Rastad and Dobson (2020) also favored shareholder resolutions as an effective instrument for promoting gender diversity in corporate boardrooms. They further compared resolutions withdrawn by shareholders and those voted on in the annual meeting and found that withdrawn resolutions are more effective in improving gender diversity on corporate boards than those voted ones. Withdrawn resolutions usually signal that the shareholders have succeeded in forcing the management to agree with the proposed resolution agenda. Thus, the mere presence of shareholder resolutions is an effective tool to influence board diversity.

Notably, these studies emphasize gender as the relevant diversity dimension and argue that shareholders are increasingly favorable to gender-diverse boards. However, these findings may differ when female directors also concurrently represent other minority status groups.

Table 9.1   Summary of illustrative studies on the relationship between board diversity and shareholder activism

Study (Year)	Board diversity dimension	Theory	Sample/method	Main argument
Berns and Williams (2021)	Gender	Agency theory and expectation violation theory	S&P 1500 firms over 2010–17; regression analysis	Boards that are gender homogenous are more likely to receive shareholder resolutions for diversity issues. This relationship becomes less pronounced when the CEO is female.
Mitra, Post, and Sauerwald (2021)	Gender	Agency theory and resource dependence theory	S&P 1500 firms over 2003–15; regression analysis	Female directors receive less shareholder dissent – defined as votes in director elections opposing a director candidate than their male counterparts. However, this effect disappears when the board is faced with agency threats.
Rastad and Dobson (2020)	Gender	Agency theory	150 U.S. firms over 1997–2013; regression analysis	Shareholder resolutions improve board diversity. Board diversity increased more in response to withdrawn shareholder resolutions than voted resolutions.
Marquardt and Wiedman (2016)	Gender	Agency theory and institutional theory	S&P 1500 firms over 1997–2011: regression analysis	Female representation in corporate boards reduces the likelihood of being targeted by shareholder diversity resolutions. Companies targeted by diversity resolutions tend to increase female board representation.
Perrault (2015)	Gender	Social network and institutional theories	U.S. firms over 2004–08; qualitative interviews	Activist shareholders play a critical role in deinstitutionalizing all-male boards.

INTERSECTIONAL CONCEPTUALIZATION OF BOARD DIVERSITY

Crenshaw (1989, 1991) originally introduced the idea of intersectionality in her study of discrimination against black women. It was based on the realization that black women's interests were not represented in either black movements (where black men sought equality with white men) or women's movements (where white women sought equality with white men) in the United States (Gopaldas, 2013). Underscoring the unique experiences of individuals with multiple dimensions of minority, Sawyer, Salter, and Thoroughgood (2013) noted that 'although being a woman and being Black may have differing levels of significance for work-related outcomes, being a Black woman carries a certain social significance that is separate from either of these identities individually' (p. 81). Crenshaw's work argued that multiple dimensions of minority status reinforce multiple intersecting identities. Thus, recent studies in this area have built on the intersectionality logic and call for consideration of differences that may appear as a duality of minority status (e.g., both gender and ethnicity minority status for an individual or group).

The idea of intersectionality is slowly started to gain momentum in diversity research (Dennison et al., 2020; Gopaldas, 2013; Gopaldas and DeRoy, 2015). While mainstream research on diversity emphasizes the aggregation of all categories (e.g., women, ethnic minorities, and people with disabilities) in defining the diversity construct, the emerging notion of "intersectional diversity" stresses the inclusion of not only all categories but also all intersections of those categories. Intersections of historically stigmatized identities are rarely visible in management and media. Thus, shareholder reactions to diversity based on dual and multiple identity categories may not be the same as to diversity based on a single dimension (e.g., gender in isolation). In the following section, we discuss how shareholders may differentially react when multiple diversity categories intersect. We focus on the intersectionality of gender and ethnicity as they are most salient in terms of visibility to the shareholders.

DUAL MINORITY ON CORPORATE BOARDS AND SHAREHOLDER RESOLUTIONS

Drawing on the perspective of intersectionality, we argue that focusing on a single diversity dimension (e.g., gender) in isolation cannot fully capture the complex nature of the relationship between board diversity and shareholder activism. Understanding diversity using the lens of intersectionality entails that diversity should be studied across multiple dimensions. So while shareholders may join other stakeholders in promoting a single dimension of diversity, particularly gender, on corporate boards, the same may not hold true if a director represents a dual minority status (Gopaldas and DeRoy, 2015). Thus, some female directors may face different reactions from shareholders than others – depending on whether or not they are associated with dual minority status. Put differently, some female directors may be perceived as minorities not only due to their gender-related attributes but also due to their membership in additional minority groups (e.g., white female versus other minority race female directors). In this regard, scholars have stressed that categorizing directors solely based on their gender runs the risk that a new form of modern discrimination will emerge – placing some females (i.e., those who belong to dual minority categories) at a more substantial disadvantage compared to those that belong in dominant ethnicity groups (e.g., Caucasian females) (Kirsch, 2018; Miller and del Carmen Triana, 2009).

Following this logic, we argue that the combination of female and ethnic minority directors can invoke stronger adverse reactions by the shareholders concerning corporate governance dimensions of corporate leadership. This is because stereotypes and tokenism effects are likely to strengthen when an individual director exposes minority status with regard to more than one attribute (e.g., both gender and ethnicity). The presence of dual minority directors on corporate boards is likely to trigger a higher number of resolutions from organizational shareholders – demonstrating the complexity of dealing with multiple dimensions of board diversity in evaluating board composition.

Proposition 1: The presence of dual minority directors (i.e., gender and ethnic minority) will lead to a higher number of shareholder governance resolutions.

THE ROLE OF INSTITUTIONAL INVESTORS

The resolutions can be submitted by single investors called "blockholders" or institutional investors such as hedge funds, pension funds, and labor unions (Ryan and Schneider, 2002). Compared to blockholders, institutional investors play a more active role in influencing corporate governance practices (Brav, Jiang, Partnoy, and Thomas, 2008). They tend to be better informed and have more negotiating power (Del Guercio and Hawkins, 1999), which is partially due to the larger size and ownership of those investors (Smith, 1996). Extant research also shows that resolutions proposed by institutional investors receive significantly higher votes of support (Denes, Karpoff, and McWilliams, 2017) and get implemented by the board of directors (Ertimur et al., 2010). Similarly, Klein and Zur (2009) found that the market reacts more favorably to campaigns led by hedge funds than those of other entrepreneurial activists.

When institutional investors raise resolutions for corporate governance issues, they signal an institutionalized need for change to other shareholders. Given that dual minority status generates tokenisms behavior and may trigger more resolutions, the presence of resolutions raised by institutional investors is likely to exacerbate this effect further, as they will signal to other shareholders that the firm's governance requires change. As such, we propose that resolutions from institutional investors may strengthen the positive relationship between dual minority boards and shareholder activism.

Proposition 2: The positive effect of the presence of dual minority directors on the number of shareholder governance resolutions filed will be stronger when they are sponsored by an institutional investor.

DUAL MINORITY DIRECTOR REPLACEMENT POST SHAREHOLDER RESOLUTIONS

An important question relates to the consequence of shareholder resolutions in inducing director dismissal. This argument is based on the line of inquiry that argues that higher shareholder activism may ultimately influence the boardroom experiences of minority directors. Namely, minority directors stand to lose boardroom influence when the firm faces negative shareholder reactions. They may bear the burden of shareholders' dissatisfaction disproportionately and ultimately face replacement (Kalogeraki and Georgakakis, 2021). At the same time, research that adopts the "female leadership advantage" logic suggests that female directors will be less likely to be replaced in situations of crisis as they garner greater trust from the labor market (Post, Latu, and Belkin, 2019). Given that activist shareholders pay increasing attention to the representation of female directors, these directors are less likely to be replaced after resolutions for altering corporate governance practices (Gupta et al., 2018). However, when dual minority status is in place, the tokenism tendencies in cases of dual minority membership may outweigh minority leadership or reputational advantage – and instead promote a higher likelihood for dual minority directors to get replaced after resolutions. This argument is supported by studies showing that dual minorities often face a disadvantage in critical conditions (Eagly and Carli, 2003) – for example, when shareholders express dissatisfaction with corporate practices (Mitra, Post, and Sauerwald, 2021). After replacement, the dual minority status director may also face increasing difficulties in being reappointed as a board member of another firm – thereby having a stronger influence on their subsequent career progress.

Proposition 3: Dual minority directors will be more likely to be replaced following an increase in shareholder governance resolutions.

Proposition 4: After replacement, dual minority directors will be less likely to be reappointed for board positions at other firms.

CONCLUSION

As shareholder activism continues to grow in the U.S. and globally, it is important to understand what increases the likelihood of firms being targeted by shareholder resolutions— a popular and institutionalized form of activism. Board diversity affects shareholders' decisions related to the governance capabilities of the firm, subsequently affecting critical organizational outcomes. While previous studies have focused on single dimensions of diversity as drivers of shareholder activism (Kang, Ding, and Charoenwong, 2010; Marquardt and Wiedman, 2016; Rastad and Dobson, 2020), this chapter calls for an intersectional approach to understanding this complex relationship.

Our chapter theorizes that shareholders may be unwilling to set aside their prejudices when boards consist of both ethnic and gender minorities and therefore express more dissatisfaction with corporate governance practices for such boards. A rise in shareholder activism may have implications for directors' subsequent career outcomes. Overall, our work contributes to ongoing debates about how shareholders evaluate and respond to board gender and racial composition. Further, we draw the attention of managers and policymakers to the dual minority status of directors (i.e., how gender diversity interacts with racial diversity to influence shareholder reactions). Future research needs to pay more attention to the configurations of multiple diversity dimensions and the ensuing shareholder response.

REFERENCES

Adams, R. B., & Ferreira, D. (2009). Women in the boardroom and their impact on governance and performance. *Journal of Financial Economics, 94*(2), 291–309.

Bansal, S., & Thenmozhi, M. (2019). Does board composition matter to institutional investors? *Journal of Emerging Market Finance, 18*(2_suppl), S238–S266.

Berns, J. P., & Williams, J. L. (2021). Calling out the laggards: shareholder activism and board gender diversity. *Gender in Management: An International Journal, 37*(1), 39–57

Black, B. S. (1998). Shareholder activism and corporate governance in the United States. In P. Newman (Ed.), *The New Palgrave Dictionary of Economics and the Law*, Vol. 3 (pp. 459–65). Palgrave Macmillan.

Brav, A., Jiang, W., Partnoy, F., & Thomas, R. (2008). Hedge fund activism, corporate governance, and firm performance. *The Journal of Finance, 63*(4), 1729–75.

Buchanan, B. G., Netter, J. M., Poulsen, A. B., & Yang, T. (2012). Shareholder proposal rules and practice: evidence from a comparison of the United States and United Kingdom. *American Business Law Journal, 49*(4), 739–803.

Cannella Jr., A. A., & Georgakakis, D. (2017). Decision diversion: the roles of leadership context and other contingencies. *Academy of Management Discoveries, 3*(4), 428–30.

Carter, D. A., Simkins, B. J., & Simpson, W. G. (2003). Corporate governance, board diversity, and firm value. *Financial Review, 38*(1), 33–53.

Chen, G., Meyer-Doyle, P., & Shi, W. (2021). Hedge fund investor activism and human capital loss. *Strategic Management Journal, 42*(12), 2328–54.

Connelly, B. L., Shi, W., & Zyung, J. (2017). Managerial response to constitutional constraints on shareholder power. *Strategic Management Journal, 38*(7), 1499–517.

Crenshaw, K. (1989). Demarginalizing the intersection of race and sex: a black feminist critique of antidiscrimination doctrine, feminist theory and antiracist politics. *University of Chicago Legal Forum*, 139–68. https://chicagounbound.uchicago.edu/cgi/viewcontent.cgi?article=1052&context=uclf.

Crenshaw, K. (1991), Mapping the margins: intersectionality, identity politics, and violence against women of color. *Stanford Law Review*, *43*(6), 1241–99.

Del Guercio, D., & Hawkins, J. (1999). The motivation and impact of pension fund activism. *Journal of Financial Economics*, *52*(3), 293–340.

Del Guercio, D., Seery, L., & Woidtke, T. (2008). Do boards pay attention when institutional investor activists "just vote no"? *Journal of Financial Economics*, *90*(1), 84–103.

Denes, M. R., Karpoff, J. M., & McWilliams, V. B. (2017). Thirty years of shareholder activism: a survey of empirical research. *Journal of Corporate Finance*, *44*, 405–24.

Dennison, M., Benschop, Y., & van den Brink, M. (2020). Rethinking diversity management: an intersectional analysis of diversity networks. *Organization Studies*, *41*(2), 219–40.

Eagly, A. H., & Carli, L. L. (2003). The female leadership advantage: an evaluation of the evidence. *The Leadership Quarterly*, *14*(6), 807–34.

Ertimur, Y., Ferri, F., & Stubben, S. R. (2010). Board of directors' responsiveness to shareholders: evidence from shareholder proposals. *Journal of Corporate Finance*, *16*(1), 53–72.

Fama, E. F., & Jensen, M. C. (1983). Separation of ownership and control. *The Journal of Law and Economics*, *26*(2), 301–25.

Georgakakis, D., Heyden, M. L., Oehmichen, J. D., & Ekanayake, U. I. (2019). Four decades of CEO–TMT interface research: a review inspired by role theory. *The Leadership Quarterly*, 101354. https://doi.org/10.1016/j.leaqua.2019.101354.

Gillan, S. L., & Starks, L. T. (2000). Corporate governance proposals and shareholder activism: the role of institutional investors. *Journal of Financial Economics*, *57*(2), 275–305.

Gillan, S. L., & Starks, L. T. (2009). The evolution of shareholder activism in the United States. In D. H. Chew & S. L. Gillan (Eds.), *U.S. Corporate Governance* (pp. 202–40). Columbia University Press.

Gopaldas, A. (2013). Intersectionality 101. *Journal of Public Policy & Marketing*, *32*(1_ suppl), 90–94.

Gopaldas, A., & DeRoy, G. (2015). An intersectional approach to diversity research. *Consumption Markets & Culture*, *18*(4), 333–64.

Goranova, M., Abouk, R., Nystrom, P. C., & Soofi, E. S. (2017). Corporate governance antecedents to shareholder activism: a zero-inflated process. *Strategic Management Journal*, *38*(2), 415–35.

Goranova, M., & Ryan, L. V. (2014). Shareholder activism: a multidisciplinary review. *Journal of Management*, *40*(5), 1230–68.

Greenwood, R., & Schor, M. (2009). Investor activism and takeovers. *Journal of Financial Economics*, *92*(3), 362–75.

Guest, P. M. (2019). Does board ethnic diversity impact board monitoring outcomes? *British Journal of Management*, *30*(1), 53–74.

Gupta, V. K., Han, S., Mortal, S. C., Silveri, S. D., & Turban, D. B. (2018). Do women CEOs face greater threat of shareholder activism compared to male CEOs? A role congruity perspective. *Journal of Applied Psychology*, *103*(2), 228.

Hillman, A. J., & Dalziel, T. (2003). Boards of directors and firm performance: integrating agency and resource dependence perspectives. *Academy of Management Review*, *28*(3), 383–96.

Hillman, A. J., Shropshire, C., Certo, S. T., Dalton, D. R., & Dalton, C. M. (2011). What I like about you: a multilevel study of shareholder discontent with director monitoring. *Organization Science*, *22*(3), 675–87.

Ibarra, H. (1993). Personal networks of women and minorities in management: a conceptual framework. *Academy of Management Review*, *18*(1), 56–87.

Kang, E., Ding, D. K., & Charoenwong, C. (2010). Investor reaction to women directors. *Journal of Business Research*, *63*(8), 888–94.

Kalogeraki, O., & Georgakakis, D. (2021). Friend or Foe? CEO gender, political ideology, and gender-pay disparities in executive compensation. *Long Range Planning*. https://doi.org/10.1016/j.lrp.2021.102126.

Karpoff, J. M., Malatesta, P. H., & Walkling, R. A. (1996). Corporate governance and shareholder initiatives: empirical evidence. *Journal of Financial Economics*, *42*(3), 365–95.

Kirsch, A. (2018). The gender composition of corporate boards: a review and research agenda. *The Leadership Quarterly*, *29*(2), 346–64.

Klein, A., & Zur, E. (2009). Entrepreneurial shareholder activism: hedge funds and other private investors. *The Journal of Finance*, *64*(1), 187–229.

Lee, M. K., Gupta, A., & Hambrick, D. (2020). The distinct effects of wealth-and CSR-oriented shareholder unrest on CEO career outcomes: a new lens on settling up and executive job demands. *Academy of Management Journal*, *65*(1). https://doi.org/10.5465/amj.2019.1346.

Ljungqvist, A., & Raff, K. (2021). When does board diversity benefit shareholders? Strategic deadlock as a commitment to monitor. *Strategic Deadlock as a Commitment to Monitor (July 28, 2021). Swedish House of Finance Research Paper* (20–24).

Marquardt, C., & Wiedman, C. (2016). Can shareholder activism improve gender diversity on corporate boards? *Corporate Governance: An International Review*, *24*(4), 443–61.

Miller, T., & del Carmen Triana, M. (2009). Demographic diversity in the boardroom: mediators of the board diversity–firm performance relationship. *Journal of Management Studies*, *46*(5), 755–86.

Mitra, A., Post, C., & Sauerwald, S. (2021). Evaluating board candidates: a threat-contingency model of shareholder dissent against female director candidates. *Organization Science*, *32*(1), 86–110.

Nielsen, S., & Huse, M. (2010). The contribution of women on boards of directors: going beyond the surface. *Corporate Governance: An International Review*, *18*(2), 136–48.

Oehmichen, J., Heyden, M. L., Georgakakis, D., & Volberda, H. W. (2017). Boards of directors and organizational ambidexterity in knowledge-intensive firms. *The International Journal of Human Resource Management*, *28*(2), 283–306.

Perrault, E. (2015). Why does board gender diversity matter and how do we get there? The role of shareholder activism in deinstitutionalizing old boys' networks. *Journal of Business Ethics*, *128*(1), 149–65.

Post, C., Latu, I. M., & Belkin, L. Y. (2019). A female leadership trust advantage in times of crisis: under what conditions?. *Psychology of Women Quarterly*, *43*(2), 215–31.

Rastad, M., & Dobson, J. (2020). Gender diversity on corporate boards: evaluating the effectiveness of shareholder activism. *The Quarterly Review of Economics and Finance*. https://doi.org/10.1016/j.qref.2020.09.007.

Rehbein, K., Waddock, S., & Graves, S. B. (2004). Understanding shareholder activism: which corporations are targeted? *Business & Society*, *43*(3), 239–67.

Ryan, L. V., & Schneider, M. (2002). The antecedents of institutional investor activism. *Academy of Management Review*, *27*(4), 554–73.

Sawyer, K., Salter, N., & Thoroughgood, C. (2013). Studying individual identities is good, but examining intersectionality is better. *Industrial and Organizational Psychology*, *6*(1), 80–84.

Shleifer, A., & Vishny, R. W. (1986). Large shareholders and corporate control. *Journal of Political Economy*, *94*(3, Part 1), 461–88.

Singh, V. (2007). Ethnic diversity on top corporate boards: a resource dependency perspective. *The International Journal of Human Resource Management*, *18*(12), 2128–46.

Smith, M. P. (1996). Shareholder activism by institutional investors: evidence from CalPERS. *The Journal of Finance*, *51*(1), 227–52.

Tee, C. M., & Rassiah, P. (2020). Ethnic board diversity, earnings quality and institutional investors: evidence from Malaysian corporate boards. *Accounting & Finance, 60*(4), 4257–90.

Terjesen, S., Sealy, R., & Singh, V. (2009). Women directors on corporate boards: a review and research agenda. *Corporate Governance: An International Review, 17*(3), 320–37.

10. Competing inequalities, inclusion and intersectionality: the role of gender, culture and marginal groups for leadership positions

Vartika Chandra Saman

I was working with IIM Bangalore on a project on women in boardrooms in India. While collecting the data around the topic, I could not find a single woman from Scheduled Caste (SC) background. Articles 341 of the Constitution of India define as to who would be Scheduled Castes with respect to any State or Union Territory. Dalits or Schedule Castes (SCs) were considered as 'untouchables' and have been excluded from public places and business, and are being denied rights and privileges enjoyed by upper castes. According to the 2011 Census, the SCs constitute 16.6 percent of the total population, or approximately 167 million people in India. However, the popular anti-caste movements have used the term 'dalit' for Scheduled Caste and this has a political connotation (Roychowdhury, 2018). I have chosen to use dalit instead of Scheduled Caste for all my research papers.

The number of women in boardrooms in India is meager but women from disadvantaged castes and backgrounds are absent. This made me think a lot as to why that is. Where are these women? Are they not interested in taking up leadership positions? If not, why? In addition, if yes, why are not there any women? Corporate governance is dominated by upper castes, which means that the way in which companies are governed (rules, policies and practices) is also dominated by the same caste. This leaves behind the 'lower caste' as they are not part of the boards, CEOs and top leadership positions. Sociologists, political scientists and historians have extensively analyzed the pertinent questions but comprehensive investigation from involvement of marginalized groups is still at a nascent stage from a corporate governance perspective. The situation is grimmer when one looks at the condition of 'lower caste' women in top leadership positions.

When Morten Huse asked me to contribute a chapter on 'diversity and corporate governance', I was more than happy to contribute on this topic. As for India, it remains relatively neglected by comparative research because of the relative lack of statistical data. So, I targeted only ten women entrepreneurs from the dalit community to be interviewed for my study as I wanted to work around their personal life and business life stories. I thought I had enough time. Guess what – I did not.

It took me weeks to connect to people who could connect me to these women. The Covid-19 situation made things worse as getting a response from people on phone and emails has always been difficult in India. Once I had some phone numbers and email IDs of my first connections (who were supposed to connect me to these women), I started to call them. Most of them did not respond after a few calls from my side, and most of them responded saying "Sorry, but there are no dalit women as entrepreneurs." Some said, "Do you want to interview a few dalit women working in small shops or vegetable vendors as there is none in the leadership position?" Some suggested one or two famous names but the contact details were not available. It became a routine for me during my bus ride (while going to my office and returning) to call these people and ask if they had any contacts.

Meanwhile, many questions were arising in my mind. Is it so difficult to find ten dalit women entrepreneurs from a population of around 97.9 million dalit women? Why does nobody ask these questions? Why are there so few studies around it? Coming from one of the leading universities in Asia, if I cannot find these women through my network then how difficult would it be for research scholars coming from smaller cities and universities to study this topic? At last, I could find two women who agreed to be interviewed but they were busy, and I was just a few weeks away from my deadline. Having no options left to interview these women, I reformulated the structure of my chapter and decided to investigate the topic through available data and five in-depth interviews. However, this experience also helped me to reformulate my study and ask relevant questions.

With the following background, this study explores the relationship between caste and entrepreneurships and the intersectionality of gender and caste in business. The present study takes the case of dalit women as they are at the bottom of the caste hierarchy. This study argues that discrimination against dalit women and their unfavorable inclusion in the markets is carved out and sustained at the intersection of gender, caste, culture and modern market structure in India. Therefore, diversity in workplaces cannot be understood within the rigid boundaries of one single identity but has to be understood through the lens of intersectionality. The following section will try to define caste and its relationship with business (especially in the context of dalits) in order to understand its relationship with gender.

UNDERSTANDING CASTE AND BUSINESS

Caste is the biggest social reality of India and touches almost every aspect of one's life, such as renting a house (Thorat et al., 2015) or accessibility to relief after disasters (Aldrich, 2010). It is one of the oldest surviving social systems and has been described as a 3,500-year-old institution (Bidner & Eswaran, 2015). One of the salient features of caste system is discrimination. This discrimination divides people into rigid hierarchical groups based on their occupation (Deshpande, 2012). It dictates the customary social, political and economic relationships. Dr. Ambedkar, a dalit and the chair of the drafting committee of the Constitution of India, recognized that the economy is the basis of the caste system. According to him, the features of the caste system are the division of Hindus into social groups called caste. It involves assignment of social, civic, political, economic and religious rights. The rights are assigned in a hierarchical manner. Dr. Ambedkar called it 'graded inequality.' He also argued that the caste system has a philosophical base in religion. The religious philosophy of Hinduism provides a justification for the caste system and denial of all the economic rights to the dalits (Hiwrale, 2020).

The principle of individual choice is violated in the caste system. The caste system also puts a low value on 'physical' work, as compared to 'mental' work, with the result that the dignity of physical labor is nearly absent in the work ethics of the caste system (Madheswaran & Singhari, 2016). Looking into the historical evolution of the caste system, the prominent scholar and social activist Gail Omvedt writes that Vedic and Indus civilization had no caste system. The caste system took centuries to develop into a rigid institution and silently became the hegemonic feature of Indian society. She further adds that the caste system was promoted as a theory to organize society and thus is thus more prescriptive than descriptive. The dominant class used their interpretations from ancient scriptures such as the Vedas and Manusmriti. A person born in a particular caste has to decide her/his occupation based on their caste. Hence, caste is described as an absolute exclusionary institution. What makes it even deeper is the justification provided by the religious scriptures (Omvedt, 2005).

THE ECONOMICS OF CASTE AND DALITS IN BUSINESS

Historically, dalits have been a deprived and marginalized community, facing many forms of exclusion. The term 'dalit,' literally means oppressed, but has acquired a new cultural connotation to mean "those who have been broken, ground down by those above them in deliberate and active way" (Shah et al., 2006). One of the strongest features of dalit identity lies in the expression of a refusal of the social domination inherited from the Brahminical system (Ilaiah, 1996).

The social origin of India's capitalist class lies in the institution of caste (Damodaran, 2008). Caste system results in growing economic inequalities because of uneven distribution of resources, access to resources such as education and health, and rewards for labor. It greatly influences the social interactions between individuals, the economic activities they conduct and the economic transactions between them, resulting in socioeconomic inequalities (Bapuji, 2015). Some studies break the popular fallacies that caste does not exist in 'modern India' and conclude that caste has not disappeared with the dawn of modernity and development. The upper caste dominates knowledge-based professions (Thomas, 2020) while the lower castes predominate in menial, hazardous and 'unskilled' work (Varman & Chakrabarti, 2004).

There are studies suggesting that enterprises started by dalits are more survivalist than entrepreneurial and the caste of the owner has a significant impact on the growth of the enterprise (Deshpande, 2013). The study of caste and how it operates in modern India in the business class has been well described in terms of complete exclusion, selective inclusion, unfavorable inclusion and selective exclusion (Thorat & Newman, 2007). Another study elaborated on the low number of dalits as entrepreneurs and argues that it is mostly because of inequality in the distribution of resources and inter-caste disparity in the ownership of private enterprises. The same pattern demonstrating inter-caste disparity in enterprise ownership has been confirmed in other studies (Iyer et al., 2013). These studies break the idea of 'meritocracy' propounded by market economies and the private sector. Another study conducted detailed interviews with human resource managers of 25 large firms in New Delhi. All the managers insisted that merit was the sole determinant in hiring decisions. Yet, every manager also said, 'family background' (including the educational level of parents) was crucial in sizing up a candidate, something which would instantly put most dalit candidates at a disadvantage. Therefore, overall, in the private sector it would seem that caste discrimination is most often motivated by what is seen as an attempt to maintain a meritocracy rather than as an explicit reference to upper caste (Newman & Jodhka, 2007). With the following background, women tend to face caste-based social and economic disparities even more in a patriarchal society like India.

THE CASE OF DALIT WOMEN ENTREPRENEURS: UNHEARD STORIES

According to Cynthia Stephen (2009), the fact is that dalit women have been victims of patriarchy as much as other women, and still suffer huge impediments to a peaceful existence, let alone the full enjoyment of their human rights. Under the circumstances, it is rare to see a dalit woman in a position of leadership, whether in the home, at work or in social or political institutions. Dalit women often are engaged in agricultural daily labor or wage labor leading to poverty, landlessness, low human dignity and poor living conditions (Jodhka & Shah, 2010). This leads to dalit women facing a dearth of life opportunity in their personal and professional lives. Women entrepreneurs are a rarity in India and few sectors are overtly dominated by males such as construction, real estate and manufacturing (Mahalingam & Kumar, 2013). However, dalit women are generally absent from every sector as entrepreneurs. Even if they are there as entrepreneurs, their businesses are either very small in size or survivalist in nature.

This section presents the findings from some of the interviews with dalit women in business. The findings elucidate how these women define their success as an entrepreneur, as well as how they have attained it and the challenges they have encountered as women and a dalit. A total number of five dalit women were interviewed by phone. The interviews were 1–1.5 hours long and the questions were semi-structured in nature. Some of the interviews were translated as the women spoke only Hindi. The women are mostly running small/medium-sized businesses with an annual turnover ranging between 200,000 and 300,000 dollars per year.

Career Success

This cohort of women generally described career success as a journey of building trust with the customers and profit-making in order to attain a sustainable balance in all aspects of their lives. The ideas that define their success as a woman were trust, honesty, straightforwardness and work–life balance. Defining trust, respondent #1 who hails from Bhagalpur district in Bihar says that "What I think is my achievement till date, has been the satisfaction of my customers." She also added, "As I am in the business which impacts women directly so I give priority to women. I have hired women as they are responsible toward their jobs. In addition, I feel comfortable with women around and vice versa. My employees can share their problems freely with me." She comes from a small town in India and started her business to support her husband. Later. she started her own business of supplying gas cylinders and transportation. She is one of the first women in the transport business from Bihar, and has received several awards for her achievements. She defines her success as "everything is important – family and work."

Respondent #2 defines her success in terms of "creating livelihood for artisans." She holds a master's degree in design and runs a textile business and design consultancy. She comes from a family of bureaucrats and remembers how her family wanted her to be a bureaucrat but she chose to become an entrepreneur. When asked why, she answered: "I wanted to create a livelihood for artisans … also I was inspired by the late Shri Kanshi Ram as he asked me to go for business."[1] She got her education from the best schools in the town and one of the best colleges in India. She also sees her success as the result of her family background: "I come from an affluent family which gives me a lot of exposure and confidence which a lot of dalits do not have."

The interviewees indicated that work–life balance is one of the strongest indications of how these women defined their career success. However, it also indicated that work–life balance is a hugely class-dependent phenomenon. Women coming from an affluent background had a support system at home (help, driver, cook) which gives them more flexibility than others. Also, women who married at a young age have other difficulties, such as becoming a mother at a young age and family expectations.

Being a Dalit Woman

Defining their life as a dalit businesswoman, all of them agreed that being a woman and from the lowest caste made the journey harder for them but there was great variation depending on the class. Remembering her school days, one said: "My other dalit friends were bullied in the school sometimes because of their caste but nobody dared to bully me. They knew my family background." However, they also recognized the fact that dalit organizations such as DICCI have also created new opportunities for dalits. Respondent #1 said: "Every businessperson's life is difficult but it is more difficult for Dalits." She added, "I was once denied to open a bank account as my father's surname made it evident that I am a dalit. I approached the higher authorities and got it done. You should know whom to approach. Everyone is not the same." Respondent #3 stated that "Discriminations still exist today but today they are much more hidden. It is not on your face but it shows when one tries to get some work done. It is easier when you belong to the business class."

Most of the respondents think that education can make a lot of difference as they believe that dalit women are the most marginalized community. Respondent #2 made a very interesting point when she said, "I think it is not just about being dalit. The business in India is dominated by baniyas.[2] Therefore, for anyone who is a non-baniya, it is difficult for him or her to survive. It is difficult to procure raw materials as they always prefer and help other baniya. However, it is more difficult for a dalit woman because of the socio-economic conditions."

Overcoming Barriers

Participants valued the availability of three particular opportunities for navigating their challenging workplace: self-belief, belief in customers and supporting partners. Self-belief is vital to advancing to overcome barriers and the respondents regarded it as a vital component to develop confidence in their career success. Respondent #2 said: "I always believed in myself and grew as a confident woman. It can also be because of my family background." Also, when asked if they could imagine themselves not being an entrepreneur, all of them said that they do not regret being an entrepreneur at all. This optimistic mindset was reflected in their responses, stating that they were motivated and satisfied by jobs in which they could affect change, and make a difference to their life and their society. Respondent #5 said: "I have never regretted being an entrepreneur as it gave me an opportunity to create jobs for others. It gives a lot of satisfaction."

Talking about how customers' trust helps them to grow as an entrepreneur, respondent #1 said: "I always believe in myself and in my customers in times of crisis. My customers also pay me in advance when needed. This is because I value them as my family." Respondent #2 elaborated in the following way: "My biggest strength are my customers. I am into textiles and designing and have fixed customers who will always come to me no matter what. This gives me a lot of stability as nobody can take away my talent as a designer."

Partners who are supportive of the respondents' careers played an integral role in this process. Respondent #5 stated: "We were in Dubai before I started my business. After coming back to India, my husband encouraged me to start a business. I think an international exposure and my husband's support helped me a lot to establish my business." Asked how the international exposure helped her, she added: "Staying abroad helped me to understand the tastes of the foreigners. I started with the export business of brass decorations. I export as well as have retail shops in India too."

The interviews also indicated that women's career barriers are both imposed upon them and by them, whether consciously or subconsciously. Respondent #1 said: "You know what is expected from a woman in our society. I did all that was required from me as a daughter-in-law, wife and sister-in-law. I thought I should help my husband in the business and engage myself as I was almost free from my responsibilities." She also added: "I got an award for my achievements as an entrepreneur as I am one of only few women in the transport business but I couldn't go and attend the function in person. My husband went and received the award on my behalf." When I asked why, she added: "My son was not well and I had to take care of him as a mother."

Networking

Networking gives women the opportunity to collaborate with others, support each other and share information within secure spaces and brings a corresponding growth in social capital, a factor that drives career advancement for the individual (Ibarra, 1993; Chen et al., 2012). Most of the women interviewed mentioned networking as one of the most important factors contributing to a successful career. Respondent #4 mentioned: "Networking is one of the most important things in business. If you know anyone who is part of your business community, it helps a lot." Respondent #1 pointed out how networking helped her to grow as a person and an entrepreneur: "I got to know one of the active members of DICCI[3] and it really helped me to grow my business. The members helped me to expand my business. It did not only help me with the business expansion but also to meet people from our community (caste) and help each other and motivate each other. It means a lot." All the respondents have appreciated the importance of organizations like DICCI as it gives a stage to dalit entrepreneurs to help each other, learn and network. Respondents also mentioned that a formal organization like DICCI gives them a space to participate and network more frequently and freely.

The respondents spoke of networking as a tool, which provided support by assisting in the expansion of business, showing an interdependence between these two and strengthening interpersonal connections. Respondent #3 explained: "It is difficult for dalit community to grow as an entrepreneur as we lack social asset in the form of networking." A very important study has examined the toxic relationship between status hierarchies and friendship mechanisms in the Indian caste system (Bhardwaj et al., 2021). This has been further supported by respondent #1 saying, "Networking is core but somehow I miss some events and informal meetings due to my family responsibilities. However, my family is my strength in times of distress."

Dalit Employees Versus Dalit Employer

When asked if they hire dalits or prefer dalit employees, most of the interviewees said they want to hire dalits but the problem is that there are very few dalit professionals due to low education level and lack of 'attributes fit for a corporate world.' Respondent #2 stated: "Although the economic condition of dalits today is better, their overall social condition remains poor which leads to low confidence in them. They have some inferiority complex as Dalits." She further elaborated: "I cannot afford as a startup and small business owner to hire dalit designers as they are expensive. You will get a non-dalit with same qualifications at a lower wage rate. I thus end up hiring a non-dalit as cost is important in business."

Respondent #1 elaborated: "I want to hire dalits but there are very few applications from dalit communities for the position of managers or operators. There are many for drivers and menial jobs." Asked about why she prefers to hire dalits, she replied: "They are the ones who are the poorest in my area. I can also trust them more as they are from the same community and we know each other better. The hiring manager is a dalit too." Respondent #5 said: "Sometimes we need to hire dalits consciously as this can bring some change in the society. Network plays an important role while hiring."

DISCUSSION

Several studies show that the business world is still dominated by social hierarchies. The historical unequal distribution of resources and power has led to a complex socioeconomic structure. The literature discussed in this chapter indicates that women and dalits have always been a marginal section in the society and excluded from the mainstream. The literature on the topic supported by the interview of the dalit entrepreneurs suggests that it is difficult for a woman to be an entrepreneur as it is a male-dominated arena but it is 'much more' difficult if one is a dalit woman. Thus, our understanding about overlapping identities will help us to question our superficial understanding of diversity. Diversity in the workplace or market cannot be understood without understanding the intersections of different identities. The interviews indicated that business is dominated by few castes in India and it is difficult for other castes to enter the market. However, dalit women are the most marginalized because of their socioeconomic status in society. The social and economic system is trapped by prejudices, rigidity and convenient exclusion. There has been some progress but caste and gender is still the biggest social realities, which has a huge impact on one's position in society.

The interviews with dalit women entrepreneurs also made me reflect back and think about my Ph.D. thesis where I interviewed Norwegian women board members. I interviewed 31 women directors for my Ph.D. on 'Gender-quotas in Norwegian Public Limited Companies, 2003–15' in the year 2017. Although the gender gap is huge between India and Norway in terms of political empowerment, economic participation and opportunity, educational attainment and health and survival (World Economic Forum, 2020), some similarities can be observed between women directors in Norway and dalit women entrepreneurs in India. I am going to discuss similarities as differences are more evident and focused between these two countries.

One important similarity is 'work–life balance' and how women in both countries see it. Both sets of women from India and Norway define success as a 'balance' between work and family life. Interestingly, dalit women entrepreneurs mentioned 'helpers (nannies, cooks and cleaners) as their support at home whereas Norwegian women mentioned the role of parental leave and kindergartens as support systems.

Both sets of women also mentioned the 'role of partners' in their success. Both Indian and Norwegian women mentioned that it is very important to have a supporting partner to achieve a successful career.

The other similarity is how 'class' matters and has a huge impact on networking. Both sets of women from Norway and India mentioned that networking is much easier if one comes from a business/influential family, although, a large number of women from different family backgrounds joined the boardroom after the implementation of gender-quotas in Norway. Many women in Norway stated that a formal quota system has led to professionalization. This makes networking easy for them. Networking does not happen at odd timings and odd places. In a similar way, dalit women entrepreneurs mentioned that organizations like DICCI make networking more formal, which helps them to participate regularly.

CONCLUSION

This study contributes to set an agenda for a new wave of diversity research. I have asked questions such as: Are social caste hierarchies being replaced by competing equalities? What is the experience of dalit women as entrepreneurs? What happens when there are overlapping identities? Why is it important to understand diversity in the context of different identities?

To draw a conclusion from the above study of available research and contemporary scenarios, it can be stated that not enough research is available to answer the question of impact of dalit women on corporate governance. In reality, there are not sufficient data sets available to formulate a conclusive study.

However, it is important to talk about diversity from a point of intersectionality as it helps to understand the problem in a better way. While exploring the relationship between gender and caste, this chapter finds that 'class' also plays an important role. First, the dalit women entrepreneurs, who came from affluent families, give credit to the quota system in India. This is a system in which their parents got help to get into a good and reputable job. Second, it also challenges the idea of meritocracy, as a candidate is rarely judged on formal qualifications alone. It is much deeper and is attached to one's gender, caste and class. Thus, it is important to talk about dalit women in leadership positions because it will help to set an agenda for diversity in the workplace. Finally, it will help the business environment in the country to be molded towards being friendlier in regard to marginalized communities. The findings suggest that studying overlapping identities helps to understand the concept of diversity in a better way.

NOTES

1.   One of the biggest dalit leaders of India. More can be read at: https://www.thequint.com/news/politics/kanshi-ram-india-dalit-movement-mayawati-bsp.

2. Baniya is derived from the Sanskrit word 'banijya,' meaning commerce. It is the most dominant business caste in India. See: https://www.livemint.com/Opinion/tDR JXCAEsoYMxdtSnZDoGJ/The-peculiar-pedigree-of-the-business-class.html.
3. The Dalit Indian Chamber of Commerce and Industry (DICCI) is an Indian association that promotes business enterprises for dalits. More information can be obtained at: https://dicci.in/.

REFERENCES

Aldrich, D. P. (2010). Separate and unequal: post-tsunami aid distribution in Southern India. *Social Science Quarterly*, 1369–89. https://doi.org/10.1111/j.1540-6237.2010.00736.x.

Bapuji, H. (2015). Individuals, interactions and institutions: how economic inequality affects organizations. *Human Relations*, 1059–83. https://psycnet.apa.org/doi/10.1177/0018726715584804.

Bhardwaj, A., Mishra, S. K., Qureshi, I., Kumar, K. K., Konrad, A. M., Seidel, M.-D. L., & Bhatt, B. (2021). Bridging caste divides: middle-status ambivalence, elite closure, and lower-status social withdrawal. *Journal of Management Studies*, 2111–36. https://doi.org/10.1111/joms.12763.

Bidner, C., & Eswaran, M. (2015). A gender-based theory of the origin of the caste system of India. *Journal of Development Economics*, *114*(C), 142–58. https://econpapers.repec.org/scripts/redir.pf?u=https%3A%2F%2Fdoi.org%2F10.1016%252Fj.jdeveco.2014.12.006;h=repec:eee:deveco:v:114:y:2015:i:c:p:142-158.

Chen, A., Doherty, N., & Vinnicombe, S. (2012). Developing women's career competencies through an EMBA. *Gender in Management*, *27*(4), 232–48. https://doi.org/10.1108/17542411211244786.

Damodaran, H. (2008). *India's New Capitalists: Caste, Business, and Industry in a Modern Nation.* Palgrave Macmillan.

Deshpande, A. (2012). *The Grammar of Caste: Economic Discrimination in Contemporary India.* Oxford Scholarship Online. https://doi.org/10.1093/acprof:oso/9780198072034.001.0001.

Deshpande, S. (2013). Caste and castelessness: towards a biography of the 'general category'. *Economic & Political Weekly*, *48*(15), April 13. https://www.epw.in/journal/2013/15/perspectives/caste-and-castelessness.html.

Hiwrale, A. (2020). Caste: understanding the nuances from Ambedkar's expositions. *Journal of Social Inclusion Studies*, 1–19. https://doi.org/10.1177/2394481120944772.

Ibarra, H. (1993). Personal networks of women and minorities in management: a conceptual framework. *The Academy of Management Review*, *8*(1), 56–87. https://doi.org/10.2307/258823.

Ilaiah, K. (1996). *Why I Am Not a Hindu: A Sudra Critique of Hindutva Philosophy, Culture, and Political Economy*. Calcutta: Samya Prakashan.

Iyer, L., Khanna, T., & Varshney, A. (2013). Caste and entrepreneurship in India. *Economic & Political Weekly*, *48*, 52–60.

Jodhka, S. S., & Shah, G. (2010). Comparative contexts of discrimination: caste and untouchability in South Asia. *Economic & Political Weekly*, *45*(48), 99–106. http://www.jstor.org/stable/25764189.

Madheswaran, S., & Singhari, S. (2016). Social exclusion and caste discrimination in public and private sectors in India: a decomposition analysis. *The Indian Journal of Labour Economics*, *59*(2), 175–201. https://econpapers.repec.org/scripts/redir.pf?u=https%3A%2F%2Fdoi.org%2F10.1007%252Fs41027-017-0053-8;h=repec:spr:ijlaec:v:59:y:2016:i:2:d:10.1007_s41027-017-0053-8.

Mahalingam, T., & Kumar, K. P. (2013). Why women entrepreneurs are rare in India & what challenges they face (E. Bureau, editor). *The Economic Times*, January 6. https://economictimes.indiatimes.com/news/company/corporate-trends/why-women -entrepreneurs-are-rare-in-india-what-challenges-they-face/articleshow/17903377.cms ?from=mdr.

Newman, K., & Jodhka, S. S. (2007). In the name of globalisation: meritocracy, productivity and the hidden language of caste. *Economic & Political Weekly*, *42*(41), October 13. https:// www.epw.in/journal/2007/41/caste-and-economic-discrimination-special-issues-specials/ name-globalisation.html.

Office of the Registrar General & Census Commissioner (2011). *2011 Census Data.* Delhi: Ministry of Home Affairs.

Omvedt, G. (2005). Women in governance in South Asia. *Economic and Political Weekly*, *40*, 4746–52. https://www.jstor.org/stable/4417361.

Roychowdhury, A. (2018). Why Dalits want to hold on to Dalit, not Harijan, not SC. *The Indian Express,* September 5. https://indianexpress.com/article/research/dalit-scheduled -caste-information-and-broadcasting-media-5341220/.

Shah, G., Mander, H., Thorat, S., Deshpande, S., & Baviskar, A. (2006). *Untouchability in Rural India*. New Delhi; Thousand Oaks, CA: Sage Publications.

Stephen, C. (2009). Feminism and dalit women in India. November 16, Countercurrents.org. https://www.countercurrents.org/stephen161109.htm.

Thomas, R. (2020). Brahmins as scientists and science as Brahmins' calling: caste in an Indian scientific research institute. *Public Understanding of Science*, 1–13. https://doi.org/10 .1177/0963662520903690.

Thorat, S., Banerjee, A., Mishra, V. K., & Rizvi, F. (2015). Urban rental housing market: caste and religion matters in access. *Economic and Political Weekly*, 47–53. http://www.jstor.org/ stable/24482557.

Thorat, S., & Newman, K. S. (2007). Caste and economic discrimination: causes, consequences and remedies. *Economic & Political Weekly*, *42*(41), October 13. https://www.epw .in/journal/2007/41/caste-and-economic-discrimination-special-issues-specials/caste-and -economic.

Varman, R., & Chakrabarti, M. (2004). Contradictions of democracy in a workers' cooperative. *Organization Studies*, *25*(2), 183–208. https://doi.org/10.1177%2F0170840604036913.

World Economic Forum (2020). Global gender gap report. https://www.weforum.org/reports/ gender-gap-2020-report-100-years-pay-equality/.

11. Diversity and leadership in the South Pacific: intersectionality at play on Fijian boards of directors

Caitlin Harm Nam, Ana Naulu, Baljeet Singh and Sabina Tasheva

Research on boards and diversity has spanned several decades and generated a large amount of empirical findings and theoretical insights (Hillman, 2015; Johnson, Schnatterly, & Hill, 2013). Research on gender diversity, in particular, has drawn significant attention and generated vivid discussions in industry and academia. At the same time, researchers suggest that current conceptualizations and investigations of board diversity need to progress beyond gender (Mendiratta, 2019; Nielsen, 2012) and focus on other relevant attributes as well as on intersectionality of gender and other relevant characteristics (Bennouri, Chtioui, Nagati, & Nekhili, 2018; Nielsen & Huse, 2010). This chapter addresses this call by looking at the intersectionality of gender and ethnicity in the context of Fijian boards of directors. Moreover, by building upon insights of the cross-cultural and national differences in gender diversity, we explore how the specificities of the context of the South Pacific, and Fiji in particular, influence the gender and ethnic composition of boards.

HISTORICAL OVERVIEW OF WOMEN IN LEADERSHIP IN FIJI

Fiji is a Small Island Developing State in the South Pacific region with a population of 889,300. It is a multi-ethnic state comprising two main ethnic groups of indigenous Fijians and Indo-Fijians. Other ethnic groups include Rotumans, Europeans, Chinese, mixed race and Pacific islands origins as well as expatriates of various nationalities. Fiji has developed a more industrialized and urbanized economy compared to many Pacific states, but gaps to achieving gender parity remain and Fiji still largely remains a male-dominated society. Women are largely underrepresented and absent from executive-level management, board level and local government positions.

Historically, leadership roles in Fiji were assumed under a chiefly system, led by indigenous Fijian (iTaukei) chiefs that were predominantly male (Chattier, 2015; Eti-Tofinga, Douglas, & Singh, 2017). Women at that time were regarded as holding a low status unless they were from a chiefly ancestry, with their roles in the community restricted to childbearing and caretaking (Eti-Tofinga, Douglas, & Singh, 2017; Reddy, 2000). Such stereotypes were exacerbated by Fiji's colonial period where men's rights preceded in aspects of decision-making, resource management and property ownership. This was largely because of early colonial administrative policies to protect indigenous Fijians by giving precedence to traditional structures of chieftainship and culture preservation. While attempting to do this, colonial authorities also simultaneously sought to develop the economic potential of the colony. This led to securing cheap labour from India in the form of indentured labourers, which saw the emergence of the early Indo-Fijian community. These early communities, along with other racial groups, generally lived in separate communities and continued to do so even when former indentured labourers began to settle down in towns and lease land from indigenous owners (Eti-Tofinga, Douglas & Singh, 2017). As such, relations between these communities were dictated by policies which cast a rigid combination of ethnic and gender boundaries, having a profound impact on most indigenous and Indo-Fijian women.

Subsequently, Fiji became a sovereign state in 1970 after 96 years of substantial transformation under British colonial rule. The Fijian Constitution adopted at independence promoted human rights, movement towards equality, democracy, non-discrimination based on gender or race, and the empowerment of disadvantaged. However, deeply rooted ethnic divisions between indigenous Fijians and Indo-Fijians began to rise, leading to a series of coups in 1987 and 2000. The political upheavals were a double-edged sword for women in Fiji, with the impacts varying based on ethnicity, class, religion, age and location. On the one hand, though women were still widely regarded as subordinate, the 1987 coup was a catalyst for change with an increasing demand by women to redress gender inequality concerns at the national level. There was greater prominence in both direct and indirect agency in the form of women's strikes and union activities, political party participation, feminist groups, other new social movements, and business involvement. The post-coup period also witnessed more iTaukei women moving up the civil service and most non-governmental organizations (NGOs) promoting (mostly indigenous) women in politics, when race and the protection of indigenous paramountcy were predominant themes. Notably, Imrana Jalal (1997) contends that indigenous women have accessed the public realm more successfully than Indo-Fijian women because of linkages through traditional chiefly power. The impacts for Indo-Fijian women during this period was more profound as discriminatory employment practices restricted Indo-Fijian women's access to and participation in paid employment.

In modern-day Fiji, leadership roles are still heavily male dominated and can, in retrospect, be attributed to the baggage of colonialism, culture, and the post-coup regimes. Women still remain underrepresented in the workforce, on company boards and executive teams, and in business but significant effort has been made to 'balance the scales'. Fiji's commitment to gender equality is evident in its Constitution, government policies and international commitments, including its ratification of the UN Convention on the Elimination of all Forms of Discrimination Against Women (CEDAW), which explicitly requires Fiji to encourage gender parity and improve women's rights in all aspects of the state. Sustainable Development Goal (SDG) 5 set a target to achieve this by 2030, requiring all convening states to ensure that women have full participation and equal opportunities for leadership at all levels of decision-making in political, economic, and public life. Today, there is no clear path to achieving greater gender equality but such national commitments can induce an environment for shifting attitudes towards women in Fiji.

Through donor funding and International Development Institutions, NGOs have played a pivotal role in these efforts by implementing initiatives aimed at 'mainstreaming' gender policies and increasing women's participation in leadership roles. Since the 1980s, following the ratification of CEDAW and the Beijing Platform for Action, NGOs through their close proximity with the grassroots (Mehra, 1997) have facilitated social transformation through a combination of activities including policy reform to create enabling institutional environments (such as family-friendly HR policies, merit-based recruitment, and promotion policies), training to upskill and empower women and networking programmes aimed at facilitating information exchange and the creation of critical mass (Srivastava & Austin, 2012; Torchia, Calabrò & Huse, 2011).

Regional organizations, primarily the Pacific Islands Forum, have also played a significant role through developed action plans, and more recently the Pacific Leaders Gender Equality Declaration in 2012. The empowerment of women in leadership remains a pertinent goal within initiatives and programmes of international development agencies and NGOs. However, there remains a lack of monitoring and evaluation mechanisms to access the outcomes of these initiatives. In order to build more targeted and efficient policies and initiatives in the future, the importance of collecting and compiling high-quality gender-disaggregated data cannot be overemphasized.

Women have had an increasing presence in professional categories such as law, medicine, architecture, veterinary services, and scientific research, although men still dominate these fields. As Leckie (2000) notes, the public sector continues to attract many well-educated women, mostly in nursing, teaching, and clerical jobs. This can be attributed to the fact women are, for the most part, concentrated in 'feminine' jobs, tending to involve responsibilities for caring. One obvious explanation is that women are socialized as young children to specialize in traditionally female tasks. However, increasing numbers of women are now able to transgress and negotiate traditional gender roles, with achievements in education and employment.

In order to achieve equal representation of men and women in leadership roles, there needs to be continued effort, not only for gender equality, but also for continued economic growth. With increasing external and social pressure, and more pathways to leadership roles being made available, Fiji is starting to see a gradual increase of women representation in senior management and leadership. For instance, in 2019, the South Pacific Stock Exchange (SPX) introduced on its continued listing requirements that listed companies were recommended to adopt a policy on promotion of gender diversity at board level. Appropriate motivation and dedicated action are critical to sustaining and promoting women's equal representation as leaders in the Pacific. This development follows closely the worldwide trend of introducing various measures for increasing the number of women in leadership and adopting corporate governance guidelines for increased diversity on corporate boards.

PRIOR RESEARCH ON GENDER AND ETHNICITY IN LEADERSHIP IN FIJI

Existing reports and literature on women in business and in leadership roles in Fiji in particular are limited (Fiji Women's Rights Movement, 2020; Pacific Private Sector Development Initiative, 2021). According to results published by the Asian Development Bank (ADB), women were found to occupy 32 per cent of managerial positions in Fiji in 2011. A recent study conducted by the Fiji Women's Rights Movement on state-owned enterprises (the sample includes commercially driven, non-commercial, statutory bodies, commissions & entities), revealed that of 192 board members in 38 boards, women comprised only 21 per cent of all directors. Ten of the 38 boards were found to have less than 30 per cent women representation, with 16 boards or 42 per cent of the 38 boards having no women at all. The study also found that women held Chairperson positions on 7 out of 38 of the boards, or only 18 per cent of the companies had a female Board Chair. Other descriptive statistics were notably that women had greater representation in the non-commercial sector, having 27 per cent women on boards, as compared to the commercial sector, where there was 19 per cent women. Of the 38 boards, indigenous Fijians were found to be under-represented, comprising only 32 per cent of board membership, and 37 per cent of the boards having less than 30 per cent indigenous Fijian participation. Indo-Fijians made up 42 per cent of board members, whilst other ethnic groups hold 26 per cent, percentages which were largely male dominated.

Separate from the study conducted by the Fiji Women's Rights Movement, the Pacific Private Sector Development Initiative (PSDI) used a sample of 309 business organizations in the 14 Pacific developing member countries of the ADB. This included the number and proportion of women as board directors, board chairs, CEOs, and senior management personnel of industry associations, publicly listed companies, and other private sector organizations, such as provident funds, super-annuation funds, non-listed companies, and state-owned enterprises (SOEs). Using a sample of 50 business organizations for Fiji, it was found that 27 per cent of boards had no representation of women and 51 per cent had more than 0 per cent but fewer than 30 per cent women directors. Just 23 per cent of all boards had more than 30 per cent representation of women. Overall, women make up 20 per cent of directors of boards in Fiji, which is broadly in line with the regional average of 21 per cent. Women were found to comprise 12 per cent of board chairs and 20 per cent of deputy chair roles.

Additionally, the study revealed that the representation of women in the sample was largely driven by publicly listed companies (PLCs) as compared to state-owned enterprises (SOEs), with 24 per cent of board directors in PLCs, but just 12 per cent of directors in SOEs. Similarly, women comprise just 5 per cent of SOE board chairs, but the rate is more than twice as high in PLCs, where women hold 11 per cent of the board chairs (Pacific Private Sector Development Initiative, 2021).

It is notable that these prior studies examined very narrowly specific characteristics of women in leadership in Fiji by using data from different groups of entities. For instance, the report by the Fiji Women's Rights Movement only examined data on SOEs. Likewise, the study by The Pacific Private Sector Development Initiative was based on a mix of organizations, specifically 19 public listed companies, 3 industry associations, 19 public listed companies, and 9 other private sector organizations. Moreover, most of the existing studies on Fiji did not address issues such as ethnicity and representation of women on boards in different industries. In our study, by comparison, 50 per cent of the sample was based on the private sector, which appears to be underrepresented in prior research despite being one of the largest sectors in Fiji in terms of the number of companies. This study also provides information on the ethnic composition of women on boards as well as the representation of women on boards per industry. As a result, our findings are likely to differ from prior research due to the difference in the type of companies used in the sample.

SAMPLE AND DATA

Our initial sample consisted of the 200 largest companies in Fiji (based on number of employees). The list of companies was obtained from the Fiji Bureau of Statistics in February 2021. Adopting the methodology of the Australian Census of Women in Leadership (EOWA, 2012), data on the company's board members and executive teams was retrieved from annual reports and company websites. A survey was sent to the selected 200 companies representing private companies, PLCs, and SOEs. We asked companies to verify the data obtained from secondary sources and to provide additional information, where possible. In this chapter, we present data that was available for 50 companies or 25 per cent of our initial sample. Based on the information provided by the Bureau of Statistics, we were able to identify the type of organization and nature of ownership.

RESULTS AND DISCUSSION

The results present data on 50 companies including 25 private companies, 7 PLCs, and 18 SOEs (Table 11.1). Our sample consisted of 242 board members. Among the 50 companies, the average board size was found to be 4.8.

Overall, women are largely underrepresented, accounting for only 15.7 per cent of directors of boards in the sample. The average number of women per board is 0.74 per company, indicating that on average less than one board member is a woman, which is low compared to average members per board and international standards. This is also comparatively lower than the regional average of 21 per cent (Pacific Private Sector Development Initiative, 2021).

Table 11.1   *Breakdown of the number and percentage of women on the board by ownership type*

	Private Co.	PLC	SOE	Total
Number of companies	25	7	18	50
Total no. of directors on board	77	38	127	242
Average size of board	3.1	5.4	7.1	4.8
Average no. of women on board	0.28	0.9	1.4	0.74
% of women on board	9.3	15.7	20	15.7
% of firms with zero women on board	75	37.5	52.6	60.8
% of firms with one women on board	20.8	50	21.1	25.5
% of firms with two women on board	4.2	12.5	15.8	9.8
% of firms with three or more women on board	0	0	10.5	3.9

Private companies in the sample were found to have the lowest number of women representation with an average percentage of 9.3 per cent and an average number of 0.28 women per board. Of the private companies in the sample, 75 per cent had no women with board membership, 20.8 per cent with one woman on the board and 4.2 per cent with 2 women on the board. The underrepresentation of women on the board of directors of the private companies can be attributed to stereotypical roles of women in society. Most of the traditional private companies in Fiji are family-owned and are mostly inherited by male members of the family. However, recently more women are taking up business opportunities as a result of gender empowerment initiatives provided by the government and development partners. However, most of the women-owned businesses that emerged out of government women-empowerment schemes are small and micro-enterprises and hence, did not meet the criteria of our sampling framework.

In comparison, PLCs were found to have better representation with an average percentage of 15.7 per cent women on the boards, and an average number of 0.9 per board. In the sample, 37.5 per cent of PLCs had no women on the board, compared to SOEs where 52.6 per cent of boards had no women; 50 per cent of PLCs had one woman on the board, and 12.5 per cent had 2 women on the board. This is largely due to the recommendation made by the SPX in 2019 that continued listed entities are recommended to adopt policies that promote gender diversity on the board level and to regularly report on progress.

SOEs were found to have the greatest amount of women representation in the sample compared to PLCs and private companies, with 20 per cent women representation on the management board and an average of 1.4 women per board. In the sample, 21.1 per cent of the SOEs had one woman on the board, and 15.8 per cent had 2 women on the board. Furthermore, no private companies or PLCs in the sample had more than 2 women on the board, whereas 10.5 per cent of SOEs had at least 3 women on the board. This is a common trend within the Pacific where a majority of female board appointments are made by the state which may be due to the increasing societal pressure to address gender diversity, and international commitments including the ratification of the UN CEDAW and the UN 1995 Beijing Platform of Action (Pacific Islands Forum Secretariat, 2013; Fiji Women's Rights Movement, 2020).

Table 11.2 presents the distribution of women in the sample over different industries. It shows that the highest percentage of women on boards in the sample were associated with the accommodation, education, and manufacturing industries. A possible explanation for these results could be attributed to resource dependence theory where firms appoint women as board members because it makes their board representative of key stakeholders. One would expect that an industry with a high proportion of female employees is likely to correspond to a higher number of women on boards (Hillman, Shropshire, & Cannella, 2007; Oehmichen, Rapp, & Wolff, 2012). In Fiji, this corresponds to the high participation rates of women in tourism, teaching and retail.

Table 11.2   Breakdown of boards by industry and percentage of women

Industry	Total no. of Directors	Percentage of women on the board
Agriculture	15	0
Accommodation	2	50
Construction	6	0
Education	47	32
Electricity	5	0
Information	24	12.5
Manufacturing	50	20
Mining	5	10
Transport	29	10
Wholesale and retail	57	10

On the other hand, mining, transport, and wholesale and retail industries were found to each have 10 per cent of women on boards, while the information industry had 12.5 per cent. Construction, agriculture, and electricity industries were found to have no women on the board. This underrepresentation of women is a common thread for such industries as they are generally perceived as a man's domain. In particular, the underrepresentation of women in the agriculture industry is of serious concern, given the growing level of food insecurity. More women should be encouraged to take up business leadership roles in agriculture-related industries.

Table 11.3   Distribution of employees by size

		Board Members		Women on Board		
No. of employees	No. of companies	Total	Average	Total	Average	% Women
1–100	11	42	3.8	5	0.5	11
100–500	22	76	3.5	7	0.3	9.2
500–1000	11	59	5.4	9	0.8	15.2
1000–1500	4	18	4.5	2	0.5	11
1500–2000	1	30	30	9	9	30
>2000	1	17	17	6	6	35

The distribution of companies by size is reported in Table 11.3. In our sample, 11 out of 50 companies employed less than 100 employees, consisted of 42 directors and had an average of 3.8 directors per board. Within this group of companies, there were 5 women directors with an average of 0.5 women per board. Similarly, 22 out of 50 firms studied employed between 100 and 500 people. This group of companies consisted of 76 directors with an average of 3.5 directors per board. More importantly, this group had the lowest representation of women on boards – only 9.2 per cent of the board members consisted of women, with an average 0.3 women per board. A possible explanation for the low representation of women on the board of small to medium-sized firms might be that most of these firms are family-owned and have a tendency to be managed by male family members in Fiji. This finding is contrary to those of Oehmichen, Rapp and Wolff (2012) in the case of Germany and Ruigrok, Peck and Tacheva (2007) in Switzerland. However, our findings are consistent with the lower representation of women on the board of private enterprises noted earlier.

Table 11.3 also shows that companies that have over 500 employees on average have a higher percentage of women on their boards. Existing research implies that this may be due to societal expectations, where larger and more visible firms in the public eye are under pressure from key stakeholders to have gender-diverse boards.

Table 11.4   Classification of board members by racial category

	Indo-Fijian		iTaukei		Others	
	No.	%	No.	%	No.	%
Total	123	55.0	45	18.6	64	26.4
Private company	48	62.3	9	11.7	20	26.0
Publicly listed company	26	68.4	6	15.8	6	15.8
State-owned enterprise	49	41.9	30	25.6	38	32.5

Table 11.4 illustrates the composition of board members in the sample by three major racial categories: (1) Indigenous Fijians or iTaukei, (2) Indo-Fijians, and (3) Others, which consist of Chinese, Europeans, and other racial denominations. Our findings show that 55 per cent of board members in the sample were Indo-Fijian, 18.6 per cent were iTaukei, and 26.4 per cent were from other ethnic backgrounds. Indo-Fijians were found to dominate all categories of companies, making up 49 per cent of board members in private companies, 48 per cent in publicly listed companies, and 26 per cent in state-owned enterprises, respectively. On the other hand, iTaukei have the lowest representation in the sample, with only 18.6 per cent, making up 11.7 per cent of board members in private companies, 15.8 per cent in publicly listed companies, and 25.6 per cent in state-owned enterprises. Other ethnicities were comparatively more visible, making up 26.4 per cent of the sample. The underrepresentation of iTaukei on boards is not surprising as majority of businesses in Fiji are owned by Indo-Fijians or other races. Early research suggests that the lack of indigenous Fijians in entrepreneurship may be due to the influences of a collectivist culture which has led to a 'non-entrepreneurial mindset' and increased focus on cultural solidarity.

Table 11.5   *Composition of women on boards by racial categories*

	Indo-Fijian		iTaukei		Others	
	Men	Women	Men	Women	Men	Women
Total	115	18(13.5)	28	7(15.5)	50	14(21.9)
Private company	46	2(4.1)	7	2(22.2)	16	4(20.0)
Publicly listed company	22	4(15.4)	5	1(16.6)	5	1(16.6)
State-owned enterprise	47	2(4.1)	26	4(13.3)	29	9(23.7)

Note: Figures in parentheses show the number of women board directors in each race category.

Our findings show that there is a significantly larger number of Indo-Fijian women on the board of directors compared to the iTaukei women (Table 11.5). Unsurprisingly, the percentage of women in each racial category is significantly lower than of men. The percentage of women representation on boards for Indo-Fijians, iTaukeis, and other racial groups was 13.5 per cent, 15.5 per cent, and 21.9 per cent, respectively.

Writing about the intersectionality of gender and ethnicity is not an easy task. Fiji is a multi-cultural society and as such it has variety of cultural norms of behaviour and conducting business. Discussions of ethnical and racial diversity have always been highly sensitive. Hence, it is the intention of this chapter to draw some attention to the multiple characteristics of corporate directors and, particularly, the composition of Fijian boards in terms of gender and ethnicity.

These first results provide only a snapshot of the current situation; deeper understanding of the cultural and business context is needed in order to conduct more fine-grained analysis. Future research may focus on different pathways to board memberships for women and men as well as different pathways for women (and men) with different ethnic backgrounds. This first explorations show clearly the existence of difference; it shows differences between firm type, firm size, and industry in terms of board diversity. Yet, more data and statistical analysis are needed to understand the underlying reasons and the historical developments of these trends over time. This research is the result of a first stage, pilot project of collecting data on Fijian boards on a large scale. As the data collection is being automated and repeated on an annual basis, in the future we will be able to provide a more complete picture of the corporate landscape of boards of directors and their diversity in the context of Fiji and the South Pacific.

ACKNOWLEDGMENTS

We would like to express our gratitude to the Carlsberg Foundation for providing continuous support and funding for the completion of this project. Without the generous funding of the Carlsberg Foundation, no systematic data on Women in Leadership in Fiji could be presented. We would also like to acknowledge that this project is a research collaboration between Copenhagen Business School, University of Sydney, and University of South Pacific.

REFERENCES

Asian Development Bank (2016). *Gender Statistics for the Pacific and Timor-Leste*. Manila.

Bennouri, M., Chtioui, T., Nagati, H., & Nekhili, M. (2018). Female board directorship and firm performance: what really matters? *Journal of Banking and Finance*, 88(C), 267–91.

Chattier, P. (2015). Women in the house (of parliament) in Fiji: what's gender got to do with it? *The Round Table*, 104(2), 177–88.

Equal Opportunity for Women in the Workplace Agency (2012). *2012 EOWA Australian Census of Women in Leadership*. Canberra: Australian Government.

Eti-Tofinga, B., Douglas, H., & Singh, G. (2017). Influence of evolving culture on leadership: a study of Fijian cooperatives. *European Business Review*, 29(5), 534–50.

Fiji Women's Rights Movement (2020, September). Gender equality, diversity & inclusion – leadership in Fiji government-controlled boards. http://www.fwrm.org.fj/images/fwrm2017/PDFs/research/FWRM_Gender_Diversity_Incl_GoF_Boards-Final_.pdf.

Hillman, A. J. (2015). Board diversity: beginning to unpeel the onion. *Corporate Governance: An International Review*, 23(2), 104–7.

Hillman, A. J., Shropshire, C., & Cannella, A. A. (2007). Organizational predictors of women on corporate boards. *Academy of Management Journal*, 50(4), 941–52.

Jalal, I. (1997). The status of Fiji women and the constitution. In B. V. Lal & T. R. Vakatora (Eds.), *Fiji in Transition: Research Papers of the Fiji Constitution Review Commission* (Vol. 1, pp. 80–104). Suva: School of Social and Economic Development, University of the South Pacific.

Johnson, S. G., Schnatterly, K., & Hill, A. D. (2013). Board composition beyond independence: social capital, human capital, and demographics. *Journal of Management*, 39(1), 232–62.

Leckie, J. (2000). Women in post-coup Fiji: negotiating work through old and new realities. In A. Akram-Lodhi (Ed.), *Confronting Fiji Futures* (pp. 178–201). Asia Pacific Press.

Mehra, R. (1997). Women, empowerment, and economic development. *The Annals of the American Academy of Political and Social Science*, 554(1), 136–49.

Mendiratta, E. (2019). Not just a woman or a man: influence of team faultlines on board gender diversity-firm performance. *Academy of Management Proceedings*, 2019(1), 14224.

Nielsen, S. (2012). Diversity among senior executives and board directors. In T. Clarke & D. Branson (Eds.), *The Sage Handbook of Corporate Governance* (pp. 345–62). Sage Publications.

Nielsen, S., & Huse, M. (2010). Women directors' contribution to board decision-making and strategic involvement: the role of equality perception. *European Management Review*, 7(1), 16–29.

Oehmichen, J., Rapp, M. S., & Wolff, M. (2012). Women on German management boards: how ownership structure affects management board diversity. *Managing Diversity in Organizations*, 82(2), 95–125.

Pacific Islands Forum Secretariat (2013). Survey of Women's Representation on SOE Boards in Forum Island Countries. https://www.forumsec.org/2013/07/05/survey-of-womens-representation-on-soe-boards-in-forum-island-countries-femm/.

Pacific Private Sector Development Initiative (2021). Leadership matters: benchmarking women in business leadership in the Pacific. https://www.pacificpsdi.org/assets/Uploads/PSDI-LeadershipMatters-Web3.pdf.

Reddy, C. (2000). Women and politics in Fiji. In B. V. Lal (Ed.), *Fiji Before the Storm: Elections and the Politics of Development* (pp. 149–60). ANU Press.

Ruigrok, W., Peck, S., & Tasheva, S. (2007). Nationality and gender diversity on Swiss corporate boards. *Corporate Governance: An International Review*, 15(4), 546–57.

Srivastava, L. & Austin, M. J. (2012). Women and non-governmental organizations in developing countries. *Social Development Issues*, 34, 77–91.

Torchia, M., Calabrò, A., & Huse, M. (2011). Women directors on corporate boards: from tokenism to critical mass. *Journal of Business Ethics*, 102(2), 299–317.

PART IV

HOW DO WE UTILIZE THE BENEFITS OF DIVERSITY? RESEARCH ON BOARD DIVERSITY, PROCESSES AND DECISION-MAKING

12. Group faultlines in boards of directors: current trends and future directions

Alana Vandebeek

Although an increasing body of literature focuses on board diversity and identifies the demographic characteristics that most determine the ability of directors to fulfill their board roles, little attention has been paid to the interaction of multiple demographic attributes. Most studies on board diversity tend to examine and assess the impact of board diversity of one attribute at a time, such as gender diversity. However, directors are highly qualified individuals who possess a wide range of human and social capital (Johnson et al., 2013; Tasheva & Hillman, 2019) and thus carry a unique array of attributes, such as social category (e.g., gender, age, or race), informational (e.g., education, tenure), and deep-level attributes (e.g., personality, beliefs, and values). Focusing only on one attribute in particular is often insufficient to explain group processes (Murnighan & Lau, 2017). Boards of directors can in fact be conceptualized and dealt with as groups (Forbes & Milliken, 1999; Vandewaerde et al., 2011; Zona & Zattoni, 2007), and faultline theory suggests that the interaction of multiple demographic attributes affects group dynamics to a greater extent than single attributes, opening new avenues for examining potentially complex group dynamics (Lau & Murnighan, 1998). Taking into account the potential interactions between different diversity dimensions can have important implications for future research on board diversity (Nielsen, 2012).

Group faultlines are defined as hypothetical dividing lines that divide a group into multiple subgroups that are homogeneous in terms of a particular set of diversity attributes (Lau & Murnighan, 1998). The concept thus considers how *a bundle* of different demographic characteristics may influence group processes and performance outcomes (Thatcher & Patel, 2012). Faultlines become stronger as more attributes align, creating distinct non-overlapping subgroups within the board. The name "faultlines" is derived from the geological construct that describes the Earth's compositional crust. The composition of a group can be analogized to the Earth's multilayered, rock-based structural crust, because each group contains a number of members (e.g., rocks), each of which has a unique bundle of individual attributes. The overlap of these attributes within the group resembles the overlap of rocks of the Earth's crust, as both have faults (i.e., fractures) from one layer to the next (Lau & Murnighan, 1998). The faultline approach therefore goes beyond prior diversity research by considering not only the availability of attributes, but also the specific configuration of these attributes, as the concept of faultlines assumes a *simultaneous alignment* of multiple characteristics of group members. An example of a strong faultline is a board with two young women and two older men. The fact that the age

147

and gender of the members are aligned facilitates the formation of two homogene-ous subgroups. If the board consisted of one young woman, one young man, one older woman and one older man, the faultline would be considered weak because two homogeneous subgroups could not be formed. Thus, although the degree of diversity is the same in both compositions, the second board contains a strong fault-line. Therefore, faultline theory can shed light on the different outcomes of board diversity. To understand the role of group faultlines on the effectiveness of corporate boards, and ultimately corporate performance, it is important to understand the different types of group faultlines and the mechanisms by which they operate in the context of boards and corporate governance.

This review focuses on group faultlines in corporate boards, but also includes some relevant and interesting studies from the top management team (TMT) liter-ature. Although the TMT plays a different role than the corporate board for firm strategy, organization and performance, theoretically the effects of their team com-position on firm-level outcomes could be similar (Finkelstein et al., 2009; Nielsen, 2012). Furthermore, studies on group faultlines in boards remain rather limited, and some insights from the TMT field can be used to inspire future research on faultlines in boards. This chapter proceeds with a discussion of the various attributes that have been used for faultline measurements in corporate boards and the resulting faultline types. Next, the most recent faultline measures are reviewed, along with some inter-esting future research methods. Then, faultline mechanisms and corresponding theo-ries that can explain these mechanisms within boards are introduced, and findings of prior faultline outcomes are reviewed. Based on the review of theories and empirical findings, a conceptual framework of the effects of group faultlines in corporate boards is developed. The chapter goes on to discuss the effect of board context on group faultlines and provides some directions for future research, focusing on some unresolved faultline puzzles.

FAULTLINE ATTRIBUTES

Early faultline research has mostly considered faultlines as a function of a diverse mix of individuals' demographic attributes, ranging from attributes such as gender and age, as well as task-related attributes such as expertise or education. However, this faultlines approach has a limitation, in that "measuring a single faultline based on characteristics that reflect very different aspects of individuals may hinder inter-pretation of its effect" (Hutzschenreuter & Horstkotte, 2013:719), which can make exact theorizing very difficult (Bezrukova et al., 2009). Therefore, recent faultline literature distinguishes between faultlines based on social category attributes, which involve a particular social identity (e.g., gender, age, race), and faultlines based on informational attributes, which are work-related and revolve around knowledge (e.g., education, work experience; Bezrukova & Uparna, 2009; Chung et al., 2015; Jehn et al., 2008; Jehn & Rupert, 2008).

Within board research, there are both studies that examine faultlines based on social category attributes, such as age and gender (i.e., Ali & Ayoko, 2020; Vandebeek et al., 2021) and studies that examine faultlines based on informational attributes, such as type of directorship, tenure, functional or financial background (i.e., Barroso-Castro et al., 2020; Kaczmarek et al., 2012b; Tuggle et al., 2010). A number of studies also use a mix of diverse attributes, including a wide range of variables (i.e., Kaczmarek et al., 2012a; Liu & Van Peteghem, 2019; Wu et al., 2021). For example, Van Peteghem et al. (2018) measure faultlines based on director independence, director financial expertise, multiple board memberships, career horizon and incentives, board tenure, share ownership and gender. Other studies consider family membership (Vandebeek et al., 2021; Vandebeek et al., 2016), stakeholder representation (Crucke & Knockaert, 2016; Crucke et al., 2015) or other factional affiliations (Veltrop et al., 2015) as important director attributes. Table 12.1 summarizes the different attributes used in these studies.

Recently, however, in addition to social category and informational faultlines, researchers are calling for work on faultlines based on deep-level attributes. Deep-level attributes are characteristics that are not immediately observable, but rather discovered more slowly, such as personality, interests, and values (Murnighan & Lau, 2017). Therefore, these faultlines may only come to light after a longer period of time, such as after the directors have worked together for a while and interact regularly. It has already been shown that diversity in terms of personality of board members can have a positive impact on the level of cognitive conflict and creativity (Torchia et al., 2015). However, if there is alignment of directors' personality and other individual characteristics, personality can be a source of faultlines. In addition, especially in the setting of family firms, faultlines in boards may be based on emotions felt by board members, such as the degree of emotional ownership they feel (Björnberg & Nicholson, 2012). This could play an important role, for example, in multi-generational family firms. Future research could therefore examine the heterogeneity within the family director group itself and consider further sub-configuration of family directors (e.g., when members of different family generations serve on the board) (Basco et al., 2019). It could also be that non-family minority shareholders form a certain coalition to protect their own interests (Bammens et al., 2011). Lastly, it could be interesting to consider the director's social capital as a source of faultlines. Network ties, relationships, and personal or professional contacts of a director might only be discovered after some time, but could also lead to social categorization processes as they may be related, for example, to status gain (Geletkanycz & Boyd, 2011; Tasheva & Hillman, 2019).

MEASURES AND METHODS

There has been an evolution in the development of faultline measures in faultline research, which is also reflected within faultline research in the field of boards and TMTs. Early faultline studies have captured faultlines using, for example, the ratio of family to nonfamily members (Minichilli et al., 2010), the ratio of executive to nonexecutive members (Basco & Voordeckers, 2015), or a combination of the prior two ratios (Basco et al., 2019). Currently, however, there are a number of different faultline measures that can capture faultline strength more accurately, by considering multiple attributes simultaneously. Some board scholars use latent class-clustering techniques (e.g., Tuggle et al., 2010; Van Peteghem et al., 2018), but others use some of the faultline measures developed within the faultline domain, such as the faultline algorithm Fau developed by Thatcher et al. (2003) (i.e., Crucke & Knockaert, 2016; Kaczmarek et al., 2012b) or the *FLS* method of Shaw (2004) (i.e., Vandebeek et al., 2016; Wu et al., 2021). The latter two measures capture the strength of group faultlines (i.e., how cleanly a board splits into subgroups), but some scholars use measures that can also measure faultline distance or width (i.e., how far apart the subgroups are). A recently developed measure, and one that is increasingly being used (i.e., Barroso-Castro et al., 2020; Vandebeek et al., 2021), is the average sil-houette width (ASW) measure, developed by Meyer and Glenz (2013), which can also identify the number of subgroups and subgroup membership. To choose which faultline measure is most appropriate for your specific research setting, Meyer et al. (2014) proposed a decision tree that can help scholars decide. According to the authors, there are a number of important factors when choosing a faultline measure. First, a researcher must know whether more than two subgroups are possible within the groups being studied, and whether the demographic attributes being studied are categorical (e.g., gender, nationality) or numerical (e.g., age, tenure) (Meyer et al., 2014). In addition, the researcher needs to know which team member belongs to which subgroup and the corresponding subgroup sizes, and whether the groups can have more than 10 members (Meyer et al., 2014). Depending on the combination of these factors, researchers can choose from different faultline measures developed within the faultline domain.[1]

Although most board studies use archival data or survey data to measure faultlines, there are other interesting research methods that can complement the extant literature. For example, the use of experiments, simulations or video recordings of real corpo-rate boards could enable us to build theory and gain a better understanding of the internal dynamics of subgroup processes. Furthermore, qualitative research designs are needed to capture the underlying psychological factors that underlie the effects of faultlines and subgroup formation. Lastly, longitudinal research designs could help examine faultline development over time, which to date remains an unresolved fault-line puzzle (Murnighan & Lau, 2017). For example, by tracking a particular board over time, researchers could examine whether subgroups become stronger over time or dissolve rather rapidly. It may be that subgroups become more or less entrenched over time, depending on the extent to which group members agree on the existence and composition of strong and stable subgroups (Meister et al., 2020).

FAULTLINE MECHANISMS

The main theoretical basis behind the concept of group faultlines was initially built on social identity and social categorization theories (Ashforth & Mael, 1989; Hogg & Terry, 2000; Tajfel & Turner, 2004). Members' characteristics are used for social categorization, leading to in-group/out-group categorizations. Strong faultlines can lead to recurring and salient subgroups, which in turn may become a very likely basis for self-identity and social categorization, because group members will perceive themselves as a category (Lau & Murnighan, 1998). When some subgroup members share common identity, values, and characteristics, they tend to interact more with these subgroup members and favour and trust their group members more than individuals from other groups (Lau & Murnighan, 2005). Therefore, board members may shift their primary focus from the board as a whole to their more homogeneous subgroups, resulting in strong subgroup identification. When these dynamics are active, a number of mechanisms may come into play, such as members favouring interaction with their own subgroup members rather than with the whole group.

A number of board scholars have examined the mechanisms behind faultline effects in boards. Most board studies that consider the concept of faultlines use the main theoretical basis of social identity and social categorization theories and similarity attraction,[2] reporting processes such as relationship conflicts and tensions, a decrease in intergroup trust and respect, and less information sharing, thus compromising the quality of board decision-making. However, because empirical findings within faultline research have been relatively inconsistent, particularly with respect to informational faultline research (i.e., with studies reporting positive effects (e.g., Rupert et al., 2016), negative effects (e.g., Bezrukova et al., 2012), or even no effects on organizational outcomes (e.g., Chung et al., 2015)), future research should look at different theoretical explanations that take into account the nature of alignment, and specifically the type of demographics responsible for alignment, such as social category versus informational (Bezrukova et al., 2009).

FAULTLINE OUTCOMES

A number of different faultline outcomes have been observed within board research. For example, Tuggle et al. (2010) report that boards with strong faultlines will spend less discussion time on entrepreneurial issues. Vandebeek et al. (2016) and Crucke and Knockaert (2016) found negative faultline effects on board task performance. Van Peteghem et al. (2018) indicate that boards with strong faultlines are associated with lower firm performance, lower CEO turnover-performance sensitivity, and higher abnormal CEO compensation. Vandebeek et al. (2021) show that social category faultlines moderate the performance–CEO-dismissal relationship. Veltrop et al. (2015) found that factional demographic faultlines negatively impact board performance, measured as perceived board effectiveness, and financial return on investment. Kaczmarek et al. (2012b) reported negative effects on firm performance, and Wu et al. (2021) found a negative relationship with strategic change.

Although the nature of board tasks differs from tasks performed by the TMT (Finkelstein et al., 2009), there are some interesting faultline studies within the TMT literature that may provide inspiration for board faultline research. For example, faultlines within the TMT are also linked to firm performance (e.g., Cooper et al., 2014; Georgakakis et al., 2017; van Knippenberg et al., 2011), post-succession performance (Georgakakis & Buyl, 2020), or strategic change (Richard et al., 2019), but other interesting faultline outcomes have also been examined. For instance, Barkema and Shvyrkov (2007) found that strong faultline settings in TMTs decreased the likelihood that firms would invest in new geographic areas as opposed to investing in familiar locations. Hutzschenreuter and Horstkotte (2013) found that task-related faultline strength helps TMTs during an expansion period to cope with the complexity inherent in expanding into new product areas, and in this way contribute to the debate whether different types of faultlines require different theoretical explanations. Ndofor et al. (2015) explain that inconclusive findings for the effect of TMT heterogeneity can be a result of the failure to model faultlines. The authors find that if TMT heterogeneity yields strong faultlines, the positive effect of TMT heterogeneity on converting resources to action is weakened, while the negative effect on converting resources to performance is further strengthened. Ou et al. (2017) show that individual leaders' ability to retain subordinates can be undermined by faultlines within the leadership team to which they belong. Li and Jones (2019) found that TMTs with strong faultlines take fewer and simpler competitive actions. Lastly, Calabrò et al. (2020) examined the moderating effects of TMT faultlines on the relationship between entrepreneurial orientation and family firm performance.

Within boards, there are still a number of interesting faultline outcomes to observe. For example, we still know little about the effects of faultlines on behavioural (dis) integration (Li & Hambrick, 2005), group morale (Thatcher et al., 2003), psychological safety (Edmondson, 1999), or learning behavior (Gibson & Vermeulen, 2003). Furthermore, Merchant and Pick (2010) describe a number of blind spots, biases, and other pathologies in the boardroom that can be influenced by the presence of faultlines. For example, faultlines can impact group polarization (i.e., "the tendency for groups to reach collective decisions that are more extreme than the decisions the individual group members would choose to make individually" (Merchant & Pick, 2010:41)), groupthink (Choi & Kim, 1999), or pluralistic ignorance (Westphal & Bednar, 2005). Therefore, the field could benefit from shifting its focus from common performance measures such as firm performance to a more behavioral approach and examining the actual behavior of boards (Huse, 2005; van Ees et al., 2009) (Figure 12.1).

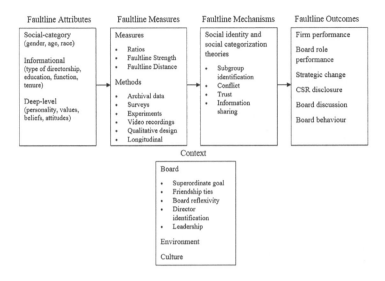

Figure 12.1   Theoretical framework of the consequences of board faultlines

EFFECT OF BOARD CONTEXT ON GROUP FAULTLINES

Prior research has argued that the effects of faultlines depend highly on contextual conditions (Meyer et al., 2014), and most board scholars incorporate contextual board conditions when studying faultlines because it is relevant to reconciling some of the mixed findings from past faultline research and understanding the boundary conditions of group faultline effects. Moreover, the inclusion of contextual effects can contribute to theoretical developments within board faultline research. In most cases, board context can facilitate or hamper communication between subgroups and thus ameliorate or attenuate the negative effects of group faultlines. Therefore, it could be said that there might be some "faultline management tactics" that revolve around installing a superordinate goal or friendship ties (Locke & Latham, 2002; Murnighan & Lau, 2017; Ren et al., 2015; Richter et al., 2006). For example, Vandebeek et al. (2016) found that the negative effect of faultlines on board role performance is reversed when boards use formal board evaluations. Board evaluation brings many positive effects, such as contributing to a collective team identity by bringing attention back to the overall superordinate goal of the board. In the same vein, Crucke and Knockaert (2016) found that having clear and shared organizational goals as a board can attenuate the negative effects of faultlines, and Veltrop et al. (2015) report an ameliorating effect of board reflexivity (i.e., "the extent to which group members overtly reflect upon, and communicate about the group's objectives, strategies and processes, and adapt them to current or anticipated circumstances" (West et al., 1997:296)) on faultline activation. Tuggle et al. (2010) found that meeting informality could allow members of different groups on a board to better understand or accept the ideas of other groups, allowing for more open meetings and thus reducing the negative relationship between strong faultlines and attention to entrepreneurial issues. Kaczmarek et al. (2012b) demonstrate that the condition of a busy board and CEO tenure can exacerbate the negative effects of faultlines, while executive pay contingency ameliorated board faultline effects through its positive effects on board cohesion. Lastly, Vandebeek et al. (2021) examined how two board contingencies – the presence of board evaluation and the number of board committees – affect how social category faultlines moderate the performance–CEO-dismissal relationship. Beyond the board context, scholars have also looked at other contextual conditions. For example, Wu et al. (2021) found that faultlines are negatively related to strategic change at low environmental complexity, environmental dynamism, and environmental munificence, but positively related to strategic change at high environmental complexity, environmental dynamism, and environmental munificence.

Interesting avenues that future research might explore is director's identification with their different identities, such as with the organization or with being a CEO (Hillman et al., 2008). Another important factor lies in the leadership of the board. For example, shared leadership (Vandewaerde et al., 2011) or leader inclusion within subgroups (Meyer et al., 2015) could play an important role in diminishing tensions between subgroups, thereby reducing the negative impact of faultlines on the board. In addition, there is still a lack of studies that consider the effect of cultural differences. Most studies have been conducted in America and Europe (Thatcher & Patel, 2012), but it could be that, for example, in less individualistic cultures, subgroups may form based on very different attributes. Thus, there is still much to discover, using creative and innovative research designs, to get a more complete picture of the effect of group faultlines in boards.

Table 12.1   Prior empirical analysis of faultlines in boards and TMTs

Paper	Faultline attributes	Faultline Measures	Faultline Outcomes
Panel A: Papers examining faultlines in boards			
Barroso-Castro et al. (2020)	Type of directorship, director tenure	Average silhouette width (ASW) measure (Meyer & Glenz, 2013)	Faultlines moderate the relationship between board resource variety and firm international activity
Crucke and Knockaert (2016)	Stakeholder group represented, gender, age	Fau (Thatcher et al., 2003)	Faultline strength is negatively related to board service performance
Kaczmarek et al. (2012b)	Age, gender, nationality, the type of directorship, educational degree, board tenure, financial background	Fau (Thatcher et al., 2003)	Faultlines negatively impact firm performance
Tuggle et al. (2010)	Tenure, functional background, and the firm/industry background of directors on a board	Latent class-clustering technique specifically developed for mixed-type data	Strong faultlines in boards of directors reduced the psychological safety required to discuss sensitive entrepreneurial issues
Van Peteghem et al. (2018)	Director independence, director financial expertise, multiple board memberships, career horizon and incentives (age >65), gender, board tenure, share ownership	Clustering process (following general setup of Thatcher et al. (2003) and Bezrukova et al. (2009))	Boards with strong faultlines are associated with lower firm performance, lower CEO turnover-performance sensitivity, and higher abnormal CEO compensation
Vandebeek et al. (2016)	Family membership, type of directorship, gender	FLS (Shaw, 2004)	Faultlines negatively impact board control and service role performance
Vandebeek et al. (2021)	Family membership, gender, age	ASW measure (Meyer & Glenz, 2013)	The negative relationship between firm performance and the likelihood of CEO dismissal is significantly weaker when boards experience social category faultlines

Paper	Faultline attributes	Faultline Measures	Faultline Outcomes
Veltrop et al. (2015)	Factional affiliations, gender, age	A combination of faultline split strength (i.e., how cleanly a board splits into two factional groups) and faultline distance or width (i.e., how far the factional groups are apart) (Bezrukova et al., 2009; Bezrukova et al., 2012; Zanutto et al., 2011)	Factional demographic faultlines negatively affect board performance, measured as perceived board effectiveness, and financial return on investment
Wu et al. (2021)	Educational level, age, tenure, functional category, nationality	FLS (Shaw, 2004)	Gender faultline strength of a board of directors is negatively related to strategic change
Panel B: Papers examining faultlines in TMTs			
Barkema and Shvyrkov (2007)	Age, gender, education type and level	Latent cluster analysis and recommendations by Lau and Murnighan (1998)	Strong faultline settings in TMTs decrease the likelihood that firms would invest in new geographic areas as opposed to investing in familiar locations
Calabrò et al. (2020)	Age, gender, family membership, experience, functional background, education	FLS (Shaw, 2004)	Strong identity-based faultlines (IBFs) negatively moderate the entrepreneurial orientation–family firm performance relationship. Conversely, strong knowledge-based faultlines (KBFs) amplify the positive effect of EO on FF performance
Cooper et al. (2014)	Educational and functional background, tenure	Fau (Thatcher et al., 2003)	Informational faultline strength positively affects firm performance under low environmental dynamism, high complexity, and high munificence, but it negatively affects firm performance under high environmental dynamism, low complexity, and low munificence
Georgakakis and Buyl (2020)	Post-succession TMT entry, gender and nationality	FLS (Shaw, 2004)	Post-succession factional faultlines strength has a negative effect on subsequent firm performance.

Paper	Faultline attributes	Faultline Measures	Faultline Outcomes
Georgakakis et al. (2017)	Functional background and international experience	Fau (Thatcher et al., 2003)	The performance effect of knowledge-based TMT faultlines is significantly altered when the leader of the TMT (i.e., the CEO): (a) socio-demographically resembles incumbent executives, (b) possesses a diverse career background, and (c) shares common socialization experience with other TMT members
Hutzschenreuter and Horstkotte (2013)	Organizational tenure and educational specialization versus age and nationality	Fau (Thatcher et al., 2003)	Task-related faultlines within the TMT help the TMT cope with product expansion while bio-demographic faultlines hinder it
Li and Jones (2019)	Age, gender, ethnicity, tenure, and functional background	ASW measure (Meyer & Glenz, 2013)	TMTs with strong faultlines take fewer and simpler competitive actions
Ndofor et al. (2015)	Age, tenure, and functional background	Fau (Thatcher et al., 2003)	When TMT heterogeneity yields strong faultlines, the positive effect of TMT heterogeneity on converting resources to action is weakened, while the negative effect on converting resources to performance is further strengthened
Ou et al. (2017)	Age, gender, education level, education specialization, company tenure, and team tenure	Fau (Thatcher et al., 2003)	Faultlines in TMTs exert cross-level effects attenuating how humble executives sustain middle managers' job satisfaction, and how job dissatisfaction drives their voluntary turnover
Richard et al. (2019)	Gender, age, educational level, functional background, and tenure	FLS (Shaw, 2004)	TMT relationship-related faultline strength (especially educational-level) negatively influences strategic change whereas TMT task-related faultline strength positively affects strategic change

NOTES

1. For a more detailed overview of all faultline measures developed within the faultline domain, see Meyer et al. (2014).
2. See, for example, Ali & Ayoko (2020); Barroso-Castro et al. (2020); Crucke & Knockaert (2016); Crucke et al. (2015); Kaczmarek et al. (2012b); Tuggle et al. (2010); Van Peteghem et al. (2018); Vandebeek et al. (2021); Vandebeek et al. (2016); Veltrop et al. (2015); Wu et al. (2021).

REFERENCES

Ali, M., & Ayoko, O. B. (2020). The impact of board size on board demographic faultlines. *Corporate Governance: The International Journal of Business in Society*, 20(7), 1205–22.

Ashforth, B. E., & Mael, F. (1989). Social identity theory and the organization. *Academy of Management Review*, 14(1), 20–39.

Bammens, Y., Voordeckers, W., & Van Gils, A. (2011). Boards of directors in family businesses: a literature review and research agenda. *International Journal of Management Reviews*, 13(2), 134–52.

Barkema, H. G., & Shvyrkov, O. (2007). Does top management team diversity promote or hamper foreign expansion? *Strategic Management Journal*, 28(7), 663–80.

Barroso-Castro, C., Pérez-Calero, L., Vecino-Gravel, J. D., & del Mar Villegas-Periñán, M. (2020). The challenge of board composition: effects of board resource variety and faultlines on the degree of a firm's international activity. *Long Range Planning*. https://doi.org/10.1016/j.lrp.2020.102047.

Basco, R., Campopiano, G., Calabrò, A., & Kraus, S. (2019). They are not all the same! Investigating the effect of executive versus non-executive family board members on firm performance. *Journal of Small Business Management*, 57(2), 637–57.

Basco, R., & Voordeckers, W. (2015). The relationship between the board of directors and firm performance in private family firms: a test of the demographic versus behavioral approach. *Journal of Management & Organization*, 21(4), 1–25.

Bezrukova, K., Jehn, K., Zanutto, E., & Thatcher, S. (2009). Do workgroup faultlines help or hurt? A moderated model of faultlines, team identification, and group performance. *Organization Science*, 20(1), 35–50.

Bezrukova, K., Thatcher, S. M. B., Jehn, K. A., & Spell, C. S. (2012). The effects of alignments: examining group faultlines, organizational cultures, and performance. *Journal of Applied Psychology*, 97(1), 77–92.

Bezrukova, K., & Uparna, J. (2009). Group splits and culture shifts: a new map of the creativity terrain. In M. A. Neale, B. Mannix, & J. Goncalo (Eds.), *Research on Managing Groups and Teams*, vol. 12: 161–91. Stamford, CT: JAI Press.

Björnberg, Å., & Nicholson, N. (2012). Emotional ownership: the next generation's relationship with the family firm. *Family Business Review*, 25(4), 374–90.

Calabrò, A., Santulli, R., Torchia, M., & Gallucci, C. (2020). Entrepreneurial orientation and family firm performance: the moderating role of TMT identity-based and knowledge-based faultlines. *Entrepreneurship Theory and Practice*, 45(4), 838–66.

Choi, J. N., & Kim, M. U. (1999). The organizational application of groupthink and its limitations in organizations. *Journal of Applied Psychology*, 84(2), 297.

Chung, Y., Liao, H., Jackson, S. E., Subramony, M., Colakoglu, S., & Jiang, Y. (2015). Cracking but not breaking: joint effects of faultline strength and diversity climate on loyal behavior. *Academy of Management Journal*, 58(5), 1495–515.

Cooper, D., Patel, P. C., & Thatcher, S. M. (2014). It depends: environmental context and the effects of faultlines on top management team performance. *Organization Science*, 25(2), 633–52.

Crucke, S., & Knockaert, M. (2016). When stakeholder representation leads to faultlines: a study of board service performance in social enterprises. *Journal of Management Studies*, 53(5), 768–93.

Crucke, S., Moray, N., & Vallet, N. (2015). Internal representation and factional faultlines as antecedents for board performance in social enterprises. *Annals of Public and Cooperative Economics*, 86(2), 385–400.

Edmondson, A. (1999). Psychological safety and learning behavior in work teams. *Administrative Science Quarterly*, 44(2), 350–83.

Finkelstein, S., Hambrick, D. C., & Cannella Jr., A. A. (2009). *Strategic Leadership: Theory and Research on Executives, Top Management Teams, and Boards*. New York, NY: Oxford University Press.

Forbes, D. P., & Milliken, F. J. (1999). Cognition and corporate governance: understanding boards of directors as strategic decision-making groups. *Academy of Management Review*, 24(3), 489–505.

Geletkanycz, M. A., & Boyd, B. K. (2011). CEO outside directorships and firm performance: a reconciliation of agency and embeddedness views. *Academy of Management Journal*, 54(2), 335–52.

Georgakakis, D., & Buyl, T. (2020). Guardians of the previous regime: post-CEO succession factional subgroups and firm performance. *Long Range Planning*, 53(3), 1–15.

Georgakakis, D., Greve, P., & Ruigrok, W. (2017). Top management team faultlines and firm performance: examining the CEO-TMT interface. *The Leadership Quarterly*, 28(6), 741–58.

Gibson, C., & Vermeulen, F. (2003). A healthy divide: subgroups as a stimulus for team learning behavior. *Administrative Science Quarterly*, 48(2), 202–39.

Hillman, A. J., Nicholson, G., & Shropshire, C. (2008). Directors' multiple identities, identification, and board monitoring and resource provision. *Organization Science*, 19(3), 441–56.

Hogg, M. A., & Terry, D. J. (2000). Social identity and self-categorization processes in organizational contexts. *Academy of Management Review*, 25(1), 121–40.

Huse, M. (2005). Accountability and creating accountability: a framework for exploring behavioural perspectives of corporate governance. *British Journal of Management*, 16(1), S65–S79.

Hutzschenreuter, T., & Horstkotte, J. (2013). Performance effects of top management team demographic faultlines in the process of product diversification. *Strategic Management Journal*, 34(6), 704–26.

Jehn, K. A., Bezrukova, K., & Thatcher, S. (2008). Conflict, diversity, and faultlines in workgroups. In C. K. W. D. Dreu & M. J. Gelfand (Eds.), *The Organizational Frontiers Series: The Psychology of Conflict and Conflict Management in Organizations*, 179–210. Mahwah, NJ: Taylor & Francis Group/Lawrence Erlbaum Associates.

Jehn, K. A., & Rupert, J. (2008). Group faultlines and team learning: how to benefit from different perspectives. In M. London & V. Sessa (Eds.), *Work Group Learning: Understanding, Improving & Assessing How Groups Learn in Organizations*, 121–49. Mahwah, NJ: Lawrence Erlbaum Asssociates.

Johnson, S. G., Schnatterly, K., & Hill, A. D. (2013). Board composition beyond independence: social capital, human capital, and demographics. *Journal of Management*, 39(1), 232–62.

Kaczmarek, S., Kimino, S., & Pye, A. (2012a). Antecedents of board composition: the role of nomination committees. *Corporate Governance: An International Review*, 20(5), 474–89.

Kaczmarek, S., Kimino, S., & Pye, A. (2012b). Board task-related faultlines and firm performance: a decade of evidence. *Corporate Governance: An International Review*, 20(3), 337–51.

Lau, D. C., & Murnighan, J. K. (1998). Demographic diversity and faultlines: the compositional dynamics of organizational groups. *Academy of Management Review*, 23(2), 325–40.

Lau, D. C., & Murnighan, J. K. (2005). Interactions within groups and subgroups: the effects of demographic faultlines. *Academy of Management Journal*, 48(4), 645–59.

Li, J., & Hambrick, D. C. (2005). Factional groups: a new vantage on demographic faultlines, conflict, and disintegration in work teams. *Academy of Management Journal*, 48(5), 794–813.

Li, M., & Jones, C. D. (2019). The effects of TMT faultlines and CEO-TMT power disparity on competitive behavior and firm performance. *Group & Organization Management*, 44(5), 874–914.

Liu, X. K., & Van Peteghem, M. (2019). Faultlines among senior executives, internal control and corporate disclosure. *Internal Control and Corporate Disclosure* (July 1, 2019). http://dx.doi.org/10.2139/ssrn.3758138.

Locke, E. A., & Latham, G. P. (2002). Building a practically useful theory of goal setting and task motivation: a 35-year odyssey. *American Psychologist*, 57(9), 705–17.

Meister, A., Thatcher, S. M., Park, J., & Maltarich, M. (2020). Toward a temporal theory of faultlines and subgroup entrenchment. *Journal of Management Studies*, 57(8), 1473–501.

Merchant, K. A., & Pick, K. (2010). *Blind Spots, Biases, and Other Pathologies in the Boardroom*. New York, NY: Business Expert Press.

Meyer, B., & Glenz, A. (2013). Team faultline measures: a computational comparison and a new approach to multiple subgroups. *Organizational Research Methods*, 16(3), 393–424.

Meyer, B., Glenz, A., Antino, M., Rico, R., & González-Romá, V. (2014). Faultlines and subgroups: a meta-review and measurement guide. *Small Group Research*, 45(6), 633–70.

Meyer, B., Shemla, M., Li, J., & Wegge, J. (2015). On the same side of the faultline: inclusion in the leader's subgroup and employee performance. *Journal of Management Studies*, 52(3), 354–80.

Minichilli, A., Corbetta, G., & MacMillan, I. C. (2010). Top management teams in family-controlled companies: 'familiness', 'faultlines', and their impact on financial performance. *Journal of Management Studies*, 47(2), 205–22.

Murnighan, J. K., & Lau, D. C. (2017). *Faultlines*. Oxford, UK: Oxford University Press.

Ndofor, H. A., Sirmon, D. G., & He, X. (2015). Utilizing the firm's resources: how TMT heterogeneity and resulting faultlines affect TMT tasks. *Strategic Management Journal*, 36(11), 1656–74.

Nielsen, S. (2012). Diversity among senior executives and board directors. In T. Clarke & D. Branson (Eds.), *The Sage Handbook of Corporate Governance*, 345–62. London, UK: SAGE.

Ou, A. Y., Seo, J., Choi, D., & Hom, P. W. (2017). When can humble top executives retain middle managers? The moderating role of top management team faultlines. *Academy of Management Journal*, 60(5), 1915–31.

Ren, H., Gray, B., & Harrison, D. A. (2015). Triggering faultline effects in teams: the importance of bridging friendship ties and breaching animosity ties. *Organization Science*, 26(2), 390–404.

Richard, O. C., Wu, J., Markoczy, L. A., & Chung, Y. (2019). Top management team demographic-faultline strength and strategic change: what role does environmental dynamism play? *Strategic Management Journal*, 40(6), 987–1009.

Richter, A. W., West, M. A., Van Dick, R., & Dawson, J. F. (2006). Boundary spanners' identification, intergroup contact, and effective intergroup relations. *Academy of Management Journal*, 49(6), 1252–69.

Rupert, J., Blomme, R. J., Dragt, M. J., & Jehn, K. (2016). Being different, but close: how and when faultlines enhance team learning. *European Management Review*, 13(4), 275–90.

Shaw, J. B. (2004). The development and analysis of a measure of group faultlines. *Organizational Research Methods*, 7(1), 66–100.

Tajfel, H., & Turner, J. C. (2004). The social identity theory of intergroup behavior. In S. Worchel & W. G. Austin (Eds.), *The Psychology of Intergroup Relations*, 7–24. Chicago, IL: Nelson-Hall.

Tasheva, S., & Hillman, A. J. (2019). Integrating diversity at different levels: multilevel human capital, social capital, and demographic diversity and their implications for team effectiveness. *Academy of Management Review*, 44(4), 746–65.

Thatcher, S., Jehn, K., & Zanutto, E. (2003). Cracks in diversity research: the effects of diversity faultlines on conflict and performance. *Group Decision & Negotiation*, 12(3), 217–41.

Thatcher, S., & Patel, P. (2012). Group faultlines: a review, integration, and guide to future research. *Journal of Management*, 38(4), 969–1009.

Torchia, M., Calabrò, A., & Morner, M. (2015). Board of directors' diversity, creativity, and cognitive conflict. *International Studies of Management & Organization*, 45(1), 6–24.

Tuggle, C. S., Schnatterly, K., & Johnson, R. A. (2010). Attention patterns in the boardroom: how board composition and processes affect discussion of entrepreneurial issues. *Academy of Management Journal*, 53(3), 550–71.

van Ees, H., Gabrielsson, J., & Huse, M. (2009). Toward a behavioral theory of boards and corporate governance. *Corporate Governance: An International Review*, 17(3), 307–19.

van Knippenberg, D., Dawson, J. F., West, M. A., & Homan, A. C. (2011). Diversity faultlines, shared objectives, and top management team performance. *Human Relations*, 64(3), 307–36.

Van Peteghem, M., Bruynseels, L., & Gaeremynck, A. (2018). Beyond diversity: a tale of faultlines and frictions in the board of directors. *The Accounting Review*, 93(2), 339–67.

Vandebeek, A., Voordeckers, W., Huybrechts, J., & Lambrechts, F. (2021). Corporate performance and CEO dismissal: the role of social category faultlines. *Corporate Governance: An International Review*, 29(5), 436–60.

Vandebeek, A., Voordeckers, W., Lambrechts, F., & Huybrechts, J. (2016). Board role performance and faultlines in family firms: the moderating role of formal board evaluation. *Journal of Family Business Strategy*, 7(4), 249–59.

Vandewaerde, M., Voordeckers, W., Lambrechts, F., & Bammens, Y. (2011). Board team leadership revisited: a conceptual model of shared leadership in the boardroom. *Journal of Business Ethics*, 104(3), 403–20.

Veltrop, D. B., Hermes, N., Postma, T. J. B. M., & Haan, J. (2015). A tale of two factions: why and when factional demographic faultlines hurt board performance. *Corporate Governance: An International Review*, 23(2), 145–60.

West, M. A., Garrod, S., & Carletta, J. (1997). Group decision-making and effectiveness: unexplored boundaries. In C. L. Cooper & S. E. Jackson (Eds.), *Creating Tomorrow's Organizations*, 293–317. Chichester, UK: John Wiley & Sons, Ltd.

Westphal, J. D., & Bednar, M. K. (2005). Pluralistic ignorance in corporate boards and firms' strategic persistence in response to low firm performance. *Administrative Science Quarterly*, 50(2), 262–98.

Wu, J., Triana, M. d. C., Richard, O. C., & Yu, L. (2021). Gender faultline strength on boards of directors and strategic change: the role of environmental conditions. *Group & Organization Management*, 46(3), 564–601.

Zanutto, E. L., Bezrukova, K., & Jehn, K. A. (2011). Revisiting faultline conceptualization: measuring faultline strength and distance. *Quality & Quantity*, 45(3), 701–14.

Zona, F., & Zattoni, A. (2007). Beyond the black box of demography: board processes and task effectiveness within Italian firms. *Corporate Governance: An International Review*, 15(5), 852–64.

13. Faultlines: understanding how board composition may influence team dynamics and subgroup formation in corporate boards

Esha Mendiratta

Corporate boards have long been a subject of inquiry in a range of disciplines. There is a general agreement in corporate governance literature that composition and team-level dynamics within corporate boards matter for board- and firm-level outcomes (Hillman and Dalziel, 2003; Johnson, Daily, and Ellstrand, 1996; van Ees, Gabrielson, and Huse, 2009). However, the conceptual meaning of composition, why and how this composition matters, and for which outcome variables, has been up for debate for decades (see Pugliese et al., 2009 for a review). Since board of directors sit at the helm of an organization, and have the highest legal authority and responsibility alongside top executives in most corporate governance systems, these questions and debates are both academically and practically relevant.

As high-profile decision-making groups, corporate boards perform two main functions. First, they oversee or monitor senior management, and are responsible for hiring, firing and compensating them (Hillman and Dalziel, 2003; Rindova, 1999; Zahra and Pearce, 1989). Second, they provide resources in the form of strategic advice to senior management (Johnson, Schnatterly, and Hill, 2013; Pfeffer and Salancik, 1978). To perform these complex tasks effectively, demographic and task-related characteristics of directors as individual, and the dynamics within the board resulting from how these characteristics combine at the group level are relevant. A bulk of the literature has conceptualized board-level dynamics as diversity or dispersion along one demographic or task-related characteristic (e.g. gender) to examine implications of this diversity for board level dynamics, and consequently board- and firm-level outcomes (Ferriera, 2011; Hillman, 2015). That is, the primary focus of corporate governance research has been to aggregate a specific individual-level characteristic at the board level to analyze how it influences decision-making and outcomes. While this approach is valuable, a singular focus on diversity tends to ignore the multidimensionality of directors as individuals and account for all relevant attributes and the joint effect of multiple director-level characteristics on decision-making and outcomes. One compelling framework to theorize the joint effect of multiple characteristics that has emerged in literature is group-level faultlines.

Faultlines are defined as hypothetical dividing lines that fracture a group into two or more homogenous subgroups based on the alignment of multiple individual-level characteristics (Lau and Murnighan, 1998). Given the growing interest in faultlines-based research within corporate governance literature, in this chapter, I review what we know about board- and top management team (TMT)-level faultlines and their influence of board- and firm-level outcomes. While a large body of work within organization behavior also draws on the concept of faultlines in the context of other types of teams, I specifically focus on literature on corporate boards and TMTs as dynamics within these high profile teams are likely to differ from teams at other levels within organizations. At the outset, it is important to note that specifically within corporate governance, while this body of work is emerging; it is by no means mature. Only 25 studies in general management and corporate governance journals explore faultlines, with this number increasing steadily in the last five years. Given the emerging nature of research, I attempt to synthesize what we know, but more importantly, I aim to identify productive opportunities for future CG research in the area. I start by tracing the origins of the concept and its theoretical underpinnings. I then move on to methodological focus and findings of corporate governance research drawing on the concept of faultlines. Finally, I present opportunities for CG research drawing on the faultlines framework.

FAULTLINES: CONCEPTUAL AND THEORETICAL UNDERPINNINGS

In their seminal conceptual work, Lau and Murnighan (1998) defined faultlines as "hypothetical dividing lines that may split a group into subgroups based on one or more attributes" (p. 328). The main premise behind the body of scholarship built on this concept is that it is the alignment of one or more characteristics of group members, and not only diversity with respect to single characteristics in isolation that influences group processes and outcomes. For example, consider the two boards of directors represented in Table 13.1. Board A has equal numbers of men and women, where all the men are over 55 years of age and have a finance functional background, and all the women are under 45 years old and have functional experiences in human resource management (HRM). Now consider corporate board B which also has equal representation of men and women; however, some of the women are older and some younger, and some have functional experiences in finance and some in marketing. Similarly, some men in corporate board B are young and some old, some come from a finance background and some from HRM.

From the traditional perspective of diversity focusing on individual characteristics, say gender diversity, boards A and B are indistinguishable as they have equal representation of men and women. This would imply that both boards have an equal potential of taking advantage of any gender-based differences that may exist. However, when considering multiple attributes of these two corporate boards simultaneously and how these attributes align, these two boards are significantly different, because multiple attributes in Board A align much more strongly than Board B. Consequently, Board A is likely to have a stronger subgroup formation based on stronger faultlines, whereas Board B is unlikely to form homogenous subgroups

Table 13.1   *Hypothetical board composition*

Board A	Gender	Age	Functional Background
Director A	Male	57	Finance
Director B	Male	59	Finance
Director C	Female	45	HRM
Director D	Female	47	HRM
Board B	Gender	Age	Functional Background
Director A	Male	57	Finance
Director B	Female	59	Finance
Director C	Male	45	HRM
Director D	Female	47	HRM

because of lack of alignment of board members' attributes. This strength of alignment or faultlines depends on two factors: (a) number of individual characteristics that are relevant to question being asked by the researcher, and (b) their alignment leading to two or more potentially homogenous subgroups (Lau and Murnighan, 1998). That is, faultlines within a group are stronger when there is a higher correlation between multiple attributes, leading to lower number of, and higher homogeneity within, subgroups. Moreover, theoretically, the effects of faultline strength on group- and firm-level outcomes are different from, and exist over and above those of diversity on individual characteristics (Lau and Murnighan, 1998, 2005; Thatcher and Patel, 2011).

In their seminal work, Lau and Murnighan (1998) relied predominantly on social categorization and social identity perspectives (Tajfel, 1981; Turner, 1985, 1987) to theorize the formation of faultlines based on demographic characteristics and their impact on group-level processes and outcomes. While their theoretical ideas were primarily limited to the internal environment of a group like presence and sizes of subgroups formed as a result of faultlines, they acknowledge the relevance of external conditions like the task assigned to the group, member entry and exit, and so on. Social identity perspective suggests that individuals tend to define themselves as belonging to groups with whom they share characteristics like gender or ethnicity (Tajfel, 1981; Turner, 1985, 1987). This type of identification results in individuals categorizing themselves and others into in-groups and out-groups, that is, those belonging to the same categories as themselves and those excluded from those categories. This categorization is likely to be stronger when, (a) perceived differences among in-group members are low, and (b) perceived differences between the in-group members and out-group members are high. Therefore, a group where multiple characteristics of team members align to create subgroups of similar members, who are also different from members of other subgroups, is likely to result in faultlines within the team, the strength of which is likely to increase as strength of alignment of group member attributes increases. When groups are characterized by stronger faultlines, social identification and categorization are likely to result in lower communication and higher relationship conflict between subgroups, resulting in lower exchange of ideas within the group (Thatcher and Patel, 2011, 2012).

Consistent with these initial theoretical ideas and conceptualizing boards as groups, a bulk of CG research has focused on the negative consequences of fault-lines formed based on both social category (e.g. gender, age, nationality) and task-related/informational attributes (e.g. tenure, functional background) for board- and firm-level outcomes. For instance, arguing that stronger subgroup formation within the board is likely to result in higher conflict and lower communication between subgroups, studies have suggested a negative impact of faultline strength on firm-level variables like firm performance (Georgakakis, Greve, and Ruigrok, 2017; Kaczmarek, Kimino, and Pye, 2012a; Knippenberg et al., 2011; Li and Jones, 2019; Van Peteghem, Bruynseels, and Gaeremynck, 2018), strategic change (Wu et al., 2021), novelty of investments (Barkema and Shvyrkov, 2007), innovation (Li and Liu, 2019); board-/TMT-level variables like board role performance (Vandebeek et al., 2016), group performance (Li and Hambrick, 2005a) and individual-level variables like abnormal CEO compensation (Van Peteghem et al., 2018) and middle manager job satisfaction/turnover (Ou et al., 2017).

However, following the tradition of diversity researchers, some studies have theorized the impact of faultlines based on social category characteristics and task-based or informational characteristics separately. Theoretical ideas regarding faultlines based on social categories are similar to those based on mixed attributes and predict a negative effect of faultlines on board processes and functioning (Veltrop et al., 2015). Theory on informational or task-based faultlines, however, has been much more contradictory. For instance, some studies argue that stronger informational faultlines have positive implications as they potentially lead to higher task conflict and consequently higher information processing within the board as like-mindedness within subgroups is likely to encourage information sharing and discussion (Cooper, Patel, and Thatcher, 2014; Richard et al., 2019). This may enable boards or TMTs to deal with complex tasks that are usually linked to higher strategic change (Richard et al., 2019). Others, however, follow the logic of social identification and categorization, or similarity attraction to argue for a negative effect of informational faultlines (Kaczmarek et al., 2012a; Tuggle, Schnatterly, and Johnson, 2010) on board functioning. Recently, combining these two perspectives, (Ma, Zhang, and Yin, 2021) argued for an inverted U-shaped effect of informational faultlines.

Similar inconsistencies also exist where the role of informational faultlines has been theorized as a moderator. Some argue that informational faultlines allow boards/TMTs to process task-related information better because they promote information exchange and elaboration of task-related information. As such, they allow board/TMTs to deal better with complexities associated with tasks like expanding product scope (Hutzschenreuter and Horstkotte, 2013) and enhance effects of entrepreneurial orientation (Calabrò et al., 2020) on firm-level outcomes. However, other studies suggest a negative impact of faultlines on a board's ability to use its resource variety to enhance firm performance (Barroso-Castro et al., 2020).

While much of the theoretical focus has been on the consequences of board faultlines, little attention given to developing theory on why and how faultlines are formed within the boards to begin with. Ali and Ayoko (2020) argue that board size is relevant for the formation of faultlines in that it has a U-shaped relationship with board faultline strength. They argue that in-group and out-group mechanisms associated with social categorization are likely to be stronger for small to medium-sized boards because of potential lack of cross-cutting directors. However, as the board grows in size, the probability of actors with cross-cutting attributes is likely to go up, suggesting a U-shaped relationship with faultline strength. Kaczmareck, Kimono and Pye (2012b) explore the role of nomination committees in formation of faultlines. Following the logic of similarity-attraction paradigm (Byrne, 1971), they suggest that when the CEO is present on the nomination committee, the board is likely to experience lower faultline strength as he/she is likely to prefer board members similar to him/her, leading to a more homogenous board and, consequently, weaker faultlines.

Following the original spirit of Lau and Murnighan (1998), researchers also try to capture dynamics by exploring inter-relationships between faultlines and endogenous (i.e. individual, board, firm) and exogenous (i.e. environmental) factors at multiple levels of analysis. For example, Li and Liu (2019) argue that CEO's higher status relative to TMT members and their unique role in managing the TMT has implications for how the effect of faultlines materializes for technological exploration. Viewing the relative size of subgroups as a proxy for power differences between subgroups, they argue that if the CEO belongs to the smaller subgroup when faultlines are formed, the members of this subgroup will feel more empowered to share the information they have and therefore, the positive effects of faultlines will be amplified when the CEO is a minority subgroup relative to a majority subgroup. Other studies also view the dynamics at the CEO–TMT interface like CEO–TMT power disparity (Li and Jones, 2019), CEO–TMT shared tenure and socio-demographic similarity (Georgakakis et al., 2017) as relevant for conceptualizing the impact of faultlines. At the board/TMT level, research has identified board busyness (Kaczmarek et al., 2012a), formal board evaluation (Vandebeek et al., 2016), board reflexivity (Veltrop et al., 2015), overlapping tenure (Barkema and Shvyrkov, 2007) and TMT shared objectives (Knippenberg et al., 2011) to alter the direct dynamics related to faultlines. Finally, munificence, dynamism and complexity in a firm's environment have also received some attention (Cooper et al., 2014; Richard et al., 2019).

In summary, as far as conceptualizing the direct consequences of faultlines goes, CG research has not seen much theoretical plurality and relies predominantly on social identification and social categorization perspectives to explore the consequences of faultlines for boards, TMTs and firms. Based on these lenses, CG research has consistently proposed negative consequences of faultlines based on social category characteristics alone, or ones comprising both social category and informational attributes. However, theory on faultlines based on informational attributes alone has been somewhat inconsistent and contradictory. There have also been some attempts to explore how the dynamics linked to faultlines are shaped by factors at multiple levels of analysis like the CEO, CEO–TMT/board interface, TMT/board and the firm's environment.

EMPIRICAL FINDINGS: FAULTLINES OF WHAT, WHOM AND HOW?

Consistent with theoretical ideas, early CG research examined both social category and informational/task-based attributes together as relevant for measuring faultlines. For example, examining joint venture management groups, Li and Hambrick (2005a) show that strong faultlines based on age, tenure, gender and nationality between two management groups engaging in a joint venture are associated with higher emotional conflict, task conflict and behavioral disintegration. The measurement of faultlines for most studies since then has also included both social category and informational/task-based attributes in one measure. However, there are studies that measure faultlines based on social category attributes only (Ali and Ayoko, 2020; Veltrop et al., 2015) and informational attributes only (Barroso-Castro et al., 2020; Cooper et al., 2014; Georgakakis et al., 2017; Kaczmarek et al., 2012a). Moreover, in line with arguing for different theoretical mechanisms for the impact of social category and informational faultlines, some studies have also used two separate measures for faultlines based on these groupings of attributes (Calabrò et al., 2020; Hutzschenreuter and Horstkotte, 2013; Ma et al., 2021; Richard et al., 2019). The most commonly used attributes (in decreasing order) are age (16 studies), tenure (16), sex (15), functional background (11) and education type or level (9). Less often used are financial expertise (2), family membership (2), director independence (2), nationality (2) and international experience (1). Not surprisingly, considering the relative homogenous nature of corporate boards and TMTs with respect to ethnicity, ethnicity has only been included in the construction of faultlines in one study (Li and Jones, 2019). Typically, studies use quantitative methods to examine the consequences of faultlines on outcome variables at different levels of analysis.

Outcome variables studied vary from firm-level variables like firm performance (Georgakakis et al., 2017; Hutzschenreuter and Horstkotte, 2013; Kaczmarek et al., 2012a; Knippenberg et al., 2011; Van Peteghem et al., 2018), board-level variables like discussion of entrepreneurial issues (Tuggle et al., 2010), performance (Li and Hambrick, 2005a; Vandebeek et al., 2016) and board effectiveness (Veltrop et al., 2015) to individual variables like abnormal CEO compensation (Van Peteghem et al., 2018) and middle manager job satisfaction and voluntary turnover (Ou et al., 2017). Moreover, given the varied nature of outcome variables studied, there is no consistency in the attributes included in the construction of faultlines for different levels of analysis of the outcome variables. Even for the same outcome variable, construction of faultlines is based on different characteristics, mostly for theoretical reasons. For instance, Georgakakis et al. (2017) construct the faultline measure using functional background and international experience to examine its role in explaining performance of multinational companies. Considering the importance of international experience of TMT members for multinational companies, they consider it a critical attribute for formation and activation of faultlines in TMTs. However, Cooper et al. (2014) explore the influence of faultlines based on education, functional background and tenure on firm performance because they consider these attributes to be the most relevant for firm performance theoretically. Finally, CG researchers study faultlines formed within both TMTs and boards, which also makes drawing conclusions challenging.

Another contentious methodological issue is the calculation of faultline strength. By far the most commonly used method has been the one developed by Thatcher et al. (2003). Their method can be viewed as a variance-based cluster analysis with a forced two-cluster solution. That is, it is a variance-based approach that gives a numeric value to a two-subgroup split defined as the largest ratio of between-subgroup variance over the total group variance of attributes. While a complete review of all measures used is beyond the scope of this review and has been conducted elsewhere (Meyer and Glenz, 2013), two things are worth noting. First, the forced two-group solution creates challenges to measure faultlines within boards. Since corporate boards typically tend to be larger teams of over 10 regardless of one-tier or two-tier corporate governance systems, more than two homogenous subgroups are plausible. It is important to determine this correct number of subgroups that maximizes the split between subgroups as it is likely to reduce the faultline strength in boards (Meyer and Glenz, 2013; Shaw, 2004; Thatcher and Patel, 2011). The two-subgroup solution method may be appropriate when researchers are only interested in faultlines based on two characteristics (Georgakakis et al., 2017); however, it is unlikely to be able to capture dynamics within the board when faultlines are based on three or more characteristics. As such, using this a priori restriction of two subgroups may lead to results that are removed from the reality of corporate boards. Second, for this measure, when variables are continuous (e.g. age, tenure), they need to be artificially categorized, leading to loss of measurement validity, and lead to under- or over-estimation of faultlines (Knippenberg et al., 2011). Recent work recognizes these limitations and uses alternative measures that address these challenges (Li and Liu, 2019; Xie, Wang, and Qi, 2015).

In summary, at this point there is not enough overlap between studies in terms of outcomes studied, attributes included in the construction of faultlines and the team studied (TMT or board) to make conclusions about faultlines based on which attributes are likely to have the strongest impact on which outcome. This conclusion is also echoed in team-level faultlines studies conducted primarily within the organization behavior and human resource management fields (Thatcher and Patel, 2012). Moreover, there is a need for wider use of methods such as those developed by Meyer and Glenz (2013) for measuring faultlines to better capture dynamics created by multiple subgroups.

FUTURE OPPORTUNITIES FOR CG RESEARCH USING FAULTLINES

Corporate boards are unique groups that have been demographically homogenous historically. This demographic composition is now changing slowly because of external institutional pressures, both through direct governmental interventions in the form of gender quotas, and softer pressures in the form of mandatory target-setting (Kirsch, 2018; Terjesen and Sealy, 2016). Moreover, since the start of the 21st century, corporate governance debates and discussions have paid increasing attention to broader societal challenges like climate change, workers' rights and so on. In order to progressively move toward addressing these challenges, there is pressure on board of directors to add certain types of expertise to boards (e.g. environmental expertise) that may not necessarily contribute to maximizing shareholder returns in the short-term (Beurden and Gossling, 2008; Walls, Berrone, and Phan, 2012). These developments have significant implications for corporate governance research using faultlines as a framework to examine board-level dynamics in terms of theoretical plurality, management of faultlines-related dynamics and methodological issues.

Drawing on Theoretical Insights from Other Disciplines

While social identification and categorization lenses from social psychology have provided a basis for theorization so far, there are at least three paths forward that may enrich our understanding of faultlines-related dynamics in the context of boards/ TMTs. First, social psychological lenses of the categorization elaboration model (CEM) and optimal distinctiveness theory (ODT) that have been used often in fault-lines literature in organizational behavior may help CG researchers explain theorize when faultlines may have a positive impact on outcomes. With rare exceptions (Cooper et al., 2014; Knippenberg et al., 2011), CG research has not taken advantage of these rich theories that may be relevant for faultlines. CEM focuses on both social categorization (negative) and information elaboration and variety (positive) potentials of subgroupings by examining faultlines both an intra-subgroup and inter-subgroup perspective. It suggests that the negative impact of faultlines on outcomes is con-tingent on three factors: cognitive accessibility, comparative fit and normative fit (van Knippenberg, De Dreu, and Homan, 2004; van Knippenberg and van Ginkel, 2010). Cognitive accessibility is the ease with which categorization effects are activated. For example, introduction of women to boards as a result of quotas likely creates a scenario where the differences between male and female board members are easily cognitively accessible. Comparative fit is the degree with which catego-rization leads to subgroups with high intra-group similarity and high inter-group differences. Normative fit is the extent to which categorization makes sense to an individual through their frame of reference. For example, if a board member holds stereotypical beliefs about certain professions, categorization along this dimension is likely to be salient. As such, by focusing on these three mechanisms, CEM provides CG researchers with a rich lens to examine when categorization processes are likely to be less salient to create an environment ripe for unleashing the positive effects of faultlines. ODT suggests a propensity among individuals to pursue a balance between uniqueness and similarity by assimilating within subgroups and seeking distinction between subgroups (Brewer, 1991). Because individuals seek to assimilate within subgroups, and seek distinction between subgroups, ODT explains why faultlines are an equilibrium outcome and why subgroups do not dissipate entirely. Both CEM and ODT, by focusing on both intra-subgroup and inter-subgroup processes at the individual, subgroup and group level, provide a fertile ground for future theoretical exploration.

Second, the unique context of corporate boards requires CG researchers to engage with power differentials based on demographic attributes, informational attributes and roles played by board members. Engaging with status and power differences between board members has the potential to move us closer to understanding the impact of faultlines on board dynamics. Theoretical lenses like status characteristics theory (SCT) (Berger, Cohen, and Zelditch Jr., 1972) from the field of sociology may provide useful insights here. So far, almost all CG research on faultlines has assumed that subgroups formed as a result of faultlines have equal power (see Li and Liu, 2019; Xie et al., 2015 for exceptions). However, particularly in the context of corporate boards and TMTs, this may be a limiting assumption. For example, the CEO, by virtue of their role as the leader of the TMT, may shift the power balance between subgroups. If the CEO's attributes align with a certain subgroup, the opinions and voices of that subgroup may have a heavier weight within the TMT, even at very high levels of faultlines or when the subgroup that the CEO belongs to is small (Xie et al., 2015). Faultlines in such a TMT may either not get activated or may not influence outcomes much even if they are activated as the CEO's subgroup may dominate decision-making. Recent addition of minorities (based on gender, ethnicity, sexual orientation, etc.) to boards may also have very specific implications for formation of faultlines and dynamics stemming from them. For instance, if all demographic minority members form a subgroup by default because of their recent entry and historical absence from boards, they may not have as much power as the majority subgroups and they may be limited in voicing their opinions (McDonald and Westphal, 2013; Nielsen and Huse, 2010a, 2010b). This may make the decision-making process seem smooth; however, minority members may not necessarily agree with the decisions made and end up using covert power tactics, resulting in different conflict-related dynamics relative to a board that is split into groups of equal power (Lau and Murnighan, 1998). As for informational attributes, certain types of expertise like financial expertise may be associated with higher power and prestige than other types of expertise like human resource management, environmental expertise and so on. This may also have implications for how faultlines are formed and activated, and influence dynamics within the boardroom.

These relative differences in power and status among board members and their implications may be captured by lenses like status characteristics theory (SCT) more appropriately. Given the historical male dominance on corporate boards, and the role of the CEO or the Board Chair, one may assume that there is an established power and prestige order on corporate boards (Berger et al., 1998). According to SCT, this established order shapes patterns of group-level participation and interaction, with high-status individuals (and by implication, high-status subgroups linked to faultlines) being afforded the right to influence decision-making more than others (Berger et al., 1972; Magee and Galinsky, 2008). The outcomes of faultlines within such an established order are unclear. One the one hand, the lower-power subgroup (say, based on gender and functional background) may not be able to contribute much to board decision-making, lowering a board's ability to perform its functions effectively (Nielsen and Huse, 2010b). On the other hand, even at higher levels of faultlines formed by these divisions empirically, we may observe positive team outcomes if the lower-status subgroups defers to the higher-status subgroups. Similarly, how subgroup formation interacts with power afforded to a CEO or board chair is also unclear. Future researchers could take these peculiar contextual conditions of corporate boards around the world into consideration to more explicitly understand power dynamics associated with faultlines.

Finally, while much of research has focused on team-level theories to understand faultlines, there are opportunities to consider how team-level dynamics related to faultlines interact with how the board performs its most critical functions (i.e. through committees) (Kolev et al., 2019). This is particularly relevant for board-level research. Boards influence firm-level decision-making by participating in committees such as audit, nomination and remuneration committees. Many corporate governance codes and laws require firms to align board member expertise with their committee assignments (Collier and Zaman, 2005; Defond, Hann, and Hu, 2005). For example, audit committees are required to have members with financial expertise. This implies that boards perform their duties by working in subgroups based at least on some informational attributes. If these informational attributes also align with other characteristics, say, gender (see, for instance, Hillman et al., 2002; Ruigrok et al., 2007 on how female and male directors are likely differ in education and functional backgrounds), the impact of faultlines is less clear. On the one hand, this within-subgroup similarity may allow the board to perform its governance or monitoring duties effectively within committees. On the other hand, it is possible that these entrenched subgroups formed through committee assignments reduce the effectiveness of the board when decisions need to be made at board level, say, linked to resource provision or strategic decision-making. I encourage future researchers to consider this unique context of the board in theory development by bringing together CG work on board committees (Kolev et al., 2019) and team-level faultlines.

Endogenous and Exogenous Factors: Capturing Dynamics of Formation and Management of Faultlines

As the review suggests, CG researchers have attempted to explore the role of endogenous (i.e. individual, board and firm level) and exogenous (i.e. environmental) factors in the formation and management of faultlines-related dynamics. There is scope to draw from recent research to understand the role of these two categories of factors better. For instance, recent research has looked into the consequences of CEO attributes like career variety (Crossland et al., 2014) and career overlaps with the board (Tasheva and Hillman, 2019) for firm and board outcomes. Such attributes may also have implications for faultlines as CEOs with higher variety in their careers in terms of functional backgrounds, international experience, education experience and so on or with larger overlaps on such dimensions with board members across subgroups may be able to manage the impact of faultlines on boards or TMTs. Similarly, individuals other than the CEO, like lead independent directors or board chairs, may also have a role to play in managing subgroups by playing the role of integrators between subgroups. Finally, individuals with cross-cutting attributes (e.g. mixed race, dual citizenship, immigrants) may also be able to act as bridges between subgroups to offset some of the communication and coordination losses stemming from faultlines. So far, no research has looked into the role of such individuals in the context of board and TMT faultlines and it may be instructive to do so.

Given the emphasis placed by Lau and Murnighan (1998) in their seminal work, there is also additional scope to focus on exogenous factors and their influence on faultlines dynamics. One area of interest, particularly for corporate boards and TMTs, is exogenous interventions by regulators and stakeholders acting as faultline triggers. Particularly in light of evidence on corporate resistance to such interventions (Deszo, Ross, and Uribe, 2015; Gregoric et al., 2015), it would be interesting to know if policies like quotas and target-setting to improve representation of minorities on board trigger faultlines within boards/TMTs. If yes, do all boards experience activation of such faultlines or are there certain board-level features that make some boards more attuned to identifying the information variety potential of new entrants vs. social categorization potential? Does this activation also occur when minorities enter boards/TMTs organically without any regulatory or normative pressures? Also, if these policies do act as triggers, are all subgroups impacted equally by them? Board/ TMT member entry and exit is likely to alter team characteristics like size, evenness of subgroups, number of subgroups and power balances, potentially resulting in different faultline strength and compositions. Therefore, future research examining types of entry (involuntary through intervention or voluntary through organic means) and its relationship with faultline activation and management is greatly needed, given the current context of corporate boards. I now turn to missed opportunities on the methodological front.

Empirical Opportunities

There are at least four opportunities on the methodological front. First, with a few exceptions (Li and Jones, 2019; Van Peteghem et al., 2018; Xie et al., 2015), almost all CG research calculates faultlines using a two-subgroup solution. While this is appropriate in specific contexts where there are two pre-existing subgroups with varying motivations and interests like representative TMT of two joint venture teams (Li and Hambrick, 2005b) and alignments of attributes within these two subgroups is relevant, it may not be appropriate in other contexts. Lau and Murnighan's (1998) original work focused on two subgroups because such a team may be associated with particularly strong dynamics. However, for relatively large teams like boards, it is critical to determine the correct number of subgroups where the inter-subgroup differences and intra-subgroup homogeneity is maximized as higher number of sub-groups are likely to reduce the faultline strength and alter dynamics with the board/ TMT (Meyer and Glenz, 2013; Thatcher and Patel, 2011). It can thus be inaccurate to use a faultline measure with a forced restriction of two subgroups where more than two subgroups create stronger alignments. For theoretical reasons, a researcher may choose to retain or remove the boards/TMTs where more than three subgroups form. However, artificially creating only two subgroups may misrepresent and misquantify the split within the board/TMT. Meyer and Glenz (2013) provide an excellent review of all available methods to calculate faultline strength within teams. Future researchers must consider all the alternatives available and use the measure that fits their conceptualization of the faultline and is relevant to the study context, instead of using a forced two subgroup solution, which has been the tendency so far.

Second, changes in population demographic make-up have implications for how quantitative research based on archival data captures characteristics of individuals within boards/TMTs. Thatcher and Patel (2012) refer to attribute alignment clarity as the "extent to which alignment on a particular characteristic is unambiguous" (p. 993). For example, alignment of attributes is clear if the board/TMT has subgroups based on gender and race and all members are either men or women and all belong a single race (i.e. are not mixed race). However, as the demographic composition of population changes because of migration, it may be challenging to assign attributes to individuals unambiguously. Similarly, variety in careers in terms of functional backgrounds, for example, creates challenges for assigning individuals to single categories. Consider individuals who are of mixed race, immigrants, dual citizens and so on. Any categorization by the researcher may alter faultline strength. For example, categorizing a dual citizen of the U.S. and Netherlands as American may create different subgroups and faultline strength than categorizing them as Dutch. Research suggests that depending on the extent to which this individual knows about, identifies with and internalizes more than one national culture, this individual may perceive themselves as American, Dutch or multicultural (Vora et al., 2019). Similarly, board/TMT members with high intrapersonal functional or educational diversity may either identify with their dominant background or intrapersonal variety (Tasheva and Hillman, 2019). How they are categorized by the researchers influences the strength of the faultline and subgroup membership. However, if this categorization is not aligned with what these individuals identify with, calculated faultlines may capture board dynamics inadequately. Future research may consider theoretically and empirically distinguishing between individuals who exhibit high attribute alignment clarity vs. those who do not, instead of artificially assigning categories to them. Moreover, although difficult for researchers (Hambrick, 2007), studies with greater access to boards/TMTs may be able to capture such nuances through use of primary data, as opposed to secondary, archival data.

Third, much of CG research needs to pay attention to correlation between attributes used to create faultlines. The assumption behind faultlines measures is that the attributes used to construct faultlines are independent. However, for boards, this assumption may be violated. For example, women and racial minorities who are recent entrants to boards/TMTs, organizational tenure is likely to be lower than men. This high correlation between gender and tenure implies that the faultlines measure may overestimate the strength of faultlines and their impact on board- and firm-level outcomes. Similarly, many studies use both age and tenure in their measure of faultlines. These two attributes are likely to show high dependence as longer tenures necessitate higher age; however, shorter tenures do not necessitate lower age. Such correlations and interdependencies can be taken into account by using approaches that apply Mahalanobis distance instead of Euclidean distance (Meyer and Glenz, 2013).

Finally, there is scope to expand both attributes considered and empirical settings used in CG research on faultlines. As pointed earlier, following team-level research, almost all studies construct their faultlines measure based on general social category and/or informational attributes like gender, age, tenure, functional background. Moreover, a bulk of the research in the space has focused on developed countries in the Global North. Expanding research to countries outside of these empirical settings opens up a rich avenue of research, particularly in the context of boards and TMTs as corporate governance differs across countries and regions (Oehmichen, 2018). For example, evidence suggests that Asian emerging markets have higher rates of managerial ownership (Rajagopalan and Zhang, 2008) to make up for weak formal institutions (Bertrand et al., 2008). Other types of owners like the state and families are also more prominent in such contexts, and representatives of these owners routinely sit on the boards and TMTs (Witt and Redding, 2014). Faultlines formed on the basis of such board/TMT member associations may impact both monitoring and resource provision abilities of board members, and strategic decision-making discretion of TMT members. Whether faultlines are formed and activated in such contexts, based on which attributes, their triggers, and consequences are all worthwhile questions for CG researchers to examine.

CONCLUSION

In conclusion, faultlines, a team-level construct, is becoming increasingly important to study board and TMT dynamics. This chapter shows that initial progress has been made by CG researchers in terms of examining the consequences of, and dynamics associated with, faultlines within boards and TMTs. Several outcomes at multiple levels of analysis have been examined, and the role of endogenous and exogenous factors in impacting the influence of faultlines has also been acknowledged. Some progress is also being made by recent research in terms of measurement of faultlines. Despite progress made, there are rich avenues of research with questions that still need to be explored, particularly in the context of historically male dominated corporate boards and TMTs whose compositions are changing slowly because of external interventions. Three paths seem particularly relevant and interesting: drawing theoretical insights from sociology and other CG research, analyzing the influence of changing population demographics and introduction of minorities on faultlines formation and associated dynamics, and reconsidering faultlines measures in terms of relevant attributes and number of subgroups. It is surprising that CG researchers have not paid attention to these issues yet, since Lau and Murnighan (1998) discussed issues of power, member entry and exit, and attribute alignment clarity in their seminal theoretical work. I hope that this chapter acts as a launching pad for the next phase of CG research on faultlines.

REFERENCES

Ali M, Ayoko OB. 2020. The impact of board size on board demographic faultlines. *Corporate Governance* 20(7): 1205–22.

Barkema HG, Shvyrkov O. 2007. Does top management team diversity promote or hamper foreign expansion? *Strategic Management Journal* 28(7): 663–80.

Barroso-Castro C, Pérez-Calero L, Vecino-Gravel JD, Villegas-Periñán M del M. 2020. The challenge of board composition: effects of board resource variety and faultlines on the degree of a firm's international activity. *Long Range Planning* (January). https://doi.org/10.1016/j.lrp.2020.102047.

Berger J, Cohen BP, Zelditch Jr. M. 1972. Status characteristics and social interaction. *American Sociological Review* 37(3): 241–55.

Berger J, Ridgeway CL, Fisek MH, Norman RZ. 1998. The legitimation and delegitimation of power and prestige orders. *American Sociological Review* 63(3): 379–405.

Bertrand M, Johnson S, Samphantharak K, Schoar A. 2008. Mixing family with business: a study of Thai business groups and the families behind them. *Journal of Financial Economics* 88(3): 466–98.

Beurden PV, Gossling T. 2008. The worth of values – a literature review on the relation between corporate social and financial performance. *Journal of Business Ethics* 82(407). https://doi.org/10.1007/s10551-008-9894-x.

Brewer MB. 1991. The social self: on being the same and different at the same time. *Personality and Social Psychology Bulletin* 17: 475–82.

Byrne DE. 1971. *The Attraction Paradigm*. Academic Press: San Diego, CA.

Calabrò A, Santulli R, Torchia M, Gallucci C. 2020. Entrepreneurial orientation and family firm performance: the moderating role of TMT identity-based and knowledge-based faultlines. *Entrepreneurship: Theory and Practice*. https://doi.org/10.1177/1042258720973997.

Collier P, Zaman M. 2005. Convergence in European corporate governance: the audit committee concept. *Corporate Governance: An International Review* 13(6): 753–68.

Cooper D, Patel PC, Thatcher SMB. 2014. It depends: environmental context and the effects of faultlines on top management team performance. *Organization Science* 25(2): 633–52.

Crossland C, Hiller NJ, Zyung J, Hambrick DC. 2014. CEO career variety: effects on firm-level strategic and social novelty. *Academy of Management Journal* 57(3): 652–74.

Defond ML, Hann RH, Hu X. 2005. Does the market value financial expertise on audit committees of boards of directors? *Journal of Accounting Research* 43(2): 153–93.

Deszo CL, Ross DG, Uribe J. 2015. Is there an implicit quota on women in top management? A large sample statistical analysis. *Strategic Management Journal* 37: 98–115.

Ferriera D. 2011. Board diversity. In Kent Baker H, Anderson RC (eds), *Corporate Governance: A Synthesis of Theory, Research, and Practice*, 225–42. John Wiley and Sons Ltd: Hobolen, NJ.

Georgakakis D, Greve P, Ruigrok W. 2017. Top management team faultlines and firm performance: examining the CEO-TMT interface. *Leadership Quarterly* 28(6): 741–58.

Gregoric A, Oxelheim L, Randoy T, Thomsen S. 2015. Resistance to change in the corporate elite: female directors' appointments onto Nordic boards. *Journal of Business Ethics* 141: 267–87.

Hambrick DC. 2007. Upper echelons theory: an update. *Academy of Management Review* 32(2): 334–43.

Hillman A. 2015. Board diversity: beginning to unpeel the onion. *Corporate Governance: An International Review* 23(2): 104–7.

Hillman A, Cannella AA, Harris IC. 2002. Women and racial minorities in the boardroom: how do directors differ? *Journal of Management* 28: 747–63.

Hillman A, Dalziel T. 2003. Boards of directors and firm performance: integrating agency and resource dependence perspectives. *Academy of Management Review* 28(3): 383–96.

Hutzschenreuter T, Horstkotte J. 2013. Performance effects of the top management team demographic faultlines in the process of product diversification. *Strategic Management Journal* 34: 704–26.

Johnson JL, Daily CM, Ellstrand AE. 1996. Boards of directors: a review and research agenda. *Journal of Management* 22(3): 409–38.

Johnson SG, Schnatterly K, Hill AD. 2013. Board composition beyond independence: social capital, human capital, and demographics. *Journal of Management* 39(1): 232–62.

Kaczmarek S, Kimino S, Pye A. 2012a. Board task-related faultlines and firm performance: a decade of evidence. *Corporate Governance: An International Review* 20(4): 337–51.

Kaczmarek S, Kimino S, Pye A. 2012b. Antecedents of board composition: the role of nomination committees. *Corporate Governance: An International Review* 20(5): 474–89.

Kirsch A. 2018. The gender composition of corporate boards: a review and research agenda. *Leadership Quarterly* 29(2): 346–64. https://doi.org/10.1016/j.leaqua.2017.06.001.

Knippenberg DV., Dawson JF, West MA, Homan AC. 2011. Diversity faultlines, shared objectives, and top management team performance. *Human Relations* 64(3): 307–36.

Kolev KD, Wangrow DB, Barket III VL, Schepker DJ. 2019. Board committees in corporate governance: a cross-disciplinary review and agenda for the future. *Journal of Management Studies* 56(6): 1138–93.

Lau DC, Murnighan JK. 1998. Demographic diversity and faultlines: the compositional dynamics of organizational groups. *Academy of Management Review* 23(2): 325–40.

Lau DC, Murnighan LK. 2005. Interactions within groups and subgroups: the effects of demographic faultlines. *Academy of Management Journal* 48(4): 645–59.

Li J, Hambrick DC. 2005a. Factional groups: a new vantage on demographic faultlines, conflict, and disintegration in work teams. *Academy of Management Journal* 48: 794–813.

Li J, Hambrick DC. 2005b. Factional groups: a new vantage on demographic faultlines, conflict, and disintegration in work teams. *Academy of Management Journal* 48(5): 794–813.

Li M, Jones CD. 2019. The effects of TMT faultlines and CEO-TMT power disparity on competitive behavior and firm performance. *Group and Organization Management* 44(5): 874–914.

Li M, Liu KC. 2019. Let's explore with a divided team! The effects of top management team demographic faultlines on technological exploration. *Journal of Management and Organization*. https://doi.org/10.1017/jmo.2019.87.

Ma Y, Zhang Q, Yin Q. 2021. Top management team faultlines, green technology innovation and firm financial performance. *Journal of Environmental Management*. https://doi.org/10.1016/j.jenvman.2021.112095.

Magee JC, Galinsky AD. 2008. Social hierarchy: the self-reinforcing nature of power and status. *Academy of Management Annals* 2(1): 351–98.

McDonald ML, Westphal JD. 2013. Access denied: low mentoring of women and minority first-time directors and its negative effects on appointments to additional boards. *Academy of Management Journal* 56(4): 1169–98.

Meyer B, Glenz A. 2013. Team faultline measures: a computational comparison and a new approach to multiple subgroups. *Organization Research Methods* 16(3): 393–424.

Nielsen S, Huse M. 2010a. The contribution of women on boards of directors: going beyond the surface. *Corporate Governance: An International Review* 81(2): 136–48.

Nielsen S, Huse M. 2010b. Women directors' contribution to board decision-making and strategic involvement: the role of equality perception. *European Management Review* 7(1): 16–29.

Oehmichen J. 2018. East meets west—corporate governance in Asian emerging markets: a literature review and research agenda. *International Business Review* 27(2): 465–80.

Ou AY, Seo JJ, Choi D, Hom PW. 2017. When can humble top executives retain middle managers? The moderating role of top management team faultlines. *Academy of Management Journal* 60(5): 1915–31.

Pfeffer J, Salancik G. 1978. *The External Control of Organizations: A Resource Dependence Perspective.* Harper & Row: New York.

Pugliese A et al. 2009. Boards of directors' contribution to strategy: a literature review and research agenda. *Corporate Governance: An International Review* 17(3): 292–306.

Rajagopalan N, Zhang Y. 2008. Corporate governance reforms in China and India: challenges and opportunities. *Business Horizons* 51(1): 55–64.

Richard OC, Wu J, Markoczy LA, Chung Y. 2019. Top management team demographic-faultline strength and strategic change: what role does environmental dynamism play? *Strategic Management Journal* 40(6): 987–1009.

Rindova VP. 1999. What corporate boards have to do with strategy: a cognitive perspective. *Journal of Management Studies* 36(7): 953–75.

Ruigrok W, Peck S, Tacheva S. 2007. Nationality and gender diversity on Swiss corporate boards. *Corporate Governance: An International Review* 15(4): 546–57.

Shaw JS. 2004. The development and analysis of a measure of group faultlines. *Organization Research Methods* 7: 66–100.

Tajfel H. 1981. *Social Identity and Intergroup Relations.* Cambridge University Press: Cambridge, UK.

Tasheva S, Hillman A. 2019. Integrating diversity at different levels: multilevel human capital, social capital, and demographic diversity and their implications for team effectiveness. *Academy of Management Review* 44(4): 746–65.

Terjesen S, Sealy R. 2016. Board gender quotas: exploring ethical tensions from a multi-theoretical perspective. *Business Ethics Quarterly* 26(1): 23–65.

Thatcher SMB, Jehn KA, Zanutto E. 2003. Cracks in diversity research: the effects of diversity faultlines on conflict and performance. *Group Decision and Negotiation* 12: 217–41.

Thatcher SMB, Patel PC. 2011. Demographic faultlines: a meta-analysis of the literature. *Journal of Applied Psychology* 96(6): 1119–39.

Thatcher SMB, Patel PC. 2012. Group faultlines: a review, integration, and guide to future research. *Journal of Management* 38(4): 969–1009.

Tuggle CS, Schnatterly K, Johnson RA. 2010. Attention patterns in the boardroom: how board composition and processes affect discussion of entrepreneurial issues. *Academy of Management Journal* 53(3): 550–71.

Turner JC. 1985. Social categorization and the self-concept: a social cognitive theory of a group. *Advances in Group Processes* 2: 77–121.

Turner JC. 1987. Introducing the problem: individual and group. In Turner JC, Hogg MA, Oakes PJ, Reicher SD (eds.), *Rediscovering the Social Group: A Self-Categorization Theory,* 1–18. Blackwell Publishing: Oxford, UK.

van Ees H, Gabrielson J, Huse M. 2009. Toward a behavioral theory of boards and corporate governance. *Corporate Governance: An International Review* 17(3). https://doi.org/10.1111/j.1467-8683.2009.00741.x.

van Knippenberg D, De Dreu CKW, Homan AC. 2004. Work group diversity and group performance: an integrative model and research agenda. *Journal of Applied Psychology* 89: 1008–22.

van Knippenberg D, van Ginkel WP. 2010. The categorization-elaboration model of work group diversity: wielding the double-edged sword. In Crisp RJ (ed.), *The Psychology of Social and Cultural Diversity*, 255–80. Blackwell Publishing: Chichester, UK.

Van Peteghem M, Bruynseels L, Gaeremynck A. 2018. Beyond diversity: a tale of faultlines and frictions in the board of directors. *Accounting Review* 93(2): 339–67.

Vandebeek A, Voordeckers W, Lambrechts F, Huybrechts J. 2016. Board role performance and faultlines in family firms: the moderating role of formal board evaluation. *Journal of Family Business Strategy* 7(4): 249–59. http://dx.doi.org/10.1016/j.jfbs.2016.10.002.

Veltrop DB, Hermes N, Postma TJBM, de Haan J. 2015. A tale of two factions: why and when factional demographic faultlines hurt board performance. *Corporate Governance: An International Review* 23(2): 145–60.

Vora D et al. 2019. Multiculturalism within individuals: a review, critique, and agenda for future research. *Journal of International Business Studies* 50: 499–524.

Walls J, Berrone P, Phan PH. 2012. Corporate governance and environmental performance: is there really a link? *Strategic Management Journal* 33: 885–913.

Witt M, Redding G (eds). 2014. *The Oxford Handbook of Asian Business Systems*. Oxford University Press: Oxford.

Wu J, Triana M del C, Richard OC, Yu L. 2021. Gender faultline strength on boards of directors and strategic change: the role of environmental conditions. *Group and Organization Management*: 1–38. https://doi.org/10.1177/1059601121992889.

Xie XY, Wang WL, Qi ZJ. 2015. The effects of TMT faultline configuration on a firm's short-term performance and innovation activities. *Journal of Management and Organization* 21(5): 558–72.

Zahra SA, Pearce JA. 1989. Board of directors and corporate financial performance: a review and integrative model. *Journal of Management* 15: 244–91.

14. Diversity, board dynamics and board tasks: an introduction to the theory of proportions

Sara De Masi and Agnieszka Slomka-Golebiowska

What is meant by diversity? The diversity debate has two main dimensions. On the one side, it is about different types of diversity (Tasheva and Hillman, 2019). Diversity might be defined as heterogeneity among group members. It has an infinite number of attributes ranging from age to nationality, from religious background to functional background, from task skills to relational skills and from political preference to sexual preference (Milliken and Martins, 1996; Kang et al. 2007). Most of the contributions in this book are about that. The other dimension of diversity is about a proportion of diversity. This is what our chapter is about.

Using an attribute of the diversity, the proportion identifies two subgroups: a minority and a majority. The importance and novelty of our approach lies in the argument that there is not an optimal proportion of minority subgroup to reach adequate level of diversity in order to improve board dynamics and thus enhance board group decision-making. Thus, we argue that a different proportion between a minority and a dominant subgroup may trigger shifts in board dynamics that affect performance of board tasks. Different proportions are required to utilize various skills, specific knowledge and attitude within a boardroom depending on sets of board task. Board attentiveness and questioning management decisions are needed to perform board monitoring tasks. In order to induce the board to be more attentive, the mere presence of the minority might be sufficient to lead to a change in the behaviour of a dominant subgroup. Put differently, in the case of board strategy tasks, a variety of knowledge and open discussions are needed to achieve these tasks. The board would be more likely to use this variety of knowledge when the proportion between a dominant and a minority subgroup becomes less skewed and more balanced. At this point, a dominant group becomes open to be influenced by the minority and to redefine its own views. This is because, at this point, the dominant group (which is now a majority) is seeing the minority as a legitimized part of the group. We argue that the numerical proportions between a majority and a minority subgroups can be seen as a source of perceived (or given) legitimization. This legitimation is not vested in a single person, but it is vested in a subgroup itself. In the case of the set of advisory tasks, the use of knowledge and skills to perform these tasks depends on the social ties and social recognition that individual board members have. The proportion between a minority and a dominant subgroup within the boardroom might not affect strongly the performance of advisory tasks.

The theory of proportions can be empirically applied to studies on the topic of boards to understand how a proportion of various types of diversity triggers board dynamics and thus enhances board tasks. Our contribution is to show how the theory of proportions helps us to exploit the benefits of diversity. Specifically, we present arguments showing that specific sets of board tasks, or specific board process would require different board dynamics that are triggered by different proportions between a minority and a dominant subgroup. These proportions cannot be taken for granted and applied to every context. We argue that different proportions trigger a shift of board dynamics. Different board dynamics are required to enhance performance of various sets of board tasks. Moreover, the specific proportions which are needed to change the dynamics between a minority and a majority are identified as tipping points. Searching for these tipping points is the challenge for future research.

The chapter is organized in the following sections. First, we discuss board tasks and the different types of knowledge and attitude that each board task requires. We then present the different dynamics that each board task has, followed by a section in which we develop the theory of proportions. Another section applies this to the board context. Finally, we discuss the implications of the theory and offer our conclusions.

BOARD TASKS: DIFFERENT TYPES OF KNOWLEDGE AND DIFFERENT TYPES OF BOARD BEHAVIOUR

Boards are complicated animals, and they perform different sets of tasks. Different states of dynamics are needed to perform different sets of tasks. Scholars have widely discussed these tasks. They have provided several taxonomies and have identified the behaviour-enhancing performance of each board task. Early studies focused on board monitoring tasks (Zahra and Pearce, 1989). This focus on board monitoring tasks evolved during the end of the 1980s and in the 1990s, together with the development of agency theory and the corporate governance concept. More recently, board strategy and advisory tasks have received renewed attention (Machold and Farquhar, 2013; Åberg et al., 2019).

Board tasks are of the varying nature and they require different individual board members' involvement inside and outside of the boardroom, different types of knowledge, skills and different attitudes. Monitoring tasks require individual attentiveness during and outside board meetings. Inside the boardroom, directors are expected to show their attentiveness by expressing their opinions, making comments and questioning management decisions. Board members may also need a specific knowledge and skills to perform certain tasks. Monitoring tasks involves control of budgeting and financial statements, control of the execution of strategies, control of the behaviour of the CEO and top management and oversight of firm engagement towards CSR activities (Huse, Nielsen and Hagen, 2009). Hence, a diverse pool of knowledge is needed to effectively perform these tasks.

Board strategy tasks are related to the discussion about how a firm should compete in the marketplace, which opportunities should be exploited and which threats should be avoided or eventually minimized (McNulty and Pettigrew, 1999; Hendry et al. 2010). The knowledge essential to perform these tasks is difficult to identify a priori. For these tasks, individual board members might not possess all of the relevant knowledge and information needed. Therefore, working as a group has a stronger impact on board task performance than the efforts of individual board members. "Diversity of thought" is vital for performing this set of tasks.

The third set of board tasks refers to advisory tasks. This involves serving as a sounding board for important management decisions as well as providing advice and counselling for top management. The specific knowledge seems to be one of the main conditions needed to fulfil these tasks (Forbes and Milliken, 1999; Hamidi and Machold, 2020). This is because a management team's search for advice usually calls for very specific knowledge with a limited timeframe in which to acquire it. Advisory tasks might not be affected by group-think as much as other board tasks. It requires that an individual board member is considered a valuable asset because she/he has very specific competences and knowledge, although the most important is that her/his position on the board is recognized in this way. Thus, board member reputation matters.

BOARD TASK PERFORMANCE URGED BY BOARD DYNAMICS

Sitting on boards can be incredibly invigorating. It broadens your horizons as you get to meet astute people with diverse experiences and backgrounds that help you grow in capabilities through cooperative behaviour. Therefore, performance of board tasks seems to be driven not only by the variety of board members' knowledge, skills, expertise (Rindova, 1999) and the attitude of board members, but also by the ability of boards to collectively use these individual diverse contributions. "Effective boards might best be described as those that amount to more than a summing of individual contributions and where the dynamic of different people working together in a board-level way genuinely adds value to the organization" (Pye and Pettigrew, 2005, p. S32). In many cases, boards fail to effectively work as they do not tap into the collective board behaviour from diversified competencies, abilities, personal traits and qualities, experiences and professional networks of their individual members (Kaufman and Englander, 2005; Khanna et al., 2014).

Monitoring tasks starts outside of the boardroom. Board members scrutinize carefully all materials handed for the board meetings. Additionally, they find on their own relevant information related to points included in the forthcoming board agenda. They prepare conscientiously for the board meetings, not wishing to be caught out with inaccuracies. During meetings, board members are expected to show their attentiveness by expressing freely their opinions and questioning management decisions. This behaviour may only occur if an individual specific board member feels accepted as a group member. The main challenge comes when boards are dominated by one subgroup that differentiates themselves based on one attribute, often easily observable like gender, age or race (Kanter, 1977; Tajfel and Turner, 1986) or an interaction of multiple attributes (see Chapter 12 in this *Handbook* on faultlines). Individuals favour those who are similar to them (Goodreau, Kitts and Morris, 2009). Such a categorization, or even stereotyping, creates isolation, discomfort and lack of confidence among board members, who are not members of a dominant group. Subgroups that are highly underrepresented may be under constant pressure and maintain a low profile, not raising questions or opinions and not challenging the executives which is a core responsibility within monitoring tasks. Thus, the contribution from a minority subgroup is hindered or not utilized at all (Kanter, 1977; Izraeli, 2000; Huse and Solberg, 2006).

As the proportion of minority representatives increases, pressure from a dominant subgroup begins to lessen. Minority representatives feel more accepted, and they are more inclined to be active during the board meetings. They also are more comfortable asking diligent and interrogative questions of the management team as they tend not to quickly acknowledge information passed to them without reflection. The more represented a minority subgroup is, the more its members view other peers as allies who can support their comments or query decisions made or proposed by management. Therefore, they are more likely to question conventional wisdom, give critical perspectives or challenge managerial proposals or decisions. At this stage, the members of a dominant subgroup tend to alter their board routines and follow the behaviour of a minority subgroup inside the boardroom.

To perform strategy tasks, boards needs to engage in discussions and debates. When a minority subgroup is underrepresented, its members are rather silent and reluctant to voice their opinions. A dominant subgroup is not inclusive and does not take into account issues raised by a minority subgroup. In this case, group thinking dominates. Increasing a proportion of a minority subgroup raises its comfort and confidence. A minority subgroup engages more easily in debates, despite differences in viewpoints, and thus invigorates discussions in the boardroom (Zahra and Pearce, 1989; Burke, 1997). Boards with a greater proportion of a minority representation adopt a broader perspective when making strategic decisions (Miller and Triana, 2009). Board members identify broader alternatives, producing "diversity of thought". They are more prone to generate different viewpoints during strategic decision-making (Golden and Zajac, 2001; Minichilli et al., 2009). Thus, boards become more creative and innovative in designing and preparing strategic issues. The more strongly a minority subgroup feels about their engagement in the board strategic activities, the more they are involved in sequence of activities related to the strategy, starting from the strategy design, its development, and eventually its implementation.

The use of knowledge and skills is especially relevant for advisory tasks (Bankewitz, 2018). In the board setting, one can differentiate between general business knowledge and firm-specific knowledge (Forbes and Milliken, 1999). General business knowledge refers to prior board experience and general executive experience. Board members' specific expertise includes knowledge about firm industry, business model and operations, technology and an understanding of the firm's strengths and weaknesses. Utilization of firm knowledge for board advisory tasks takes the form of individual consultation. Social ties with the executives increases the extent of useful knowledge and skills. Consultation with the individual board member might increase the quality of decisions taken by management (Hillman et al., 2000). Thus, the proportion between a minority and a dominant subgroup in the boardroom does not strongly affect the performance of advisory tasks.

Board tasks, the types of knowledge that are required and the board dynamics needed to effectively perform the tasks are summarized in Table 14.1.

Table 14.1   Tasks, knowledge, dynamics

Board tasks	Where	Type of knowledge	Board dynamics
Monitoring tasks	Inside and outside the boardroom	• Individual attentiveness • Questioning management decisions • Specific knowledge on a specific topic	• Feeling of acceptance in the group • Speaking-up behaviour the behaviour of the minority affects the behaviour of the dominant group
Strategy tasks	Inside the boardroom	• Difficult to identify a priori • Need to share knowledge among board members	• Risk of group-thinking • Minority should have a strong feeling of acceptance and engagement
Advisory tasks	Outside the boardroom	• Very specific knowledge with limited timeframe in which to acquire it	• Individual consultation • Importance of social ties and recognition

DEVELOPMENT OF THE THEORY OF PROPORTIONS

Different proportions between a minority and a dominant subgroup triggers different board dynamics, impacting differently on board performance. Prior scholars have focused on the conditions under which a minority becomes visible and able to impact a dominant subgroup. Their aim was to identify the minimum absolute number of members that forms a minority subgroup that is necessary to make a minority not marginalized, but valued in the board context (Erkut et al., 2008; Konrad et al., 2008; Torchia et al., 2011). Testing the case of having one person, two persons and three persons, previous scholars show that reaching at least three persons within a minority subgroup (called the critical mass) changes the working style of a whole group, making the minority more comfortable, reducing the sense of isolation within a group. The main findings of those studies are that reaching the critical mass of three people of a socially distinct identity is necessary to give voice to a minority in the boardroom and hence, to have its contribution impactful. Although, on the one hand, the critical mass can be particularly beneficial for creating behavioural change, on the other hand this absolute number of at least three members of a minority might not universally explain every shift in the interactions between a minority and a dominant subgroup. We argue that specific sets of board tasks, or specific board process, would require different states of board dynamics that are triggered not by the absolute number of a minority, but by various proportions between a minority and a dominant subgroup – what we refer to as tipping points. When a tipping point is reached, the minority can affect the dynamics of the group, its culture and its behaviour. Not only does the minority group begin to become individually differentiated, but its presence also changes the behaviour of a dominant subgroup. Searching for these tipping points is a challenge for future research. We argue that not a single tipping point can be universally applied to shift board dynamics and consequently enhance the performance of all board tasks. Different tipping points are required to utilize various skills, specific knowledge and attitudes within the boardroom, depending on the particular set of board tasks.

Our attempt to develop the theory of proportions builds on the seminal work of Rosabeth M. Kanter (1977). She looks at the effects of a dominant subgroup on a minority subgroup. In her arguments, the main focus is on the proportions between a minority and a dominant subgroup rather than the absolute number of the minority. She argues that the relative numbers (called the proportional representation) of socially and culturally different people in a group shape the group interactions. Using the case of women in the upper levels of organizations, she discusses how the relative numbers interfere with how men or women can usually behave. She proposes four different groups according to the different proportional representations between a minority and a dominant subgroup. First, uniform group – 100:0 – has only one kind of person, one significant social type. The second group is skewed and is formed when the proportion falls to 85:15. It means that a minority might reach up to 15 per cent (called tokens); however, a numerical dominant social type still controls the whole group and its culture. Next, there is a tilted group with proportions of 65:35,which is moving towards a less extreme distribution. Finally, at about 60:40 and down to 50:50, is the balanced group where a majority and a minority subgroup might not generate actual type-based identifications.

This theory suggests that the benefits (or the costs) of the diversity might give different results according to the proportions between a minority and a dominant group. Kanter (1977) predicts that any minority group should start to be visible somewhere in the tilted group as tokenism disappears and minority members can ally to influence the group's culture. She neither empirically tests her theory nor gives any precision about the exact proportional representation for various group settings. The groups identified by Kanter, based on the certain ranges of proportions, cannot be applied to every context. We argue for certain tipping points that are triggers for board dynamic shifts required to perform specific sets of board tasks. Various sets of board tasks require different board dynamics.

APPLICATION: PROPORTIONS CANNOT BE TAKEN FOR GRANTED

To clarify our arguments on the power of the proportions, we will here use the case of women on boards. The debates about women on boards are not the latest, but still due to the very slow pace of change on boards it is necessary to collect empirical evidence to strengthen the rationales for gender diversity on boards. Women board members have been considered a minority in the context of boards as their numerical representation has always been quite limited. The introduction of gender board quota laws in many countries has forced an increase in the numerical representation of women, creating different proportions between men and women in the boardroom. In this section we discuss how the theory of proportions might change board dynamics of each board task using the case of women on boards.

As discussed in the previous sections, monitoring tasks require attentiveness during and outside board meetings. In the case of a homogenous group, group-thinking and social loafing behaviour would be very likely to occur. Gender diversity might be needed to induce the group to be more attentive. Some scholars have found that the mere presence of a woman on boards changes the behaviour of men (Huse and Solberg, 2006; Adams and Ferreira, 2009). Other studies show that women on boards are more motivated to fulfil their board duties than men (Konrad et al., 2008) and they tend to ask questions (Bilimoria and Huse, 1997; Bilimoria and Wheeler, 2000). This behaviour induces men to change their attitude and being more committment to accomplish their board's duties. Hence, in order to trigger a change, the mere presence of the minority would be sufficient to lead to a change in the behaviour of a dominant group.

Strategy tasks require that the board has a pool of different knowledge and multiple opinions that can provide different perspectives. The presence of a variety of knowledge and the use of such knowledge is the key to effectively perform-ing strategy tasks. Research documents (Post and Byron, 2015; De Masi et al., 2021) that women directors are more likely to have a non-executive experience or non-business-related background. This diversity in terms of experience and back-ground can potentially produce alternative perspectives on strategic issues, leading to more options and better decisions. This diversity of alternatives and perspectives should not be obscured by group thinking. In order to have the men on boards be able to use the knowledge and opinions coming from the minority (women on boards), the proportion between men and the women should become less skewed and more balanced. With this new proportion, the dominant group (identified in the subgroup of male directors) moves from being dominant to a majority. At this point, male directors start to consider women directors as a valuable asset for board activities and board decisions. The different (and eventually opposite) points of views brought by women are taken seriously from the men on the board. In other words, at this point, the majority (of male directors) is open to be influenced by the minority (of women directors) and to redefine its own views, using the knowledge and the opinions coming from the minority. As a result, the women's view might be adopted by the men or eventually it might be used to modify, or integrate with, the men's opinion. This is because at this point, women on boards gain legitimization and their view is recognized as legitimate. The numerical proportions between the men and women on the board can be seen as a source of perceived (or given) legitimization. This legitimation is not vested in a single person, but it is vested in the minority as a group.

In the case of board advisory tasks, which deals with providing advice and coun-selling for top management, the proportions between men and women on boards might be not as relevant as in the case of monitoring and strategy tasks. Usually, top management search for advice, asking board members with not only very specific business knowledge, but also those that are highly recognized and with high esteem. These attributes might not be earned through the proportion between men and women on boards. Moreover, usually this advice is sought without waiting for a board meeting but rather taking an initiative outside the boardroom. For this reason, board advisory tasks might not require group efforts as it is in case of board monitoring and board strategy tasks. Women are not very likely to belong to the well-established business networks. They might be perceived as an outsider or as having less specific business expertise and experience (Huse et al., 2009; Bøhren and Staubo, 2016; Gabaldon et al., 2018). Thus, they are not likely to be asked for advice from manage-ment on an individual basis.

DISCUSSION

The theory of proportions applied to the board context suggests important reflec-tions. Firstly, the corporate governance literature about board diversity has focused mainly on the presence of a single attribute among directors, showing the positive (or negative) consequences of having directors with this specific attribute. In our chapter, we argue that the benefits of the diversity depends not on the presence of this specific attribute, but on the proportion between the two subgroups that this single attribute might form. Different proportions create different board dynamics which can lead to different board outcomes. We want to move forward the discussion about the benefits of the diversity, stepping back from the idea that *one size fits all*. We provide arguments that each board task requires different dynamics that are trigged by a specific proportion between a minority and a majority subgroup. To effectively perform monitoring tasks, it is enough to reach a proportion between minority and a majority subgroup which makes the minority representatives less isolated and more inclined to speak-up during meetings. In the case of strategy tasks, not only should the minority feel free to voice its opinions, but the majority should be able to hear these different opinions. This would be possible when the proportion between men and the women becomes less skewed and more balanced. In the case of advisory tasks, the proportion between the majority and the minority might be not so rele-vant (Slomka-Golebiowska et al., 2022). These findings should be considered by policy-makers around the world. Many governments have implemented gender quota laws, identifying different thresholds of women directors that a board should meet. Our chapter suggests that identifying the specific proportion between women and men within the board depends on which board tasks should be improved. Secondly, the theory of proportions can be applied to other types of diversity, generalizing beyond men and women on boards, and apply it to other types of diversity. As we discussed at the beginning of this chapter, diversity is defined considering visible or not observable attributes among members. These attributes might create two subgroups within boards. Hence, other proportions, based on other types of diversity, might be present. For example, having specific experience (i.e. financial experience, legal experience and so on) or not might create two subgroups, because it might group two different social types. How specific background or experience might change the dynamics of each board task is a challenge for future research. Board activities require interactions among the two subgroups. Different types of board member diversity may facilitate or make more difficult such interactions, affecting the board's capacity to work as a cohesive group. Given that boards are rather small, prestigious groups with social structures subject to political, cognitive, power and personal dynamics, the effects of board dynamics, driven by changes in proportions, on board tasks can be stronger than in other socially diversified groups. Furthermore, an individual board member may be member of more than one subgroup. Depending on the firm or board settings, certain attributes might be stronger. In technological firms that are growing very quickly, the age of board members might be a stronger attribute than gender to form two subgroups. Thus, subgroups are not always permanent. The diversity of proportion impacts which types of diversity shape to the largest extent the state of board dynamics that affect board task performance.

Thirdly, in analysing the benefits (or the costs) of diversity, research should consider the proportion between a minority and a majority subgroup that a specific attribute creates, looking at different outcomes and different contexts. In our chapter, we focus on a board of directors and on specific sets of board tasks. Future research might consider other tasks or other decisions that a board takes on, such as risk appetite or CSR decisions. Moreover, corporate boards are elite groups and they might work similarly as other decision-making groups. For example, the current discussion about a better balanced proportion between women and men in academia or in politics might bring interesting contexts to test the theory of proportions.

CONCLUSIONS

We have, in this chapter, theoretically and practically contributed to show how proportion is an important dimension of diversity. The theory of proportions has been developed in the board context. We have shown that each set of board tasks requires different dynamics. Specific states of board dynamics are trigged by a specific proportion between a minority and a majority subgroup. The specific proportions which are needed to change the dynamics between a minority and a majority subgroup are identified as tipping points. Each board task, and probably each board process, requires different tipping points. Boards experience considerable contextual differences. However, all boards are obliged to perform the same tasks. Their performance will be driven not just by different types of diversity attribute but also by the different proportions of those subgroups created, based on those attributes. This expands our understating about the rationale and benefits of diversity on boards.

REFERENCES

Åberg, C., Bankewitz, M., Knockaert, M. (2019). Service tasks of board of directors: a literature review and research agenda in an era of new governance practices. *European Management Journal*, 37(5), 648–63.

Adams, R. B., Ferreira, D. (2009). Women in the boardroom and their impact on governance and performance. *Journal of Financial Economics*, 94(2), 291–309.

Bankewitz, M. (2018). Board advisory tasks: the importance to differentiate between functional and firm-specific advice. *European Management Review*, 15(4), 521–39.

Bilimoria, D., Huse, M. (1997). A qualitative comparison of the boardroom experiences of U.S. and Norwegian women corporate directors. *International Review of Women and Leadership*, 3(2), 63–73.

Bilimoria, D., Wheeler, J. (2000). Women corporate directors: current research and future directions, in M. J. Davidson and R. J. Burke (Eds.), *Women in Management: Current Research Issues, Volume II*. London: Chapman.

Bøhren, Ø., Staubo, S. (2016). Mandatory gender balance and board independence. *European Financial Management*, 22, 3–30.

Burke, R. (1997). Women directors: selection, acceptance and benefits for board membership. *Corporate Governance: An International Review*, 5, 118–25.

De Masi, S., Słomka-Gołębiowska, A., Paci, A. (2021). Women on boards and monitoring tasks: an empirical application of Kanter's theory. *Management Decision*, 59(13), 56–72.

Erkut, S., Kramer, V. W., Konrad, A. M. (2008). Critical mass: does the number of women on a corporate board make a difference? In S. Vinnicombe & M. Singh (Eds.), *Women on Corporate Boards of Directors: International Research and Practice* (pp. 222–32). Cheltenham, UK and Northampton, MA, USA: Edward Elgar Publishing.

Forbes, D. P., Milliken, F. J. (1999). Cognition and corporate governance: understanding boards of directors as strategic decision-making groups. *Academy of Management Review*, 24(3), 489–505.

Gabaldon, P., Kanadlı, S. B., Bankewitz, M. (2018). How does job-related diversity affect boards' strategic participation? An information-processing approach. *Long Range Planning*, 51(6), 937–52.

Golden, B., Zajac, E. (2001). When will boards influence strategy? Inclination x power = strategic change. *Strategic Management Journal*, 22(12), 1087–111.

Goodreau, S. M., Kitts, J. A., Morris, M. (2009). Birds of a feather, or friend of a friend? Using exponential random graph models to investigate adolescent social networks. *Demography*, 46(1), 103–25.

Hamidi, D., Machold, S. (2020) Governance, boards and value co-creation: changing perspectives towards a service dominant logic. *European Management Journal*, 6, 956–66.

Hendry, K., Kiel, G., Nicholson G. (2010). How boards strategise: a strategy as practice view. *Long Range Planning*, 43, 33–56.

Hillman, A. J., Cannella, A. A., Paetzold, R. (2000). The resource dependence role of corporate directors: adaptation of board composition in response to environmental change. *Journal of Management Studies*, 37(2), 235–55.

Huse, M., Nielsen, S. T., Hagen, I. M. (2009). Women and employee-elected board members, and their contributions to board control tasks. *Journal of Business Ethics*, 89, 581–97.

Huse, M., Solberg, G. A. (2006). Gender-related boardroom dynamics: how Scandinavian women make and can make contributions on corporate boards. *Women in Management Review*, 21(2), 113–30.

Izraeli, D. (2000). Women directors in Israel, in R. Burke and M. Mattis (Eds.), *Women on Corporate Boards of Directors: International Challenges and Opportunities* (pp. 75–96), Dordrecht: Kluwer.

Kang, H., Cheng, M., Gray, S. J. (2007). Corporate governance and board composition: diversity and independence of Australian boards. *Corporate Governance: An International Review*, 15, 194–207.

Kanter, R. (1977). *Men and Women of the Corporation*. New York: Basic Books.

Kaufman, A., Englander, E. (2005). A team production model of corporate governance. *Academy of Management Perspectives*, 19, 9–22.

Khanna, P., Jones, C., Boivie, S. (2014). Director human capital, information processing demands, and board effectiveness. *Journal of Management*, 40(2), 577–85.

Konrad, A. M., Kramer, V., Erkut, S. (2008). Critical mass: the impact of three or more women on corporate boards. *Organizational Dynamics*, 37(2), 145–64.

Machold, S., Farquhar, S. (2013). Board task evolution: a longitudinal field study in the UK. *Corporate Governance: An International Review*, 2, 147–64.

McNulty, T., Pettigrew, A. (1999). Strategists on the board. *Organization Studies*, 20(1), 47–74.

Miller, T., Triana, M. (2009). Demographic diversity in the boardroom: mediators of the board diversity–firm performance relationship. *Journal of Management Studies*, 46, 755–86.

Milliken, F. J., Martins, L. L. (1996). Searching for common threads: understanding the multiple effects of diversity in organizational groups. *Academy of Management Review*, 21, 402–33.

Minichilli, A., Zattoni, A., Zona, F. (2009). Making boards effective: an empirical examination of board task performance. *British Journal of Management*, 20(1), 55–74.

Post, C., Byron, K. (2015). Women on boards and firm financial performance: a meta-analysis. *Academy of Management Journal*, 58, 1546–71.

Pye, A., Pettigrew, A. (2005), Studying board context, process and dynamics: some challenges for the future. *British Journal of Management*, 16, S27–S38.

Rindova, V. P. (1999), What corporate boards have to do with strategy: a cognitive perspective. *Journal of Management Studies*, 36, 953–75.

Slomka-Golebiowska, A., De Masi, S., Paci, P. (2022). Board dynamics and board tasks empowered by women on boards: evidence from Italy. *Management Research Review*, forthcoming.

Tajfel, H., Turner, J. C. (1986). The social identity theory of intergroup behaviour, in W. G. Worchel and S. Austin (Eds.), *Psychology of Intergroup Relations* (pp. 7–24), Chicago, IL: Nelson-Hall.

Tasheva, S., Hillman, A. (2019). Integrating diversity at different levels: multilevel human capital, social capital, and demographic diversity and their implications for team effectiveness. *Academy of Management Review*, 44, 746–65.

Torchia, M., Calabrò, A., Huse, M. (2011). Women directors on corporate boards: from tokenism to critical mass. *Journal of Business Ethics*, 102(2), 299–317.

Zahra, S. A., Pearce, J. A. (1989). Boards of directors and corporate financial performance: a review and integrative model. *Journal of Management*, 15(2), 291–334.

PART V

CONSEQUENCES FOR RESEARCH AND PRACTICE

15. Different contexts matter on different levels: plea for a deeper understanding of (responding to) (board) diversity

Andrea D. Bührmann and Katrin Hansen

Research on diversity and diversity management began its journey nearly 50 years ago in the United States. Since then, it has travelled throughout the world, shifting its focus according to workforce diversity and board diversity, business chances, societal climate, political goals and scholarly interests. Thus, research on diversity and diversity management has been diverse in itself.

Nevertheless, most studies are centred on one isolated research level (see Danowitz, 2015). This is even sometimes the case for studies on board diversity. They concentrate on boards and therefore run the risk of abstracting from other relevant contexts. Consequently, those studies fail to reflect diversity management types and their effects in a comprehensive way. To avoid this danger and to improve our understanding of board diversity as well as diversity management and its processes, we propose a more complex research design: namely a multi-level approach. This can contribute to broadening and deepening research on diversity and its management, and especially board diversity and its impact on actual and perceived human capital. Diversity in the context of boards has gained attention in research in recent years. Discussions around this subject are often driven by political programmes, such as soft and strict quota laws in the European Union (EU). This research field has produced mixed results (see Veltrop et al., 2021). Therefore, we consider a more general examination of diversity research to be important for discourses in corporate governance, as well as fruitful.

Firstly, we introduce different forms of diversity and how they interact. Secondly, we consider an intersectional framework for multi-level research on diversity management. Thirdly, we explicate these considerations based on different types of diversity management against the background of board diversity. Finally, we draw a conclusion and discuss some further research perspectives. Our starting point is the reflexive diversity research programme (Bührmann, 2021).

REFLEXIVE DIVERSITY RESEARCH

Reflexive diversity research takes up central findings of so-called positivist-functionalist and critical-emancipatory diversity research and enhances them in a constructive way. In the following, we will illustrate this using the example of research on board diversity and its impact of actual and perceived (human capital) diversity on boards.

On the one hand, positivist-functionalist diversity research mainly focuses on the economic usefulness of diversity management concepts. Businesses and entrepreneurial utility calculations are at the heart of this kind of research. Studies try to evaluate the consequences of diversity management concepts, for example comparing the number of women with entrepreneurial performance. Most studies do not relate these numbers to other metrics of workforce diversity. Moreover, they do not consider the intersectional relation of gender for example to other relevant dimensions of diversity.[1] In contrast, studies oriented towards critical-emancipatory diversity research question such a focus and study not only companies, but also other types of organizations in their social structural surroundings. These studies scrutinize the social consequences of diversity management concepts for individuals and in social developments. Thus, they often take a multi-level perspective.

Several studies show that board members "normally" have a white middle-class background. However, because of (social-)theoretical considerations, critical-emancipatory diversity research itself postulates specific categories (e.g. race, class and gender), and the different arrangements related to them, to be particularly relevant – if perhaps not always present.

Others propose to de-centre this triad of race, class and gender, beginning instead by asking which dimensions of diversity are made relevant in which context and by means of which power relations. Reflexive diversity research takes up this idea. It uses the two research programmes in order to shed light on their blind spots and sets out to transform the oppositions between the two research programmes in a dialectical perspective. In so doing, reflexive diversity research neither ontologically assumes a positively given diversity or normality, nor does it limit itself to de- or re-constructing the processes through which diversity and its dimensions (and their manifestations) are constructed. Thematically, it studies not only the ways in which diversity management or diversity policy concepts work, how they are implemented and what effects they have. In fact, it regards these explicit ways of responding to diversity as forms of social differentiation and asks why diversity is responded to at different levels. In addition, the different ways in which differentiations materialize and become institutionalized or organized are analysed in a multi-level perspective. Ultimately, reflexive diversity research concerns the intended and unintended effects of its own studies. Along with a 'second wave of critique' (Metcalfe and Woodhams, 2012, p. 78), reflexive diversity research calls for more 'performative critical diversity studies' (Zanoni et al., 2010, p. 19). These should theorize research itself as performative practice. Thus, reflexive diversity research turns into a subject of research itself. Therefore, it asks not only *what* is researched, but also *how* research is conducted, by whom, and what its consequences are. Based on this, part of reflexive diversity research design is to engage with three questions: (1) who is conducting research, what is their situation/position in the innovation system and what is their research philosophy?[2] (2) Which methodologies or methods for generating and analysing data are used and why, and what are their limitations? (3) What are the criteria of 'good' research regarding reliability and validity?

Reflexive diversity research aims to inquire into the practices of problematizing diversity and the empirical practices of diversity work. Its objective is to research the processes of constructing, de-constructing and re-constructing social practices of differentiation and their consequences. Consequently, reflexive diversity research is not content with merely pointing out the contingency of societal relationships and self-relations, but also seeks to challenge supposed certainties and/or document existing social critiques. Based on these considerations, reflexive diversity research tends to provide an epistemological as well as methodological framework for researching diversity, its dimensions and their specifications.

However, it does not presume that differences, and by extension diversity, are given and need "only" be discovered using certain scientific methods. Neither does it presume certain differences or commonalities to be "relevant", "given" or "necessary". Instead, differences – and thus, possibly the phenomenon of diversity itself – are assumed to be something that emerges primarily from an interplay of different practices and elements. However, these construction processes may have real (i.e. effective) consequences. They can, but do not necessarily, materialize in one way or another.

Following these considerations, diversity is a phenomenon brought about by different practices, which may or may not materialize. Therefore, the question is no longer which notion of diversity is "accurate", which dimensions are "relevant" and which of their materializations appear "suitable", or, of course, whether "all" diversity dimensions have been considered. Rather, the question is why diversity strategies have been implemented, and according to which criteria they are constructed. This also means that power relations become relevant. For this perspective we must also ask who has the power to make which concept of diversity emerge, and who governs the criteria relevant to its conception, implementation and processing. Therefore, the interplay between board diversity, workforce diversity and contexts that matter are of great interest.

DIFFERENT FORMS OF DIVERSITY AND THEIR INTERACTIONS

In this article we use a broad concept of diversity following Thomas, who described diversity as '*any* mixture of items characterized by differences and similarities' found within the workforce (Thomas, 1996, p. 5). This opens up discourse not only for group characteristics or demographic specifics, but also for further dimensions of diversity which might be highly relevant in the context of the workforce as well as in a board context. Such dimensions could include different 'KSAOs' (knowledge, skills, abilities and other characteristics, see Ployhart and Moliterno, 2011), such as managerial experiences and competences or board members' capabilities (see Klarner et al., 2021), attitudes towards learning, work and performance, leadership styles, habits, values and so on.

We use this broad conceptualization of diversity as a starting point to unravel a more complex understanding of diversity and responses to diversity on boards and in their various organizational environments on different levels. According to reflexive diversity research we conceptualize diversity as a social construct. Our presumption is that dimensions of diversity and their configurations are historically contingent. Therefore, contexts matter.

The relevance of a unit's diversity and the salience of various kinds of differences depend on the specific combination of differences and similarities in a situation, on the more immediate situational context, and on the broader organizational context. It is connected to societally installed arrangements such as gender arrangements, migration regimes and class orders. Thus, differences and similarities are not primarily connected with individuals but rather 'unit-level constructs' (Harrison and Klein, 2007). In particular, Harrison and Klein distinguish three different forms of diversity: separation, variety and disparity.

- *Separation* refers to the horizontal distance between positions, opinions, attitudes and values. Opposition, spatial distance and language barriers are also related to separation. Separation bears risks for group cohesion and group performance as it hinders close collaboration.
- *Variety* as category of difference concerns types of and access to information, knowledge, experiences and functional, educational and experiential background. The hopes for positive effects of a diverse workforce (e.g. creativity and improved quality of solutions) (see Cox and Blake, 1991), are based on the existence of variety in a team. On boards, different perspectives of internal and external (part-time) directors (see Veltrop et al., 2021) and experiences in corporate governance and management, capabilities such as organizing expertise, building relationships, assessing strategic activities and allocating resources (see Klarner et al., 2021) and collaboration in general are central to the variety category. However, conflicts may emerge related to the variety form of diversity as is well-known from interdisciplinary teamwork and, as most recently discussed, concerning board dynamics when outside directors are involved (Veltrop et al., 2021). And precisely this process of understanding and solving conflicts, of making fruitful use of constructive disagreement, should be recognized and valued as a source of positive effects (see Cox and Blake, 1991; Veltrop et al., 2021).
- *Disparity* refers to vertical differences in ownership of and access to valuable goods, resources and assets, in voice given and listened to. Income, status, prestige and influence are covered within this third category. In research on diversity and in diversity management (DiM) practice, social arrangements are identified as sources of disparity; the corresponding discourses focus on societal minorities and gender (see e.g. Hansen, 2021; Hansen and Seierstad, 2017; Machold et al., 2013; Nielsen and Huse, 2010). Cognitive conflicts among CEO, internal and external board members might capsize into dysfunctional board dynamics as Veltrop et al. show: '... board members visibly withdrew from the conversation, criticized each other, talked over each other, and did not engage with or seek

any further information from the CEO' (2021, pp. 211ff.). In practice, these three kinds of difference are often intertwined. Relations and interdependencies between diversity features should be acknowledged in order to respond to diversity in a goal-oriented manner (Harrison and Klein, 2007).

Research on diversity in general and on diverse boards brought up mixed results, up to the point that diversity of skills and divergent ideas might 'yield a board dynamic that may more easily spiral into dysfunction' (Veltrop et al., 2021, p. 225). Even when an organization is engaging in strategic DiM unfolding a variety of practices, we have to consider unintended consequences of diversity initiatives (Leslie, 2019).

A FRAMEWORK FOR AN INTERSECTIONAL APPROACH TO MULTI-LEVEL RESEARCH

To fully capture the phenomenon of diversity in complex social systems (such as corporations, boards, top-management teams) and to identify effective and sustainable ways of responding to it, we suggest an intersectional approach of conceptualising diversity in a multi-level model (Hansen, 2014; Hansen and Seierstad, 2017). The background to the proposal of a multi-level model is constituted by some models first discussed at different Academy of Management conferences (Ployhart and Moliterno, 2011; Devinney, 2013; Stahl and Sully de Luque, 2014).[3] The model utilized here is composed of three main levels, each containing two sub-levels.

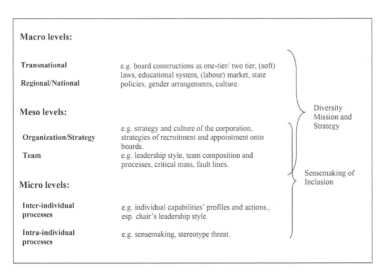

Source: Based on Hansen, 2014; Hansen and Seierstad, 2017, modified.

Figure 15.1   Diversity in a multi-level model

As can be seen in Figure 15.1, we argue that it is highly important to capture processes on different levels and especially their interplay. Devinney (2013) also hints at this as he argues that '… we can now begin asking very interesting and important questions about what goes on between and across the levels of analysis' (p. 82). This includes the combination of theories which focus on different, specific levels, such as socio-economic developments, political or economic policies, strategic management, leadership theories, and theories from corporate governance, human resource management, organizational behaviour and psychology.

It is evident that an organization's diversity strategy and mission connect macro and meso levels as a combination of "outside-in" arguments (e.g. laws, market demands, pressure from EU regulations) and "inside-out" considerations (strengths and weaknesses). Inclusion, on the other hand, links meso levels (strategies, structures, culture, team processes) with micro levels of individuals' behaviour and their sense-making related to diversity. At the same time, inclusion takes place in the context of societal developments: which aspects of diversity are seen as relevant or even dangerous depends on specific societal patterns, such as gender arrangements, migration regimes or class orders. The diversity strategy's foundations at the individual level and its effects on the individual level should be considered "micro-foundations".

In such a model, we can locate and link phenomena of diversity and its different forms and design DiM initiatives. Furthermore, we can analyse and much better understand why DiM programmes in organizations sometimes fail (Dobbin and Kalev, 2016). Unintended effects of deliberate and in themselves reasonable diversity initiatives constitute an important issue here: diversity practices themselves might generate distal effects beyond desired results such as increased representation and inclusion of targets and decreased career gaps between members of minorities and dominant groups (Leslie, 2019).

Leslie distinguishes three categories of diversity practices which might yield unintended consequences. Either as single initiative or in combination, non-discrimination practices, resource practices and accountability practices produce important, more or less strong signals of '… what the organization is like …' (Leslie, 2019, p. 6). Individuals then interpret and react to those signals. Leslie (2019, p. 6) identifies four categories of unintended consequences:

- Negative spillover, such as decreased non-target engagement,
- Backfire, such as negative diversity goal progress,
- False progress, such as improved diversity metrics without true change,
- Positive spillover, such as increased non-target engagement and ethical behaviour.

Integrating that aspect into our multi-level model, we position these initiatives on the meso level. We then look for reactions on the micro level which might create an impact on the micro level itself (increased or decreased engagement of non-target individuals, ethical behaviour), but also back up on the meso level (diversity metrics, backfire). Furthermore, Leslie inspires us to ask questions concerning signals sent to the macro level. Organizational diversity initiatives might signal a need for increased or decreased engagement of external actors (politicians, business leaders, non-governmental organizations (NGOs), etc.). These signals are registered by individuals outside the organization (micro level of other organizations) and transferred to the macro level, where they stimulate programmes, laws, and public/regional diversity initiatives. These programmes, laws and so on then return as signals to the organization's meso level.

ORGANIZATIONAL RESPONSES TO DIVERSITY

In the following section we set out to show how different types of diversity could develop in different DiM strategies on different levels. We use the approaches to DiM developed by Ely and Thomas as a widely discussed background.

Ely and Thomas (1996, 2001) highlight three different paradigms. The paradigms affect how people function in groups within the organizations as well as how likely the groups are to acknowledge the benefit of their diversity. The paradigms identified by Thomas and Ely for companies are:

- The 'Discrimination & Fairness Approach' (D&F),
- The 'Access & Legitimacy Approach' (A&L), and
- The 'Learning & Effectiveness Approach' (L&E as emerging paradigm) (Ely and Thomas, 1996).

We will present the characteristics of the three perspectives below and discuss them (see also Hansen and Seierstad, 2017; Aretz and Hansen, 2002; Bührmann, 2015; Hansen, 2014) from the perspective of business, board governance and education.[4] Obviously, our multi-level approach leads to a deeper understanding of how these paradigms really work.

Discrimination and Fairness (D&F)

The D&F paradigm is regularly initiated by board members. It is characterized by efforts to comply with legal requirements and societal demands based on ethical or strategic considerations. The D&F perspective is often based on the premise that a diverse workforce is a moral imperative to ensure fair treatment. Areas of possible discrimination are identified and named, and conflict resolution takes place. Historically discriminated groups – which are usually called minorities – are represented to a 'politically correct' quota or target and presented, but not really integrated or fully included. The phenomenon of 'glass ceiling' (Morrison et al., 1987) – especially as regards becoming a board member – is a potential consequence. Moreover, from the D&F perspective, there is often strong pressure on minorities to assimilate. Observed or assumed differences are conceptualized as disparity: majorities represent embraced normality, minorities represent tolerated deviations.

The D&F perspective can help to understand the 'glass cliff' (Ryan and Haslam, 2007) phenomenon. Glass cliffs are challenging positions which seem attractive, but are in fact extremely risky. These precarious leadership positions on boards are often offered to women. This is evident in the study of Ryan and Haslam (2007) who found: 'At the same time, by appearing to support women but actually giving them inferior positions with limited opportunities for development, those in power can deny charges of overt discrimination while ensuring that any change does not dramatically challenge the gender-based status hierarchy or rock the organizational boat too hard' (p. 558).

Organizations that build their DiM on the D&F perspective often do not really open up to new perspectives and might lose high potential from minorities who sooner or later experience that they have little chance of performance in the respective firms. Nevertheless, there are positive effects to be found in organizations adopting DiM initiatives from the D&F perspective. This includes developing specific programmes, securing appropriate communication and providing positions for minorities (to the quota/target level). Many scholars see D&F as a (first) step towards responding to diversity – understood as variety – in an inclusive way, but it does not create cultural changes. Diversity is not anchored as important in the organization, and there is often only little internal or strategic consistence. DiM has not become part of the hegemonic culture. Differences in power among the actors involved and the 'colour-blind ideology' (Ely and Thomas, 2001, p. 256) send ambiguous signals to minorities: on the one hand, belonging to a minority is portrayed as non-problematic; on the other hand, assimilation is demanded in a more or less subtle manner.

D&F activities are mostly triggered by signals or pressures from the macro level such as strong and soft laws, mainly directed towards certain dimensions of diversity such as gender, (dis-)ability or ethnic background. Units in charge are usually equal-opportunity officers or ombudspersons. Activities mainly focus on the minority individuals in order to support them in resolving challenges and to repair deficits. This follows a logic of normalization according to the model provided by members of the majority (e.g. providing institutional possibilities for child care during hours of late shifts). Existing institutional rules, processes and culture are questioned neither on the strategic level nor on the team level.

Access and Legitimacy (A&L)

The A&L perspective is often driven by a more market-oriented logic, notably competition in key markets, be it on the sales or supply side. The leading principle is to open relevant markets and to secure market shares by using similarities between customers and workforce in product development and marketing. Such strategies follow the expectation that a "fit" enables the organization to generate fruitful ideas and strategies and thereby increase market shares. The business case for diversity is clearly established within this perspective (Ely and Thomas, 2001, p. 243). Social proximity is seen as a competitive advantage on the micro level throughout interpersonal interactions between personnel and customers/suppliers/sub-contractors (e.g. cultural rapport). It is intended to strengthen the firm's – and, by extension, the board's – basis of legitimacy by mirroring the diversity of society in the organization. However, we have to critically question whether it is really society the organization seeks to mirror, or rather target groups with relevance to competition on markets.

Thus, a problematic aspect of this paradigm is its invitation to stereotyping: co-workers are often reduced to their affiliation with a certain social (minority) group and confronted with stereotype threats (Roberson and Kulik, 2007). Specific behaviours and attitudes are expected or even requested because the specific value of these co-workers is anchored in their group affiliation. It is often observed that minorities are not viewed as individuals or are not fully included, but rather functionalized regarding stereotypes they are linked with. Meanwhile, they are found to be made responsible for customer satisfaction in the respective segment or for other positive effects inside the organization. How they deal with this is left to the individual.

Nevertheless, we would be remiss not to identify positive aspects of the A&L perspective. It is often the case that minorities are given access to a considerable number of attractive positions building on the logic of the A&L paradigm of diversity management. On the other hand, those positions are no longer available for members of the dominant group. In consequence, conflicts and resistance might emerge and jeopardize the DiM concept if the positive effects are not evident.

Parallels can be drawn to Veltrop et al.'s (2021) findings: independent, external directors were invited to boards but their new and conflicting perspectives and questions were not listened to, but rather deflected in certain board settings through the dominance of the chair: '(i.e., directors were less engaged in seeking information or clarification from the CEO and withdraw from boardroom deliberations)' (p. 212).

As argued above, not all minorities are targeted but just the ones with connection to relevant markets (such as customers with buying capabilities, bottleneck sectors in supply, or certain countries). DiM intends to overcome separity (access to new target groups) and seeks to ensure variety (specific connections with markets and according to KSAOs).

Learning and Effectiveness (L&E)

The Learning and Effectiveness (L&E) (Ely and Thomas, 1996)[5] paradigm is characterized by the idea that insights, skills and experiences from a diverse workforce are potentially valuable resources for the group and, accordingly, for the organization in total. Diversity is linked to work processes and the paradigm frames diversity as holistic organizational learning and adaptive change. Variety is aimed for and the organizations are aware of the need to counterbalance disparity in order to tap into new potentials. Space is provided for all co-workers to perform by making good use of their individual experiences, skills and traits. Productive elements of diversity are emphasized and sought for. To tap into the potentials within the organization/group, formerly biased processes must be abandoned. It is evident that to fully embrace this paradigm often requires comprehensive cultural changes in the organization.

The L&E paradigm is triggered by sense-making processes (see Hansen and Seierstad, 2017) of top managers in business or presidents/rectors and their teams in academia. Boards are key in leading the sense-making process and nurturing its continuity. Those processes might be based on former DiM experiences following the F&D and/or the A&L paradigm. At the core are strategic considerations, possibly connected to corporate social responsibility (CSR) (Bührmann, 2015). For the most part, external pressures will not play a relevant role. Instead, a far-reaching process of learning and change characterizes this third approach. Rather than putting one isolated unit in charge, different actors from different levels co-manage DiM. Counter current flows as top-down requests, and arrangements from management initiate and require ongoing dialogues and practical changes.

Recently, inclusion rather than integration has been discussed and demanded as part of this paradigm. This fits with Veltrop et al.'s (2021) findings about the key function of psychological safety on diverse boards in explaining unintended effects on monitoring:

> While most of the literature and regulatory effort has focused on the attributes of individual directors, we have argued that two of the most widely supported prescriptions in governance – namely, appointing outside directors to boards and having an independent chair to counterbalance the CEO – may potentially *undermine* boardroom dynamics and thus director monitoring. In so doing, we highlight that both the chair's leadership and the psychological climate within the boardroom are key to stimulating directors' engagement in monitoring. (p. 227)

Interpreting this conclusion from our model's point of view, we can formulate that Veltrop et al. demand an inclusive approach at board level, led by a chair in a participative style, giving voice to conflicting perspectives, facilitating processes and aiming for the best results for the corporation.

Inclusion & Transformation (I&T)

Thomas' and Ely's typology has been developed further both in relation to companies and, more specifically, for the higher education sector. As a result, Bührmann (2015, 2021) has identified the I&T paradigm. We deliberately do not relate this paradigm to DiM, but to a more complex approach of *responding* to diversity.

The I&T paradigm shares several characteristics with the L&E paradigm: first, like L&E, the I&T paradigm follows the idea that diverse members' skills and experiences are potentially valuable resources for working, learning or researching groups, and therefore appreciated in the whole organization. Second, equally to the L&E paradigm, diversity and DiM are viewed as holistic organizational learning and adaptive change. Like in the L&E paradigm, a deep process of learning and change characterizes the I&T paradigm. Rather than putting isolated and often separated units in charge, different actors from different levels co-manage DiM. Thus, inclusion rather than integration has been demanded as overall objective. Inclusion follows a logic which values diversity from an ethical point of view and broadens the aim towards aspects such as the well-being of the people involved, both inside the organization and in its surroundings. Third, the top management level tries to stop formerly biased processes and discrimination in organizations. This could include enabling the organizational members to enhance their KSAOs. Fourth, there are some similarities regarding DiM measures: ongoing dialogues on enhancing and improving unbiased structures and processes are institutionalized on the meso and the micro levels, addressing both (historically discriminated) minorities and (mostly privileged not biased) majorities. The overall aim is to strengthen variety and reduce disparity. Important topics include enhancing the recruiting systems; strengthening human resource development, especially leadership evaluation; expanding childcare for students, staff and faculty; engaging with activities from the bottom to support students' initiatives such as refugee law clinics.

Yet, the I&T paradigm differs from the L&E paradigm in several aspects: the abovementioned initiatives and activities aim to transform not only the organization itself but also the organizational field. However, doing this in a systematic and sustainable way highlights the crucial differences between the L&E and the I&T paradigms. The most striking characteristic is the complex interplay between the meso level and the macro level. This includes the set of relations between the organization itself and its social environment. It also includes the impact on this environment which, in order to deserve the label "transformation", must be strong and broad enough to show a substantial effect. This requires an organization's response to diversity to be sustainable and needs a sound and stable commitment of the organization in total. We think that the strategic triggers and considerations of responsibility carries not only towards re-shaping the internal context of diversity and inclusion inside the organization, but also towards reversing the perspective and exerting influence on the external context. The unit in charge can only be top management, which has the exclusive right to represent the organization in public.

In the attempt to establish a positive cycle of interdependencies, the organization gains an active role on the macro level and takes responsibility for its environment. Ideally, a learning loop is implemented. Diversity is no longer a business or single organization case but unfolds its power in a broader social context, possibly in a powerful network of various actors. This has been missing in the other paradigms. Figure 15.2 sums up our discussion of the different types of DiM.

The types identified by Thomas and Ely have been described and analysed in detail. In contrast, the recently emerging I&T type has received little attention so far. However, a recent study by Fujimoto et al. (2019) shows that first signs of such an approach can be found with regard to corporations.

DiM type	Organizational aims	Strategies → Process logics	Tactics → Measures	Focused Levels
Discrimination & fairness	Compliance with legislation and avoidance of legal challenges	*Assimilation:* Adapting new employees to existing structures	Observing legal and ethical requirements	In reaction from government (macro-level) to individuals discriminated against (micro-level)
Access & legitimacy	Establishing and improving access to markets	*Differentiation:* Normalising the existence of 'other' employees and customer segments	Matching employees from 'other' groups to the corresponding customer segment	In adoption to market needs (macro-level) to reflection of clients with part of the staff (meso-level)
Learning & effectiveness	Structural and ethical development of the organization from an ethical and organizational perspective	*Integration:* Recognition of differences - integration of 'new' employee groups into a flexible and adaptive organization	Support programmes for certain target groups and adaptation of organizational structures and cultures	Concerning the whole organization and its culture
Inclusive & transformative	Further development of the organization AND transformation of the external environment	*Inclusion:* groups previously unaddressed now specifically included in the case of structural change	As in the learning and effectiveness type AND ongoing involvement in shaping the external environment	Concerning the whole organization and its culture and interdependences between the macro-meso- and micro-level

Source: Based on Bührmann, 2021, p. 138, modified.

Figure 15.2   Types of DiM

CONCLUSION

In this chapter, we considered a multi-level examination of diversity research to be important in order to understand the dynamics between the different levels and forms of diversity within and beyond organizations. Based on this, we developed a conceptual heuristic for discussing an intersectional framework for multi-level research on diversity (management). Based on the reflexive diversity research programme, we argued that diversity (and, consequently, the actual and perceived diversity of human capital) is not given, but the effect of diverse practices.

This implies that context and its different levels become very important. Next, we distinguished different forms of diversity: namely separation, disparity and variety. In practice, these three forms of difference are often intertwined. Therefore, relations and interdependencies among diversity features should be acknowledged in order to respond to diversity in a goal-oriented manner. After this, we introduced a framework for a multi-level research approach. Based on Hansen (2014) and Hansen and Seierstad (2017), we distinguished three levels: the macro, meso and micro. However, we focused not only on these different levels, but also on their intermediation. Here, we identified some side effects. Subsequently, we explicated these theoretical considerations – which could be viewed as a kind of heuristic framework – based on four types of diversity management. It became evident that contexts matter on different levels. Contexts must be considered in order to understand why and how diversity management concepts work, or fail to work, in a comprehensive way.

In view of these considerations about different forms of diversity and levels of research, we discussed the different ways of responding to diversity on different (organizational) levels based on divergent approaches to responding to diversity. Here we focused our deliberations on board diversity.

Based on this heuristic, there is much research still to be carried out. The following research questions should be addressed: we have addressed larger companies and especially their boards without distinguishing between different industrial sectors. The open question is: do these contexts matter, too? And if yes, to what extent? So far, we have concentrated on companies and their boards, but it remains unclear whether there are differences in other types of organizations, such as universities or public administrations. Thirdly, we do not have a systematic view on whether there are different impacts on different levels of implementing and processing diversity management strategies.

NOTES

1. Intersectionality recently emerged as an important idea within diversity research and can be understood as the need to understand a variety of factors (and experiences) related to diversity across multiple dimensions at once (e.g. class, gender, religion and race and ethnicity) (see Bührmann, 2015).
2. One especially stimulating best practice example for doing this kind of introspection is Morten Huse's sharing philosophy which is driven by open innovation, collectivity and impact (see Huse, 2020).
3. The roots of a three-level conceptual framework of gender were set by Ragins and Sundstrom as early as 1989 (Ragins and Sundstrom, 1989). We find parallel considerations from the 1980s' and 1990s' educational sciences. Thus, the structural model of socialization (Hurrelmann and Ulich, 1980) can be seen as a basis for gaining a deeper understanding of socialization processes. Nestvogel (1999, p. 389) added to this model the level of world system. In particular, Walgenbach (2012) hints at the transnational dimension of structural dominance. We are still following Nestvogel's intention while using Walgenbach's labelling.
4. In relation to higher education, Williams (2013, pp. 129–59) distinguishes – using a similar typology to that of Thomas and Ely – three different diversity management models: the affirmative action and equity model; the multicultural and inclusion model; and the learning, diversity and research model.
5. Later on, Ely and Thomas (2001) also called this paradigm Integration and Learning (I&L).

REFERENCES

Aretz, H.-J. & Hansen, K. (2002). *Diversity und Diversity-Management im Unternehmen. Eine Analyse aus systemtheoretischer Sicht.* Lit Verlag.

Bührmann, A. D. (2015). Diversitätsmanagementkonzepte im sozialwissenschaftlichen Diskurs. Befunde, Diskussionen und Perspektiven einer reflexiven Diversitätsforschung. In P. Genkova & T. Ringeisen (Eds.), *Handbuch Diversity Kompetenz: Perspektiven und Anwendungsfelder* (pp. 76–88). Wiesbaden: Springer Verlag.

Bührmann, A. D. (2021). *The Reflexive Diversity Research Programme: An Introduction.* Cambridge Scholars Press.

Cox, T. H. & Blake, S. (1991). Managing cultural diversity: implications for organizational competitiveness. *Academy of Management Review*, 5(3), 45–56. https://doi.org/10.5465/ame.1991.4274465.

Danowitz, M. A. (2015). Rethinking higher education diversity studies through a diversity management frame. In R. Bendl, I. Bleijenbergh, E. Henttonen & A. Mills (Eds.), *The Oxford Handbook of Diversity in Organizations* (pp. 357–69). Oxford University Press.

Devinney, T. M. (2013). Is microfoundational thinking critical to management thought and practice? *Academy of Management Perspectives*, 27(2), 81–4. https://doi.org/10.5465/amp.2013.0053.

Dobbin, F. & Kalev, A. (2016). Why diversity programs fail: and what works better. *Harvard Business Review*, 94(7/8), 52–60.

Ely, R. J. & Thomas, D. A. (1996). Making difference matter: a new paradigm for managing diversity. *Harvard Business Review*, September/October, 1–13.

Ely, R. J. & Thomas, D. A. (2001). Cultural diversity at work: the effects of diversity perspectives on work group processes and outcomes. *Administrative Science Quarterly*, 46(2), 229–73. https://doi.org/10.2307%2F2667087.

Fujimoto, Y., Azmat, F. & Subramaniam, N. (2019). Creating community-inclusive organizations. managerial accountability framework. *Business & Society*, 58(4), 712–48. https://doi.org/10.1177/0007650316680060.

Hansen, K. (2014). *CSR und Diversity Management: Erfolgreiche Vielfalt in Organisationen.* Springer Verlag.

Hansen, K. (2021). Nicht-elitäres Talentmanagement. In P. Genkova (Ed.), *Handbuch Globale Kompetenz*. Springer. https://doi.org/10.1007/978-3-658-30684-7_89-1.

Hansen, K. & Seierstad, C. (2017). *Corporate Social Responsibility and Diversity Management: Theoretical Approaches and Best Practices.* Springer International.

Harrison, D. A. & Klein, K. J. (2007). What's the difference? Diversity constructs as separation, variety, or disparity in organizations. *Academy of Management Review*, 32(4), 1199–228. https://doi.org/10.5465/amr.2007.26586096.

Hurrelmann, K. & Ulich, D. (1980). *Handbuch der Sozialisationsforschung.* Beltz Verlag.

Huse, M. (2020). *Resolving the Crisis in Research by Changing the Game: An Ecosystem and a Sharing Philosophy.* Cheltenham, UK and Northampton, MA, USA: Edward Elgar Publishing.

Klarner, P., Yoshikawa, T. & Hitt M. A. (2021). A capability-based view of boards: a new conceptual framework for board governance. *AoM Perspectives*, 35(1), 123–41. https://doi.org/10.5465/amp.2017.0030.

Leslie, L. M. (2019). Diversity initiative effectiveness: a typological theory of unintended consequences. *The AoM Review*, 44(3), 538–63. https://doi.org/10.5465/amr.2017.0087.

Machold, S., Huse, M., Hansen, K. & Brogi, M. (2013). *Getting Women on to Corporate Boards: A Snowball Starting in Norway.* Cheltenham, UK and Northampton, MA, USA: Edward Elgar Publishing.

Metcalfe, B. D. & Woodhams, C. (2012). Introduction. New directions of gender, diversity and organization theorizing. Re-imagining feminist post-colonialism, transnationalism and geographies of power. *International Journal of Management Reviews*, 14(2), 123–40. https://doi.org/10.1111/j.1468-2370.2012.00336.x.

Morrison, A. M., White, R. P. & Van Velsor, E. (1987). *Breaking the Glass Ceiling: Can Women Reach the Top of America's Largest Corporations?* Addison-Wesley.

Nestvogel, R. (1999). Sozialisation im "Weltsystem". *Zeitschrift für Soziologie der Erziehung und Sozialisation*, 19(4), 388–404. http://www.digizeitschriften.de/dms/img/?PID= PPN513648674_0019%7CLOG_0082.

Nielsen, S. & Huse, M. (2010). Women directors' contribution to board decision-making and strategic involvement: the role of equality perception. *European Management Review*, 7(1), 16–29. https://doi.org/10.1057/emr.2009.27.

Ployhart, R. E. & Moliterno, T. P. (2011). Emergence of the human capital resource: a multi-level model. *Academy of Management Review*, 36(1), 127–50. https://doi.org/10.5465/amr .2009.0318.

Ragins, B. R. & Sundstrom, E. (1989). Gender and power in organizations: a longitudinal perspective. *Psychological Bulletin*, 105(1), 51–88. https://doi.apa.org/doi/10.1037/0033 -2909.105.1.51.

Roberson, L. & Kulik, C. T. (2007). Stereotype threat at work. *Academy of Management Perspective*, 21(2), 24–40. https://doi.org/10.5465/amp.2007.25356510.

Ryan, M. K. & Haslam, S. A. (2007). The glass cliff: exploring the dynamics surrounding the appointment of women to precarious leadership positions. *Academy of Management Review*, 21(2), 549–72. https://doi.org/10.5465/amr.2007.24351856.

Stahl, G. K. & Sully de Luque, M. (2014). Antecedents of responsible leader behavior: a research synthesis, conceptual framework, and agenda for future research. *Academy of Management Perspectives*, 28(3), 235–54. https://doi.org/10.5465/amp.2013.0126.

Thomas, R. R. (1996). *Redefining Diversity*. AMACOM.

Veltrop, D. B., Bezemer, P.-J., Nicholson, G. & Pugliese, A. (2021). Too unsafe to monitor? How board-CEO cognitive conflict and chair leadership shape outside director monitoring. *Academy of Management Journal*, 64(1), 207–34. https://doi.org/10.5465/amj.2017.1256.

Walgenbach, K. (2012). Intersektionalität – eine Einführung. *Portal Intersektionalität*. http:// portal-intersektionalitaet.de/uploads/media/Walgenbach-Einfuehrung.pdf.

Williams, D. A. (2013). *Strategic Diversity Leadership: Activating Change and Transformation in Higher Education*. Stylus Publishing.

Zanoni, P., Janssens, M., Benshop, Y. & Nkomo, S. (2010). Guest editorial. Unpacking diversity, grasping inequality: rethinking difference through critical perspectives. *Organization*, 17(1), 9–29. https://doi.org/10.1177/1350508409350344.

16. Diversity and corporate governance: how can groundbreaking research be developed?

Morten Huse

I have recently reflected on what is excellence in research. Definitely, it has something to do with bringing our knowledge forward and to make our research relevant. I have thus also been reflecting on how research and publications about diversity and corporate governance contribute to excellence. How can research about diversity and corporate governance contribute to changing society and making a better world?

Most of my own research that has been combining diversity and corporate governance has been on the topic of women on boards. However, diversity and corporate governance goes far beyond that. Corporate governance is highly rooted in corporate stakeholder relations, and diversity includes various aspects of inclusion that do not directly relate to business-level value creation. Most research about diversity and corporate governance is relating to meso-level studies, often studies about boards of directors. When focusing on contributions that may change the world, then, I clearly indicate the need to lift studies to macro levels. Perhaps, we in a holistic way should try to integrate micro-, meso- and macro-level studies of diversity and corporate governance. This is what we have tried to do in this volume.

There are in this volume diversity contributions about women on boards (Seierstad, Åberg and Fjellvær, Chapter 3), LGBT+ persons (Özbilgin and Erbil, Chapter 4), international board members (Al-Mamun et al., Chapter 6), and about competence diversity (Seierstad, Åberg and Fjellvær, Chapter 3; Oehmicken, Weck and van Ees, Chapter 7) as well as leaders and entrepreneurs from various social classes (Saman, Chapter 10). Some of the chapters make dives into how human rights and talent potentials may clash. Some contributions even reflect on and discuss multi-level diversity and intersectionality (Bührmann and Hansen, Chapter 15; Saman, Chapter 10). There are chapters about diversity contributions in the boardroom represented by theory of proportions (De Masi and Slomka-Golebiowska, Chapter 14) and faultlines (Vandebeek, Chapter 12; Mendiratta, Chapter 13), and there are presentations about mechanisms to achieve diversity (Magnusdottir et al., Chapter 8; Seierstad et al., Chapter 3). Some of the presentations are focusing on social or societal issues (Asad et al., Chapter 9; Al-Mamun et al., Chapter 6). Most of the authors have affiliation in Europe, but some have backgrounds on other continents. The list of country affiliations includes Australia, Belgium, Denmark, Fiji, France, Germany, Iceland, India, Italy, the Netherlands, Norway, Poland, Spain, Switzerland, Turkey and the United Kingdom. Furthermore, most research about diversity and corporate governance is published by women. However, in this volume a significant number of men are contributing.

I like the possibility of combining various contributions in a book. Together they give a much broader perspective on a topic than what a single paper will do. Furthermore, the book format gives a greater freedom for the authors to present what they believe in. They are not forced into the formulaic ways in which journal articles typically need to be presented. We are getting close to what Lee (2009) and DeNisi (2010) call programmatic research. Programmatic research may be seen as a project exploring an overarching research theme. It is not each individual contribution that is the most important, but what the various individual contributions combined teach us. Programmatic research makes it possible for junior scholars to contribute together with senior scholars. It contributes to overcome various aspects of research bias, including method bias, researcher bias, cultural biases and so on.

In this final chapter, I will present reflections in lines with the programmatic research lessons. I will direct reflexive questions towards groundbreaking research, meaningful research, excellence in research and contributions to make a better world. The rest of this chapter follows in these sections. First, with the title "Making a better world and doing research with meaning", I introduce polymorphic and programmatic research. Second, under the title "Bringing knowledge forward", I summarize the individual and overall contributions of the various chapters of this book. Third, using the title "An alternative research agenda – polymorphic research about women on boards", I merge the main conclusions in the book with lessons from my own journey of exploring diversity and corporate governance. In this section, I illustrate through my introspective journey, programmatic and polymorphic research. Introspection is a process whereby I am observing my own conscious thoughts and emotions (Huse, 2020: 118). Finally, I present some challenges for future diversity and corporate governance research. I do this considering an overall commitment to develop ground-breaking research and to develop a better world.

MAKING A BETTER WORLD AND DOING RESEARCH WITH MEANING

I was influenced by the former Academy of Management (AOM) presidents Tom Lee (2009) and Angelo DeNisi (2010) to apply the programmatic research concept. Anthologies like the present book may contribute to programmatic research, while I see polymorphic research as a next step in making important, innovative and interesting research. I like the overall theme for the AOM 2022 conference "Creating a better world together". Thus, I bring that perspective with me when reflecting on meaning with our research.

Which are the most groundbreaking research contributions about diversity and corporate governance? Systematic reviews and bibliometric analyses may give some indications. Will it be highly cited articles such as the *AMR* publication by Aguilera and Jackson (2003), the *Financial Review* article by Carter, Simkins and Simpson

(2003) or Bear, Rahman and Post's article in *Journal of Business Ethics* (2010)? Will it be the programmatic research, the research stream and set of contributions around Cranfield University and Sue Vinnicombe? Sue Vinnicombe became Commander of the British Empire due to her consistent work and publications about women on boards. Her work in motivating and training younger scholars is an example to follow. Further, I think that various polymorphic approaches that are disseminated through politics and practice may be high up on the list of groundbreaking research contributions (Seierstad et al., 2017). Our research should be meaningful beyond that of giving individual credits.

I started this chapter by asking about what excellence in research is. The European Research Council defined it to have something to do with groundbreaking and path-setting. It should have an innovation potential, be independent, support the development of junior scholars and have second- and third-order impact. Programmatic research can contribute to reach these objectives, and I am seeing this volume as an inspiration for doing programmatic research.

"Most contemporary research issues and the everyday constraints imposed by a business school require a diverse skill set and multiple points of view for programmatic scholarship" (Lee, 2009: 198). Jonas Gabrielsson characterized programmatic research as poetry for scholars (Huse, 2020: 89): "The focus on single papers and their citations is too atomistic, and does not make sense when you think about the broader meaning of scholarly work and writing as engaging in a conversation." It is seldom that one publication makes an influence on theory or practice, but a stream of research, as in programmatic research, may.

Most of the contributions in this book about Diversity and Corporate Governance have been developed in interaction. Sabina Tasheva and I, as editors, have been learning and been guiding in this process. At least for me, it has been an immense and important learning process to integrate contributions from scholars in early and as well as late phases of their careers.

In his crusade for doing research with meaning, Mats Alvesson suggested that we should apply polymorphic research (Alvesson, Gabriel and Paulsen, 2017). Polymorphic means "occurring in different forms". Research can appear in different forms and not only the formulaic way we face it through the present publication pressures. The major point of polymorphic research is to open up alternative ways of thinking and writing research. In polymorphic research we break with the mainstream and explore new ways of applying theories and methods, target audiences and ways of dissemination. After more than 30 years of intensive research about diversity and corporate governance, there is a need for moving forward. We should in our research have in mind characteristics of what we see as outstanding and groundbreaking. In doing so I bring forward Alvesson's concept of polymorphic research. This means in practice to challenge existing formulaic approaches and to think out of the box.

We have in this *Handbook* combined traditional approaches to board diversity with some of the latest insights into the role of diversity in managing organizations. Through the contributions in this book, we have, in the present era of high uncertainty, illustrated the importance of the diverse resources board members are bringing to the board. Through the various contributions, we have presented various approaches to diversity research, alternative concepts of diversity and challenged existing assumptions about diversity and the consequences of diversity. However, still, we have shown how diverse backgrounds of board members contribute to firm survival, and that diversity may contribute to identifying profitable and sustainable future business avenues. In this *Handbook* we have focused on current discussions and future directions for research on diversity and corporate governance.

BRINGING KNOWLEDGE FORWARD – PROGRAMMATIC RESEARCH

The different contributions found in this book have in an integrative and holistic way, elements of programmatic research. It is not the individual chapters that are the most important. It is what is communicated by integrating the various contributions. Here are contributions that are questioning the concept of diversity; discovering the concept from various disciplinary traditions; evaluating and appreciating various aspects of diversity; approaching the issues through a variation in methodological philosophies; and seeing the challenges from a variety of national and cultural backgrounds. I have been involved as co-editor of some previous anthologies about women on boards. The main contribution of *Women on Corporate Boards of Directors* (Vinnicombe et al., 2008) was to increase the awareness and insights about international practices regarding women corporate board members. We wanted to better inform corporate, legislative and regulatory leaders and policymakers about women on corporate boards. *Getting Women on to Corporate Boards* by Machold et al. (2013) is a result of evidenced-based reflections from a workshop held in 2011. In exploring political contexts, the role of advocacy movements, experiences from women directors themselves and latest research findings, we provided a comprehensive overview of the rationales, processes and outcomes of formal approaches to gender diversity on boards. The contributions of these books are results of joint efforts. The main contribution is not the individual chapters. This is also the ambition for this book about "Diversity and Corporate Governance". In Figure 16.1, I have sorted some reflections from the book.

Figure 16.1 indicates some of the main concepts and attributes presented in the book. They need to be understood and considered in research and practice about diversity and corporate governance. Corporate governance objectives are presented with board- or firm-level definitions and with societal-level definitions. What is best for the board, for the firm or for society? What is best for the individual is also introduced. Diversity is approached from three main different perspectives: in terms of competence or capabilities; inclusion; and some structural descriptions such as intersectionality, overlapping identities, competing equalities, faultlines and proportions. Instruments for change is the concept used for describing how to achieve diversity. The reality about diversity is embedded in the society, and there are variations across nations and cultures, and the reality is not static, but dynamic. Finally, the

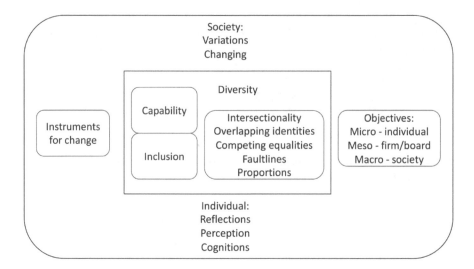

Figure 16.1   Concepts challenging diversity research and practice

understanding of diversity and its possibilities and challenges depends on individual reflections, perceptions and cognitions.

Andrea Bührmann and Katrin Hansen offer a conceptual heuristic for discussion an intersectional framework for multi-level research on diversity. They show that diversity, particularly in actual and perceived human capital diversity, is not a given. It is the effect of diverse practice. Bührmann and Hansen's work is based on a reflexive diversity approach. Vartika Chandra Saman is also focusing on intersectionality. She is asking whether social caste hierarchies are being replaced by competing equalities. What happens when there are overlapping identities? Why is it important to understand diversity in the context of different identities? She is discussing this in the context of the experience of dalit women as entrepreneurs. She investigates the question of cast and gender in contemporary Indian business.

The chapters by Andrea Bührmann and Katrin Hansen (15) and by Vartika Chandra Saman (10) show that studying overlapping identities and intersectionality helps us understand the concept of diversity in a better way. Faultlines is another concept that takes us deeper into the understanding of diversity. Faultlines are hypothetical dividing lines that fracture a group into two or more homogeneous subgroups based on the alignment of multiple individual-level characteristics. Alana Vandebeek (12) provides an overview of the literature on group faultlines in boards of directors. She provides insights for future research directions and to guide future contributions on group faultlines in boards of directors. Esha Mendiratta (13) is more specific. She reviews the literature on board and top management team-level faultlines and their influence of board- and firm-level outcomes. She argues that faultlines may be a crucial perspective for corporate governance research on board composition. Sara De Masi and Agnieszka Slomka-Golebiowska (14) show that proportions of diversity must be understood when identifying profitable and sustainable future business avenues. By applying Kanter's theory of proportion, they show in the case of gender diversity that various proportions have different impact on the performance of different board tasks.

Board diversity is not only a question of gender. And diversity should not be only something to exist. Diversity should from competence or capability perspectives also be utilized. Carl Åberg, Hilde Fjellvær and Cathrine Seierstad (5) use in their chapter different recent resource or capability theories to show how board diversity may contribute to corporate entrepreneurship and value creation. They study job-related diversity and show that this diversity can have both positive and negative impacts. Åberg, Fjellvær and Seierstad apply the concepts of dynamic capabilities, absorptive capacity and ambidexterity. Jana Oehmichen, Michelle Weck and Hans van Ees (7) show how the digitalization of our economy can have consequences for the tasks for non-executive board members. Looking at an overall demographic diversity measure based on gender, age, tenure and nationality, they found in their study from the Netherlands that non-digital directors are more diverse than digital directors.

De Masi and Slomka-Golebiowska (14) argue for how board gender diversity has impacts on board tasks. Oehmichen et al. (7) use diversity as the dependent variable, Asad et al. (9) explore how gender diversity impacts shareholder resolutions, and Al-Mamun et al. (6) explore the impact board members' international experience has on corporate social responsibility.

While Vartika Chandra Saman takes the perspective of caste and class, Mustafa Özbilgin and Cihat Erbil (4) take the case of LGBT+. They explain why the inclusion of LGBT+ is an international imperative in the boardroom diversity discussion. In their chapter, they introduce and develop a rainbow plan for change. Özbilgin and Erbil draw on the theory of heteronormativity and shows how it clashes with the talent potential and human rights of LGBT+ individuals in the workplace.

How is it possible to achieve diversity on boards? Özbilgin and Erbil make some suggestions in how to get more LGBT+ on boards, and Hildur Magnusdottir, Olaf Sigurjonsson, Arna Arnardottir and Patricia Gabaldon (8) illustrate the importance of nomination committees. They found in the case of Iceland that nomination committees may be important tools to promote and enhance accountability and diversity within boards. Cathrine Seierstad, Carl Åberg and Hilde Fjellvær (3) go into the discussion of gender quotas. However, they show that the Norwegian board gender quota regulation did not take Norway into the broader debate about diversity – neither for PLC boards nor boards in other types of organizations. Thus, board quotas must not be considered as the solution to achieving board diversity. The attention in Norway was only gender and PLC boards. They argue that there is a need for a wider board diversity debate and focus from organisations, politicians and in research.

The contributions in this *Handbook* present perspectives from several societies. Chandra Saman makes reflections from India, Nam et al. from Fiji, Seierstad et al. from Norway, Oehmicken et al. from the Netherlands, Asad et al. use data from USA, Al-Mamun et al. compare data from Malaysia, Pakistan and the Philippines, and Magnusdottir et al. use Iceland as an example.

The contributions made in this book go beyond the individual chapter. They clearly show that diversity and corporate governance is about more than input–output relations between the number of women on boards and company performance. A reflexive diversity approach is needed. Context matters, and multi-level diversity research is important to understand the dynamics between the different actual and perceived levels and forms within and beyond organizations (Bührmann and Hansen, Chapter 15).

AN ALTERNATIVE RESEARCH AGENDA – POLYMORPHIC RESEARCH ABOUT WOMEN ON BOARDS

Several of the contributions in this book show relations between board dynamics and diversity. The overall picture shows the need, not only to distinguish micro-, meso- and macro-levels understanding of diversity contributions. The levels need to be integrated holistically. However, most of my diversity research has been about women on boards. For several years I have been involved in programmatic research about women on boards. However, my large number of studies has also led me into polymorphic research on the topic.

Studies of women in boards started to receive attention during the 1980s, and it has increased ever since. However, studies of women on boards go in different directions. Firstly, I use the title women in boards when referring to the meso-level contributions women have. This means their impact in the boardroom. I will, however, also present some micro-level and macro-level reflections. I have argued for this distinction in Huse (2018a). The micro-level reflections are about the individual person, their characteristics, motivation and the board capital with which they may contribute. The macro-level studies are about the societal case – both as a context and as an objective; how that of getting women on boards may contribute to getting a better and sustainable society. I am also referring to a fourth main stream of research when understanding women on boards; that is, to explore how it may be possible to increase the number of women on boards. I argue for the importance of integrating these four perspectives.

There are, however, also other ways of sorting the research about women on boards, and some types of research may be more difficult to publish than other types. A standard reference for women on board studies is the literature review by Terjesen, Sealy and Singh (2009). They are also making micro-, meso- and macro-level distinctions. Their review was published in 2009, but the studies of women on boards have mushroomed since then. The Terjesen et al. publication has contributed significantly to this growth. There are several recent reviews about women on boards, and they tend to use more sophisticated review techniques than those used by Terjesen et al. Systematic or structured review techniques are used, some are applying meta-analyses and more recently, we find bibliometric studies. A main problem in many of the recent reviews is that research into the topic is leaning on some keywords, and typically has not been able explore many of the studies giving directions into the topic. The background and path-setting studies may use different concepts; they may not be published in leading journals; or they may have a background in other languages than English. Often, the reviews lack introspection, and reflections about the future are limited. I will therefore now include a short introspective journey of my research about women and boards. It is a journey in programmatic research.

An Introspective Journey into Research about Women on Boards

My journey started during the 1980s. I experienced in practice many of the challenges women have in the workplace, and I started my journey to support women that wanted to make a change. My research interest about women on boards started in 1989. I then made literature reviews on the topic, and I started discussing the topic and joint research projects with some featured scholars as Idie Kesner (Kesner, 1988). Several of my master's students started writing their theses about women on boards. During the 1990s, I conducted interviews with women board members. I became a mentor and discussion partner for some female change agents and made seminars for women on boards. I applied for research grants, and even got involved in national initiatives to increase the number of women on boards. My first international publication on the topic was Bilimoria and Huse (1997), and I was involved in AOM symposia about women on boards in 1998 and in 2000. During these symposia, I got accepted by the international group of women researching the topic. In particular, I worked closely with Diana Bilimoria and Sue Vinnicombe. At the 2000 symposium, I presented a paper called "A way forward" (Huse, 2000). In this paper, I analyzed the effects of various instruments to increase the number of women on boards. My conclusion was that voluntary actions did not seem to work in Norway, and that a quota regulation should be considered.

During the 1990s, I conducted several quantitative studies about boards of directors. They also included surveys. Most of them explored actual board behavior. In these studies, I tried to find positive correlations between the number of women on boards and board or company performance. Unfortunately, it was difficult to find significant results. Thus, I did not report that in my papers. However, the different sets of survey studies conducted during the 1990s led to the development of a large survey instrument about a value-creating board (Huse, 2008; Sellevoll, Huse and Hansen, 2007). This instrument was developed during the 2000s and used together with colleagues from and in several countries. The instrument and some of the data have been included in BI Norwegian Business School's research depository (BIRD). This survey contained many questions about gender, gender relations and perceptions about gender. Results from these surveys have received considerable attention.

Quotas to regulate by law gender balance on boards was suggested and implemented in Norway during the 2000s. This resulted in a rapid growth in the number of women on boards in public limited companies, not only in Norway but also in other countries. This made it possible to make more meaning of making quantitative business case studies of women on boards. However, in this period I got directly involved in two other streams of research. The first stream was to explore and understand the women that wanted to become board members. This stream I called the "golden skirts" studies. The second was to continue the exploration of how a quota regulation could be and was implemented in other countries. This is the polymorphic stream, and I used the "champagne method" as the main approach.

The "golden skirts" studies were based on various sets of interviews with women in board positions. However, we also used other sets of available data. They gained considerable attention in the international press. Who are the women getting board positions, how are they becoming board members and what are their contributions? Huse (2011), Seierstad et al. (2021) and Rigolini and Huse (2021) are some publications from these studies. In these studies, we interviewed women in various countries, and in Norway we also followed the "golden skirts" over time. We observed that the women contributed with different types of board capital, and the choice of women depended on variations in institutional pressures.

The Champagne Method and Polymorphic Research

The champagne method is an action research approach and is a polymorphic way of doing research. I am challenging existing ways of collecting data and communicating the results. Some of the processes are described in Machold et al. (2013) and Seierstad et al. (2017). For me it started in the beginning of the 1990s, but I did not formulate it until the late 2000s – almost 20 years later. The champagne method has been a way of mentoring champions for change. I have been learning from these mentorships without making formal notes or recording. However, these relationships have, on the actual topics, taught me more than any formal study. The champagne method is about trust and building deep relationships. The champagne method is close to my motto that "Life is too short to drink bad wine". It is about doing important things and to do it with people that are giving you energy. The champagne method has since 2010 dominated my research about women on boards and that of getting women on boards.

During the 1990s, I met on a regular basis with some Norwegian women that were championing getting women on board. They included me in their individual agendas. They took me into their worlds, and step by step we contributed to explore more about how to get women on boards, their perceived barriers and their thinking. In this way they helped me formulate research grant applications and to disseminate the lessons to political decision-makers. Main Norwegian newspapers featured my agenda about women on boards.

During the 2000s, I spent much time in Italy, and I began to forge partnerships with some women wanting to see gender equality progress in Italy. Some of my Italian partners, based on our ongoing meetings and discussions, suggested that we should work through Fondazione Bellisario and its leader Lella Golfo – a member of the Italian Parliament. La Sapienza professor Marina Brogi was in this period my main "champagne method"-partner. Lella needed to define her coming agenda for promoting women and gender equality. Why not get a quota regulation in Italy as in Norway? We decided to meet with Italian politicians in the Italian parliament. The attention was supported as Marina was able to get support from most of the leading press in Italy, and a panel meeting in the parliament was organized.

In 2010, various windows opened in Germany, and together with some colleagues in Norway, we had been invited to make presentations in the UK parliament. One of my "champagne methods" partners, Professor Katrin Hansen, took me into German politics and her agenda to get a quota regulation in Germany. Katrin shared with me her experiences and her networks of politicians, civil servants and women-on-boards activists. We met with and consulted politicians both at regional and federal levels, and we worked together with Frauen in die Aufsichtsräte (FidAR) and its leader Monika Schulz-Strelow on their agenda. In this period, I also accepted a five-year late career position at a German university. That made me follow the German developments closely, and I was interviewed on German television and in some of the main German newspapers.

The access and developments in Italy and Germany inspired me to continue the process. Together with colleagues at local national universities, we set up similar projects. Together with university colleagues I tried to identify partners in potential countries, and direct initiatives were taken in Austria, Israel and Denmark. However, as we got projects and good starts in Spain and Slovenia, other countries had to be kept on hold. Huse (2018b) summarizes some of the background observations in some of the countries considered. Results from the Spanish project are reported in Izquierdo, Huse and Möltner (2016) and the Slovenian project in reports from the EQPOWEREC project (Kanjuo Mrčela, 2016). In both countries we had intense discussions with politicians and business associations, including a presentation in the Slovenian parliament and the Spanish ministry of equality. We had considerable press coverage in both places.

Formal descriptions of the champagne method and polymorphic research are presented elsewhere (Huse, 2020; Huse and DeSilva, 2023). The journey is presented in Seierstad et al. (2017) and Huse (2018b). I have here showed alternative ways of collecting data and communicating results. By applying polymorphic research, I have moved from mainstream procedures and techniques to reflexive interpretations. The target audience is not the self or a narrow group of scholars, but political decision-makers.

Challenging Assumptions

Challenging assumptions may often be like "swearing in the church", and sometimes it is like being a devil's advocate. Since 1990, I have made about 150 international academic or practitioner presentations about women on boards. Many of them have been at panels, and I am sure that I have listened to more than 500 presentations about women on boards. I have also met with or have interviews with some hundreds of women being board members or those that have aspired to board memberships. About 100 are recorded or videotaped. Definitely, I have learnt much from the presentations, encounters and interviews. However, I have increasingly started to react negatively to many stereotypic presentations, for example: "All men contribute negatively, and all women contribute positively", and all women are experiencing discrimination. "Women are smarter than men, and men are making barriers for women". I know that this is far from reality, and thus I wanted to challenge these assumptions. I will contribute to creating a better world, meanwhile it is also important to destroy assumptions that are not sustainable.

I need to present some background reflections before continuing this section. I am Scandinavian and a man. My reflection would probably have been different if I had been from other regions and if I had been a woman. However, I do also think that a male Scandinavian perspective is needed as a background for the formulation of hypotheses and assumptions. My questioning comes from me as a man, being a feminist and a scholar having worked with value-creating and behavioral perspectives on boards. I have been member of boards dominated by women, and in boards with only men. Here are some of the assumptions that should be challenged:

First, during recent years, my main research and teaching has been about mentoring, women as well as men, in many countries and on several continents. I have found that it is important for research and practice to explore how the cultural differences across countries and national realities vary.

Second, the barriers women are facing vary across countries and cultures (Huse, 2014, 2018b). In some places, the reality is that men are being discriminated against. In some countries it is now impossible for men to get into boards unless they are or represent major investors. Almost all available positions of independent board members are dedicated to women. It is important for research and practice to acknowledge that women in many places do not compete with men for career positions, but with other women.

Third, do the women aspiring for board and corporate leadership positions have the same characteristics as women in general? Can it be the case that those aspiring for such positions only represent a small group of women, and that this group has different characteristics, including motivation, than women in general? It is important for research and practice to understand the characteristics of women aspiring for and becoming board members, and not only to make a comparison of general and stereotypic attributes of women and men.

Fourth, some barriers that women face are about choices in private life. Women have, more often than men, the options of not being breadwinners. Most men are taking, often by necessity, the role as breadwinners. Some women have today more freedom than men to choose alternatives to devote their lives to careers and earning money. There are men that would like to have the same choices as women to opt-out of the career or breadwinner pipeline. Furthermore, many women are raised to care for children, family and the home, often also including cleaning, laundry and cooking. Is this only something that is negative? There are many women that do not trust that their male partners are as good as them in doing that, and thus they do not properly include the men in such activities. There are many men wanting to spend more time at home, with the children and the family, and doing activities not directly related to that of being breadwinners. There are men that want to have the freedom of being "an academic housewife" (Goeke, 2020). Juliane Goeke is referring to the possibility that despite having an academic education, women as well as men may prefer to opt-out of the corporate career pipeline. It is important for research and practice to explore the importance of various holes in the corporate pipeline.

Fifth, Catherine Hakim has presented the importance of erotic capital for getting board and leadership positions, and the title of one of her books is *Erotic Capital: The Power of Attraction in the Boardroom and the Bedroom* (Hakim, 2011). However, she is also paying attention to the fact that it is not only women that may have erotic capital, but also men. On the other side we also need to pay attention to the evolution of #MeToo incidences. #MeToo is typically addressing power differences in the work-life. Men are typically seen as leaders and thus also powerful in the work-life, and men are using their power to approach women with sexual abuses or harassments. Is it likely that women when getting into leadership positions will use their power in a similar way? It will be important for research and practice to explore consequences of changing power relations.

CONTRIBUTIONS TO GROUNDBREAKING RESEARCH ABOUT DIVERSITY AND CORPORATE GOVERNANCE: DO WE CREATE A BETTER WORLD TOGETHER?

The European Research Council has defined excellence in research. It should be groundbreaking; it should be beyond the state of the art; and it should contribute to second- and third-order impact. Excellence in research should have an innovative potential and include training of students and junior faculty.

How can we develop groundbreaking research about diversity and corporate governance? In this chapter, I have leaned on some of the challenges presented in some of my own recent publications (Huse, 2018a, 2020). I am challenging for-mulaic research and scholars to explore some possibilities by using polymorphic approaches. My diversity and corporate governance research on the topic started with studies about the existence and number of women on boards, and it moved to how to get more women on boards. In later contributions, I integrated these meso-level studies with work on micro- and macro-levels. I studied the characteristics of the women aspiring for board positions and those becoming board members (Huse, 2011; Nielsen and Huse, 2010; Rigolini and Huse, 2021). During recent years, I have tried to understand national variations in discourses relating, for example, to culture, norms and regulations, and how these can be influenced. I have tried to include indigenous approaches to my understanding of women on boards. However, in this *Handbook*, we have seen the need to go beyond women on boards – even beyond the understanding of gender on boards.

In the previous section, I presented lists of directions for further research about women on boards. This list should be extended to similar research about diversity and corporate governance. We should explore the challenges facing boards, corpo-rate governance, corporations and society. There is a need to explore what diversity means taking into consideration a changing society and societal needs. We should try to have some perspectives about the future and not only about the past. We do not need to look many years ahead until we can imagine dramatic changes about boards and corporate governance issues. These could include the impacts of digitalization, migration, globalization, climate change, pandemics, economic inequality and even wars. We must also foresee the impacts of dynamic interactions. The reality is not stable. The world is not static but changing. We cannot trust that the work we did 20 years ago about diversity and corporate governance will be valid in the future. I am not only thinking about the distant future, but also the future when somebody starts citing the research we plan to do now.

As scholars, we need to be champions. We have been trained to reflect and make inferences. Our interpretations and reflections need to be communicated to those influencing or making decisions. However, as reality is fast changing, we also need to do research not only for our target groups or stakeholders, but also with them. We should reflect on the question of whether we contribute to creating a better world together.

REFERENCES

Aguilera, R. V., & Jackson, G. (2003). The cross-national diversity of corporate governance: dimensions and determinants. *Academy of Management Review, 28*(3), 447–65.

Alvesson, M., Gabriel, Y., & Paulsen, R. (2017). *Return to Meaning: A Social Science with Something to Say*. Oxford University Press.

Bear, S., Rahman, N., & Post, C. (2010). The impact of board diversity and gender composition on corporate social responsibility and firm reputation. *Journal of Business Ethics, 97*(2), 207–21.

Bilimoria, D., & Huse, M. (1997). A qualitative comparison of the boardroom experiences of US and Norwegian women corporate directors. *International Review of Women and Leadership, 3*(2), 63–76.

Carter, D. A., Simkins, B. J., & Simpson, W. G. (2003). Corporate governance, board diversity, and firm value. *Financial Review, 38*(1), 33–53.

DeNisi, A. S. (2010). 2009 presidential address: challenges and opportunities for the academy in the next decade. *The Academy of Management Review, 35*(2), 190–201.

Goeke, J. (2020). Social constructionism and the corporate talent pipeline: gaining and retaining talents (doctoral dissertation, Universität Witten/Herdecke).

Hakim, C. (2011). *Erotic Capital: The Power of Attraction in the Boardroom and the Bedroom*. Basic Books.

Huse, M. (2000). A way forward: programs to increase the number of women on corporate boards, AOM symposium presentation, Washington, DC.

Huse, M. (2008). Exploring methods and concepts in studies of board processes. In Huse, M. (Ed.), *The Value Creating Board: Corporate Governance and Organizational Behaviour* (pp. 221–33). Routledge.

Huse, M. (2011). The golden skirts: changes in board composition following gender quotas on corporate boards, Australian and New Zealand Academy Meeting, Wellington, NZ.

Huse, M. (2018a). *Value-Creating Boards: Challenges for Future Practice and Research*. Cambridge University Press.

Huse, M. (2018b). Gender in the boardroom: learnings from world-leader Norway. *FACTBase Bulletin*.

Huse, M. (2020). *Resolving the Crisis in Research by Changing the Game: An Ecosystem and a Sharing Philosophy*. Edward Elgar Publishing.

Huse, M. & DeSilva, M. (2023). Polymorphic research and boards of directors: let us make a better world together. In Cucari, N., Yamak, S., Lee, B., & De Falco, S. E. (Eds.), *Handbook of Research Methods for Corporate Governance: Innovative Methods for Future Research*. Edward Elgar Publishing.

Izquierdo, M., Huse, M., & Möltner, H. (2016). Value creating boards and gender diversity: suggestions to progress in getting women on boards in Spain. BI report. https://biopen.bi .no/bi-xmlui/bitstream/handle/11250/2408370/2016-02-Huse%20mfl_revised%20version .pdf?sequence=1&isAllowed=y.

Kanjuo Mrčela, A. (2017). Gender diversity on boards of directors in Slovenia: impending legislation to establish quotas. In Seirstad, C., Gabaldon, P., & Mensi-Klarbach, H. (Eds.), *Gender Diversity in the Boardroom* (pp. 75–102). Palgrave Macmillan.

Kesner, I. F. (1988). Directors' characteristics and committee membership: an investigation of type, occupation, tenure, and gender. *Academy of Management Journal, 31*(1), 66–84.

Lee, T. W. (2009). The management professor. *Academy of Management Review, 34*(2), 196–9.

Machold, S., Huse, M., Hansen, K., & Brogi, M. (Eds.) (2013). *Getting Women on to Corporate Boards: A Snowball Starting in Norway*. Edward Elgar Publishing.

Nielsen, S. T., & Huse, M. (2010). Women directors' contribution to board decision-making and strategic involvement: the role of equality perception. *European Management Review, 7*(1), 16–29.

Rigolini, A., & Huse, M. (2021). Women and multiple board memberships: social capital and institutional pressure. *Journal of Business Ethics, 169*(3), 443–59.

Seierstad, C., Tatli, A., Aldossari, M., & Huse, M. (2021). Broadening of the field of corporate boards and legitimate capitals: an investigation into the use of gender quotas in corporate boards in Norway. *Work, Employment and Society, 35*(4), 753–73.

Seierstad, C., Warner-Søderholm, G., Torchia, M., & Huse, M. (2017). Increasing the number of women on boards: the role of actors and processes. *Journal of Business Ethics, 141*(2), 289–315.

Sellevoll, T., Huse, M., & Hansen, C. (2007). The value creating board: results from the "Follow-up surveys" 2005/2006 in Norwegian firms. BI-report. http://web.bi.no/forskning/ papers.nsf/0/aef67d3cebee152bc125728f00496947/$FILE/2007-02-sellevoll-huse-hansen .pdf.

Terjesen, S., Sealy, R., & Singh, V. (2009). Women directors on corporate boards: a review and research agenda. *Corporate Governance: An International Review, 17*(3), 320–37.

Vinnicombe, S., Singh, V., Burke, R., Bilimoria, D., & Huse, M. (Eds.) (2008). *Women on Corporate Boards of Directors: International Research and Practice*. Edward Elgar Publishing.

Index